Franciszek Korni

The Struggle

To Pat and our two boys,
with love

Franciszek Kornicki

The Struggle

Biography of a Fighter Pilot

STRATUS

© Stratus
© Franciszek Kornicki

Published in Poland in 2008
by STRATUS s.c.
Po. Box 123,
27-600 Sandomierz 1, Poland
e-mail: office@stratusbooks.com.pl
www.stratusbooks.com.pl

UK Office:
Mushroom Model Publications,
36 Ver Road, Redbourn, AL3 7PE, UK.
e-mail: rogerw@mmpbooks.biz
http://www.mmpbooks.biz

ISBN
978-83-89450-80-7

Editorial Team
Bartłomiej Belcarz
Robert Pęczkowski
Artur Juszczak
Dariusz Karnas

Cover
Bartłomiej Belcarz
Artur Bukowski

DTP
Artur Bukowski

Special thanks
Wojtek Matusiak
Richard Kornicki

Druk: Pracownia Poligraficzna KNAP - DRUK
Stanisław Knap
Al. Jana Pawła II 37,
37-450 Stalowa Wola, Poland
tel/fax: (0 15) 844 34 12

PRINTED IN POLAND

CONTENTS

1

PART I - 1916 - 1939
EARLY YEARS IN POLAND

My Village, Wereszyn

In the middle of a round meadow, largely surrounded by woods on gently rising land - pines on one side, mixed oak, elm, beech and lime elsewhere - there was a spring such as I have never seen in all my life. It was ringed by twelve old willow trees, and was about eighteen feet by ten, oval, two feet deep, bordered by logs and very much alive. It was as if dozens and dozens of little volcanoes were erupting endlessly at the bottom; they were of different sizes, shapes and shades, constantly changing, pulsating, bubbling. As a small boy I spent many summer hours there, lying on my tummy, head cupped in my hands, elbows in the grass, watching in wonderment and dreaming of the strange happenings which were supposed to have taken place there many years ago.

The story goes that there was a small church in ancient days, precisely where the spring was, and that one day, when the church was full of people, the earth swallowed the church and everybody in it, and the spring came into being. The people were bad and this was their punishment, but they were to return to the surface of the earth after they had done their penance and gained the Almighty's pardon. Supposedly a beautiful maiden of our village would, one day, find by chance a thread near the spring and winding it up on a piece of wood, she would pull the church out of the spring with all the people in it, singing and rejoicing, and the spring would be no more.

I did not like the thought that the spring would cease to exist. It was a source of a fine stream which ran through a mile and a half of linked narrow meadows, gathering more water from the slopes of adjacent fields, until it reached the eastern part of the village. From there on, the banks became progressively higher until they formed a narrow gorge which was spanned by a wooden bridge. The water would rush under the bridge and then fan out, slow down, and join our lovely lake with unmistakable delight - there was so much water there! And the view was beautiful.

The eastern bank of the lake was lined with willow trees, their lower branches touching the water, and there were thatched cottages amongst the trees and above them. On the opposite side a road ran directly by the lake rising steadily to a height of some thirty feet above the water; it was a mud road, all roads were mud roads in our district. Five grand poplar trees grew on the high bank of the lake casting giant shadows on the water on late summer afternoons. The northern side of the lake was dammed by a wall of earth with grass, weeds, shrubs, and trees, growing here and there on the outside edge and beyond. The dam was broken in the middle by a wooden sluice: enormous oak piles, crossbars and planks regulating the level of the water. The overflow of water fell down about fifteen feet, the stream continuing on its way to join the rivers Huczwa, then Bug, and finally Wisła, on its way to the sea, where all rivers die.

The lake was also a great divide between the village and the vast landed estate of Robert Białkowski. All villagers, without exception, spoke Ukrainian at home and some Polish when they felt obliged to try it. Mr Białkowski and his estate workers at all levels spoke Polish at home and tried some Ukrainian when they felt like it. Individual farms dotted around outside the boundary of the village and the estate were owned by ethnic Poles. People had no difficulty in understanding one another for there is a great affinity between those two languages and everybody was familiar with them. The younger generation of villagers had a good working Polish which they learned at the village school.

The school was situated on the edge of the village in about two acres of grounds, one third of which was a playground. There were some high elms growing on one side of it as well as one or two right in the middle of it. In the far corner, and well hidden behind some bushes, there was a lavatory - a small construction with two lock-up compartments for boys and girls alike. There was always a race to it at the end of each period and needless to say boys usually won. The remaining two-thirds of the grounds were out of bounds to children as it was mainly an orchard, and a small vegetable and flower garden for private use by our teacher.

The wooden school building consisted of a long and narrow corridor/hall with pegs on the walls; one large classroom with benches for four or six and corresponding long multiple desks, like pews in church; and the schoolteacher's flat: all under one roof. It was the biggest building in the village apart from the wooden Orthodox church. The schoolteacher had nobody to help him, all teaching was done by himself and he ran four forms - the third and fourth in the mornings and the first and second in the afternoons. Thus the children of two forms were in the same room and their lessons were so arranged that when one form was listening to verbal instructions the other was struggling with written work. This would change during the course of any morning or afternoon several times, depending on the stage of instruction. At the end of four years every child could read and write, knew tables by heart, could add, subtract, do long division and multiplication more or less accurately, and was introduced to geometry, fractions, geography, and history. There was also a small library in the school for children and adults, which was well used and was where I borrowed my first book.

All immediate needs of the villagers, estate workers, and farmers nearby were taken care of by four Jewish families who lived in the heart of the village and ran three shops - one a general store; the second with rolls and rolls of various coloured materials, needles, buttons and ribbons; and the third a hardware shop including paraffin and leather. The fourth family were farmers - unusual for Polish Jews - but the head of the family loved the land and horses. He also provided transport with his cart and two fine greys for the three shops when needed. His wife and children were also buying and selling whatever came their way but they did not run a formal shop. The shops restocked their merchandise from one of the three nearest towns, the first two were twelve and fourteen kilometres away and were rather small, whilst the third was our district main town - Hrubieszów - and was twenty-one kilometres distant. All roads being mud roads were quite impassable in late autumn and early spring because of rain, and during the worst spells of winter, because of snow. In a really bad year these siege-like conditions could last about four months.

The estate of Mr Robert Białkowski ran to several thousands of acres of arable land, meadows, and woods. The manor house was built in the middle of beautiful grounds with unusual trees, shrubs, lawns, flower beds, and farther on behind stiff conifers there were two orchards, rows and rows of soft fruit bushes, a vegetable garden, cold frames where melons were grown, and a small overgrown reservoir where once carp were bred but it seemed that pike had taken it over. A fine straight drive, lined with giant lime trees, led to the ruins of the big house, burned to the ground in the First World War. Alas, I was too young to have ever seen it in its full glory. I wandered amongst the broken bricks, smashed tiles, wash-basins, twisted pipes, glittering pieces of glass, collapsed chunks of walls, gaping holes underneath floors, and felt very sad that it was no more. I could not understand why anybody would want to destroy something which must have been truly grand.

There were hard times for Poles after 1920 when the Polish army, organised and led by Marshal Piłsudski, defeated the Red Army, and the Soviet Union lost the war: the only war they ever lost between the 1917 revolution and their Afghanistan venture. Mr Białkowski and his family moved to a lodge, enlarged it a bit and stayed there until the Second World War.

The lodge was separated from the estate buildings by a screen of thickly planted conifers - about five rows in all - and a fence. Here too one could see the signs of war destruction with odd parts of brick walls standing here and there, but most of these buildings were restored and new wooden ones added.

The road continued in a straight line from the edge of the lake for two hundred yards, then curved and turned 90° to the left for another one hundred and fifty yards, over a small wooden bridge and forked, with one branch continuing in a westerly direction and the other turning right to the north. On both sides of the first two hundred yard stretch of the road were the estate buildings - on the right a smithy, then a small building housing a giant potato steamer providing a main ingredient for horses' winter fodder, and close to it a long solid building of brick and timber construction which was primarily a grain store, and was subdivided inside into several sections. A separate room was constructed in the centre area where rows and rows of smoked gammons, sausage rings, and strips of salt-cured pork were hanging and shelves were filled with glass and stone jars full of preserves of every variety one could think of. A most heavenly aroma percolated through the loosely fitted but heavily padlocked door, and my mouth watered whenever I found myself nearby. Further on, close to the road bend stood a 'T' shaped shed without walls housing a steam engine and threshing machine in the centre and providing a vast space for storing bales of wheat, rye, barley, or oats, prior to threshing which was always done in late autumn and winter. Big mountains of various corn bales were also built in the fields close to roads, and were later brought by carts to the threshing machine.

On the other side of the road a long low brick building was partitioned in the middle and half of it was used as stables for estate working horses and the other half as a cowshed for animals owned by the estate workers. An 'L' shaped building stood some fifty yards behind it which was a hay store, a cowshed for the estate herd, and stables for up to six horses to pull two coaches which were housed on one side of the stable. Mr Białkowski's black stallion Bartek had his own corner. The master, riding his splendid horse, was a familiar sight on most days. Between the two buildings on the side nearest the conifers and the lodge stood a hand-operated water pump and a very long trough, where all animals were watered. On the other sided a high brick wall joined the two buildings and a mountain of straw was always built against it during threshing time. The farm carts were lined in a row near a high fence separating the yard from the main road. Ploughs, and other farm implements, were under cover nearby and close to a cart-weighing machine housed in a separate little building. By the main entrance to the estate yard, almost opposite the lake dam, there was an underground ice store which was filled in winter with alternate layers of straw and large chunks of ice brought down several steps into a large, cold, and dark room. The ice lasted well into summer.

Following the left fork of the road for a hundred or so yards, one would come to two timber buildings on the left side of the road which were terraced back-to-back cottages for full-time estate workers. The first one comprised four cottages and the second eight, half of them facing south and stet north. Each of the cottages opened into a fair sized entrance hall with a stepladder to the loft. From the hall, one door led to a windowless food and general store, and the second one to a large room with one window which was a combined kitchen, living room, and bedroom. A wood-burning kitchen stove and bread oven were well designed as one unit fitting neatly into a corner of the room. Above the bread oven there was a well concealed flat space useful for drying seeds and things, and large enough for a child to sleep there. All children loved that spot because it was a sort of private place and it was always warm. The cottages had clay floors which were very hard, smooth, and surprisingly free of dust. Proud housewives would mix clean, light brown clay with water in a bucket to a runny paste and, on Saturdays, smear it with a rag on the floor. This would dry very quickly and leave a most pleasing effect for the next few days, but it was Sunday which really mattered. Two of the cottages had an additional room with its own brick-built slow combustion space heater, burning wood, of course. Close to every cottage there was always a heap of brushwood, thin branches of trees and undergrowth replenished periodically from the estate woods, to keep the kitchen fires going. Chopping wood was a never-ending job for all family members who could swing an axe.

Two piggeries were standing some distance apart, sub-divided into sections where each house-hold had its own pig or two, the oldest being fattened for the next kill. When a pig was killed all the family worked like beavers - all butchery had to be done immediately, rings of sausages were made and hung inside the cottage chimney together with gammons, on a strong wooden bar placed across the top of the chimney, where they stayed for three weeks, or longer. During the smoking period only hard wood, like oak, was allowed to be burned in the kitchen stove. Thick strips of fat, and sometimes shoulder hams, were rubbed with salt until a thin layer was formed outside, and they were hung in the food store and would last safely until consumed. Jars of drip-ping, mixed with fried onions, were produced at the same time, as well as black pudding which had to be eaten within a day or two. Nobody sold any meat to anybody; it all went into the family larder in one form or another, and was carefully rationed over a period of several months. The norm was roughly two pigs a year, one before Christmas and one before Easter.

Water was a problem; it had to be fetched by bucket from a well belonging to a farmer, across the road, no doubt by arrangement with Mr Białkowski. It was an open well, quite deep, and lined with oak beams inside. On top a four foot high wooden wall was built around it to prevent acci-dents. Some four yards from the well stood a high pole to which a long wooden bar was attached on a swivel. Tied to the outside end of the bar was a big and heavy piece of tree root which weighted that end right down to the ground. The other end was pointing to the sky, and attached to it was a rope with a bucket at its end hanging just inside the upper wall. You had to pull the rope down until the bucket hit the water, and when it was full, you would pull it up with very little effort and transfer the water from the well bucket into your own bucket and carry it home. When the water was used up, for whatever purpose, you would go to fetch another one, and another, day after day, year after year. Some people used a wooden yoke shaped to fit neatly on human shoulders, with hooks at each end, dangling on a piece of rope. You could carry two large buckets of water with this contraption, but a little balancing act was necessary in order not to spill it. The water from the well was used for cooking, washing-up, personal washing, and laundry. In warmer weather, wives and daughters carried dirty laundry to a stream nearby where they rubbed it with soap, bashed it with flat pieces of wood with handles, and dried it on lines all over the place.

Another problem was lavatories. Well, there were only two for twelve cottages; they were under one roof, semi-detached, so to speak, with very thin wooden walls between them, and about a hundred yards away. Fortunately there were bushes, trees, and deep ditches all round.

Adjacent to the cottages was a piece of land divided into plots for the private use of estate workers. The size of a plot was less than an acre. The most important crops were potatoes, white cabbage - enough to make a barrel of sauerkraut - onions, beetroot, peas, beans, ridge cucum-bers for pickling, root vegetables for winter use, poppy seeds, and salad items. Heavy work like ploughing, planting, and harvesting potatoes, was done in the 'firm's' time and with the 'firm's' equipment and horse power.

Looking south from the cottages, the ground sloped gently for about a hundred yards down towards a lively stream with a footbridge before rising again to form an 'island' with precise boundaries: to the east a high fence beyond which was a large orchard, and the rest of Mr Białkowski's sacred grounds; to the south a deep ditch and a dam running in a straight line east-west, beyond which another artificial lake extended its shallow waters over what had been a lovely meadow with a fast stream running through the middle of it; on the other two sides was a stream which ran north from the lake sluice, then curved sharply to the east and north again, thus separating the cottages from all other estate buildings.

In the middle of this 'island' was a flour-mill; by the orchard fence stood a fine single-storey house, and on the opposite side was a long shed with three walls only, providing shelter for horses and carts belonging to mill customers. The mill was quite something: several floors high, square, towering above the countryside, with an engine room stuck to one side of it, where a monstrous engine was endlessly chuffing and puffing, and its giant fly-wheel swishing furiously around and mesmerising the onlookers. The engine was powered by steam supplied from a boiler next door which burned tons and tons of logs.

Mr Białkowski, the estate owner, had a large family - three sons and three daughters. His second wife was slim, about 5'5", dark greying hair, fine features, always walked fast, always busy. There was an air of efficiency, elegance, and dignity about her; she had a kind smile but she did not smile often.

Mr Białkowski, the head of the family, was of medium height, powerfully built, rugged of face, with moustaches, high boots and breeches most of the time, riding whip in hand at first, and a walking stick in later years, a semi-feudal squire, firm but fair. I was a bit afraid of him at first, but I always liked him. The education of six children must have cost a fortune, bearing in mind that there were no state grants for anybody at any level. It seems that later on dowries for daughters, and probably further payments on account of individual shares of family fortunes, necessitated mortgaging the estate. High inflation and world-wide economic depression in the '30s made things worse. Part of the estate was sold; first hundreds and hundreds of oak trees went, and when the ground was cleared, the land was sold as well. When the children were younger and less expensive, Mr Białkowski had a manager whose name was Roman Zienkiewicz, a bachelor until he married the last governess for the youngest daughter in 1931. They left a year or so later and both found jobs in the district town, Hrubieszów; he in local government and she as a teacher. He fought with distinction under Marshal Piłsudski against the Red Army of Lenin and Trotsky in 1920, and ended his days in a German concentration camp in World War II. A few years before the war started the financial control of the estate was taken out of Mr Białkowski's hands but he carried out day to day management until he died sometime during the war.

It was said that he had a mistress. I knew her as an unmarried mother of a girl, and a boy almost my age, living in one of the cottages. She was an excellent cook and worked for the family regularly at first and part-time later. She once baked a birthday cake which was sent to me when I was away from home. I had never tasted anything so good before, nor since. We were all friends long before the cake was baked.

I have tried to sketch, as accurately as I could, the world into which I was born. I must now search my memory and continue from as far back as I can personally remember.

The Family

My parents - Łukasz and Aniela - had six sons. The first, Stanisław, died in infancy; then in 1901 came Władysław (Władek), in 1906 Feliks (Felek), in 1909 Kazimierz (Kazik), in 1911 Jan (Janek), and in 1916 me. We lived in one of the two room cottages, in front of which, fenced neatly on three sides, was my mother's little flower garden where forget-me-nots, nasturtiums, asters, and heavenly-scented stocks flourished every year.

The main entrance led into a hall, the size of a small room. Fixed to part of the wall near the main entrance door were horizontal bars on which chickens roosted at night - they were thrown out unceremoniously first thing in the morning. Next came a ladder to the loft full of hay which was fed to our three or four cows in winter. In warmer weather at least two of my elder brothers slept there. They had sheets and blankets and were expected to make a proper bed for themselves. The scent of hay was very pleasant and it was fun to sleep there. I do not think they bothered much about bed-making. One corner of the hall was occupied by a few sacks of grain - barley, wheat, rye - ready for milling, and bran for pigs. Facing the main door was the windowless bulk food store with hanging smoked sausages and gammons at times, a barrel of sauerkraut, a sack of flour, a small sack of salt and another of sugar, dry pulses, preserves, pickled vegetables, etc., as well as any household items which needed a temporary home.

Another door from the hall led to the kitchen. On entering it one would see a window on the right with a long bench/shelf underneath it, and further in the corner stood a kitchen table with two deep drawers full of cutlery and bits and pieces. Our cutlery was of iron and aluminium, we did not eat with wooden spoons any more, but some people did. Underneath the table was a wooden receptacle for vegetable parings, remnants of unusable food, etc., which were fed to the pigs. To the left of the table was a door to the next room, and next to it was the kitchen stove and bread oven unit in a corner. The rest of the room was filled with one enormous bed big enough for three boys, a bench, and a low stool. Cooking pots and pans were on top of the stove and on the shelf under the window. The next room had one table, two chairs, one bench as long as the table, one wardrobe, one huge chest with a curved lid and two double beds. The table was placed against the wall, underneath the window. On the windowsill were flower pots; a fuchsia, geranium, and rosemary were always there. The window in each room looked at my mother's small flower garden. On the walls of the second room hung two Holy pictures and one landscape with an oversize ram in the foreground. At one time my pencil and wash sketch of the flour-mill was also hanging somewhere.

It was a tight squeeze in winter. Washing in cold water was a lick-and-promise affair and periodical scrubs from head to foot in a wooden tub full of warm water were not easy to arrange as water had to be heated on top of the stove. I was the first to be thrown in as I was the smallest, and more hot water was added as the next bigger brother jumped in. We usually flooded the kitchen - to our mother's despair. In warmer weather the tub was moved to the hall, but the chickens did not like that. In summer the tub was put away and we swam in the big pond, naked of course; only the squire's mob and their friends wore swim-suits. Girls were bathing and washing in the shallower part under the watchful eyes of their mothers, and they always had something on. The brave ones would undress completely under water and splash about starkers - to a great show of disapproval by their mothers who were really more amused than annoyed.

I think my mother was the hardest working woman in the world. She cooked for seven, baked bread, washed and ironed laundry, milked two or three cows daily either in the cowshed nearby, or in their summer quarters over a mile away, made cheese and butter, fed pigs and chickens, looked after a vegetable garden, tended her flowers with love and affection, often fetched water from the well, endlessly sewed lost buttons on, repaired underwear and clothing, prepared raw flax for dressing and spinning, spun miles of thread by hand methods, without a spinning wheel, bleached newly woven lengths of linen and God knows what else.

On Sundays we all marched two and a half kilometres to church in the next village. This was a great social event, everybody wearing Sunday-best, arriving early and parading outside the church, meeting friends, talking, laughing, gossiping, and children running around and playing. And then the long sung Mass would begin, all in Latin. I did not understand it at first but the catechism classes before the first Holy Communion helped a bit. Some people had prayer books, but a lot did not. Many older people could not read. The sermons were mostly hell and damnation and I was a bit afraid of God, purgatory, and hell.

Our squire would arrive with his family in a coach, as would his equals from other estates nearby, and whilst they prayed inside the church, their coachmen looked after the horses and stayed outside - you could not leave a coach and horses unattended. Anyhow, there was nothing to stop them from saying a prayer outside the church.

Mother always hurried back after the Mass to get our lunch ready which usually consisted of *pierogi* - something like overgrown, half-moon shaped ravioli filled with a mixture of cottage cheese and potatoes or minced meat mixed with fried onions and bread crumbs. They were prepared before church and all she had to do was to boil water and drop them in for a few minutes. A plateful of *pierogi* with some melted butter poured over, or dripping with residual crackling, tasted delicious. Double quantity was usually made and we had them for supper as well, fried on both sides in a pan to a golden-brown colour. Sometimes we had a stew, or cold smoked ham or sausages, but not very often. Chickens were for laying eggs and only those which refused to do so were punished with death and provided a feast for the family on odd occasions. Eggs were food and currency - I was sent sometimes with a dozen eggs or so to buy something in the shops.

Our diet was based on vegetables. For breakfast we usually had *krupnik* which was pearl barley cooked in diluted milk with some potatoes in it - sort of white soup eaten with brown rye bread. When the family moaned about too much *krupnik*, mother would boil some eggs, or better still fried them with thin slices of smoked sausage, all mixed together; this was delicious and called *jajecznica*. A frequent lunch was cabbage soup made of fresh cabbages or sauerkraut, peas, potatoes, thickened with flour and enriched with chopped crackling and, if we were in luck, bits of smoked sausage. A plateful of that, with rye bread, was a good meal. Other lunch or supper dishes were buckwheat cooked to the same consistency as rice with bits of meat or just butter, thick lentil soup, baked pasties similar to Cornish pasties, baked potatoes with whatever was available, a rabbit stew, a hare stew, and even a carp in the poaching season. Christmas and Easter were marked by special dishes and cakes, and other sweet things, and we all looked forward to our mother's specialities. They were really good and our enthusiastic praise was genuine, which pleased her no end, but she would always say "it was nothing" and "anyhow not as good as it should have been".

Our mother was a good disciplinarian but she was always kind and loving as well as firm. She would not hesitate to resort to physical punishment on occasions when one of the younger lot overstepped the mark, but the older ones would be far worse off by the dressing-down she would administer in clear and uncompromising terms. There were certain things which were definitely not on, such as starting a fight with a smaller boy and, God forbid, boasting about the victory. But it was alright to fight a bigger boy in self-defence, even if it meant coming home with a bloody nose. Mother would not complain to anybody about that, even it she had to repair some tears in clothing, which would obviously displease her. She would demand an account of the battle, ask questions, and point out a lesson or two to be learned. When a fight was one-against-one and a brother was present he should not interfere, but he could shout advice. Everybody must fight his own fight and not rely on anybody's help. We heard that time and time again - it was good advice. If comfort was needed, the defeated warrior would get it with a loving smile but no more than was necessary to restore his equilibrium.

The first dog I remember in our home had longish white hair, was of medium height, played with everybody but obeyed nobody except my father. Her name was Figa and we all adored her. The last time I saw Figa was from some distance, she looked wild and was snarling at my eldest brother who had a shotgun in his hands and shouted at me to run home. Then I heard a shot. Poor Figa had rabies and had to die. I missed her terribly.

I can still recall the smell of fresh rye bread my mother used to bake. After wood fire cinders and ashes were quickly scraped out of the bread oven, some six large round loaves would be shoved in once a week. The flat bottom of each loaf had a lot of small cinders and ashes embedded in it, except in summer when the shaped dough was first placed on large cabbage leaves.

I made a bow and arrow using young straight shoots of hazel, a piece of string, and a small nail which I attached to the head of the arrow. I released the arrow quite accidentally - please believe me - at a distance of two yards at the back of the head of a chap who was not good, but he was not bad either. The arrow nail penetrated the skin at one side of his head and got stuck. The poor fellow ran home screaming, with my arrow dangling behind, still firmly in the target. It took me a long time to forget what followed.

I remember two popular treatments for coughs and colds, pain in the chest, and such like. One of the remedies was leeches. An old woman, looking like a witch with dark head-scarf over her grey hair, arrived with a small jar containing the hungry little beasts, picking them out with her fingers and released them on her patient's naked back. The leeches sucked the 'bad blood', swelling slowly until they had enough, and were pulled off and returned to the jar. Another remedy was a fascinating vacuum suction treatment applied to the back or chest, known in English as 'Cupping'. The same old woman would arrive with a basket containing little tumblers of just over an inch in diameter. She would light a small torch with a mop-like head, hold it in one hand, pick a tumbler with the other and approach the patient lying on his back, put the torch inside the tumbler for a second then quickly withdraw the torch and slam the tumbler down on the flesh. A degree of vacuum would be created inside the tumbler and draw the flesh in, the tumbler becoming firmly attached to the skin and sucking the illness out of the body. When a tumbler was pulled off there would be a small popping noise and ghastly purple rings on the skin.

My father was the estate coachman and frequently drove members of the squire's family and their friends to the district town, either to or from the railway, shopping; visits to friends, or other business.

The coach was usually drawn by two horses, but on rare occasions four were used, and that was quite a sight. Father handled the foursome skilfully, he was very good at it. When the coach was occupied by the younger generation only, they would nag him to let them drive, and where the road was straight and safe, he would agree. High-spirited Stephanie would immediately crack the whip and change pace to a fast trot; she loved the speed.

There was a coaching inn in town with a guest room for passengers to tidy up, stabling for horses, and cover for coaches. The distance of twenty-one kilometres could be covered in well under two hours in the summer when the road was dry and dusty, but it could take about four hours when autumn and spring rain would turn the road into a sea of mud with deep potholes into the bargain. In winter, when the snow was tightly packed, a lightweight, elegant sledge and pair would move swiftly at a fast trot with ease, bells ringing - a leather strap with several little bells was fastened around the neck of each horse - steam rising from the horses and lumps of snow flying from their hooves. An enormous rug lined with wolf fur would be wrapped under and around the feet and legs, and extending right up to the arms of passengers sitting side-by-side. My father would wear a long, warm, fur-lined coat, heavy boots, warm hat and gloves and a rug. In sub-zero temperatures ice would form on his moustache, and he would drive the horses hard as the temperature could fall rapidly, particularly at night, -20 degrees C was not uncommon.

He knew most of the coachmen stopping at the inn, and occasionally when two or three of them met they would pool their allowances together, buy some food and vodka and have a jolly lunch session, swapping stories and jokes.

He enjoyed his job and the variety it offered, he was trusted and respected and left alone to arrange his work as he saw fit. There were two coaches, a sledge, a buggy, at least five horses' harnesses, and saddles to look after. Everything had to be spick and span of course, and it was. I used to sneak into his domain and help clean and polish things.

Before I started school my father was promoted to the post of overseer, field-work excluded, having succeeded our neighbour who died suddenly. He was responsible directly to the estate manager, and his duties included distribution of animal fodder, security of stores and buildings, checking and arranging repairs of equipment and gear, horse carts and sledges, and supervision of all activities within the perimeter of the estate buildings and main yard. He carried a big bunch of keys with him.

I remember that his pay went up and mother was very pleased about it, but I do not know precisely what he earned as he was paid in kind as well as in cash. The rewards in kind included accommodation, fire wood, usage of a small plot of land, fodder and pasture for three to four cows (depending on size of family), a section in a common pig-sty for two to three pigs, a quantity of wheat, rye, and barley for bread flour, and pearl barley, and a sum of money. The working day was long. Father would rush out of the house at about six am to issue fodder for horses and supervise watering and feeding. Mother would get up at the same time, light the kitchen stove and cook breakfast. Father would come back and eat his breakfast while the horses were eating theirs. He would leave shortly after breakfast, returning home for a one hour lunch break, back to work again, and finally come home after the horses had been watered, fed and bedded. It was a long day, six days a week with Sunday morning and evening attendance to horses. There were no annual holidays in that package, but every family would be allowed to use horses and cart for a shopping expedition to town, usually twice a year. I also remember one or two visits to my aunt some considerable distance away, where we stayed two nights. My uncle was a great organist in a wealthy parish and was teaching music as well. Once he took us to an empty church and played most beautifully on an enormous organ - popular tunes and dance music. Mother did not think that was a proper thing to do in church but he assured her it was, and anyhow, how did she know that angels in heaven would not enjoy a waltz or a polka now and then?

The job of coachman went to my eldest brother Władek, a young ex-cavalry corporal. He volunteered for the Polish Forces led by General Piłsudski, an outstanding soldier, statesman, and a patriot. After the defeat of the Red Army in 1920, followed by the Riga Peace Treaty, he served for a year or so in No. 21 Cavalry Regiment (21 *Pułk Ułanów Nadwiślańskich*) and eventually returned home. He was fully employed on the estate until he succeeded his father as a coachman. He was very popular with the younger generation of the Białkowski family, they treated him like a friend. He was very good looking with black hair, classical features, nice smile, thin wiry body of about five foot five inches, agile, alert, and energetic. There was an air of competence and authority about him. His military service had made a man of him at an early age. Everybody liked him, particularly girls, but his love-life was not a happy one. The first girl he was about to marry jilted him; she would not swap the life in a large town for our village. The second one – his fiancée - died of tuberculosis. He watched her wasting away, spending every penny he earned on doctors, silently heart-broken and despairing. The third one he married and she bore him five children and died suddenly; his second wife bore him one son and outlived him.

On 1st September 1924 I started school at the age of seven years and eight months. On the first day my mother gave me a few eggs and told me to buy a pencil and an exercise book and to proceed to the village school where I was expected and would be told what to do. I went to the shop, made my purchases, and was pleased to hear that little Chaim was also starting school - but he had left home already. There were no lessons on that afternoon. Our teacher was young, married, and had a baby daughter. He explained things to us, checked the register, showed us the playground, lavatories, and out-of-bounds area. He was nice and friendly and inspired confidence. I was instantly certain that I would like him, and I did, for four years and more.

Janek, at about thirteen, was then in the fourth form; Kazik at fifteen was already doing some casual work on the estate; and Felek at eighteen was about to finish his apprenticeship at a smithy in the neighbouring village. He was living with the blacksmith's family, coming home for Sundays only. He had no pay for the first year and had to do odd jobs daily which had nothing to do with learning the trade. In fact, father had to pay a lump sum before Felek was accepted for training. Felek was very unhappy there but determined to stick it out and learn the trade well, which he did. He then found employment at another smithy within a few hundred yards from home, which had been established a couple of years before. He worked there until he was called up to do his National Service in No. 44 Infantry Regiment whose garrison town was Równo, in south eastern Poland. We did not see much of Felek during the next two years. He came home once or twice every year for a short leave, looking very smart and full of beans. Władek had no time for the infantry and called them hares. The two brothers had endless arguments about their respective arms. The pay of national servicemen was very small indeed but the food was adequate. My parents and brothers would send him money now and then, which was the normal thing to do.

The building of the flour-mill began at the time Felek was called up. The blacksmith he had been apprenticed to was offered the job as head-man in the estate smithy and as chief mechanic in charge of the flour-mill engine, after some training. He, in turn, trained Kazik to look after the engine under his supervision. It was really a simple job of checking steam pressure, oil levels, cutting logs on a circular saw, and feeding the boiler. Kazik enjoyed the job very much; it was under cover, warm in winter, and provided the opportunity of meeting a lot of people. Occasionally I would take his lunch to the engine room when there was nobody to relieve him. I was fascinated by the enormous engine and the chuffing noises coming out of the monster. I soon learned where the oil points were and I was allowed to add some oil when nobody was looking.

In summer, when the mill was closed for maintenance work, Kazik would be given other jobs such as helping with repairs of machinery and gear, mending fences, or work in orchards and gardens. He worked in the engine room for several years until he caught tuberculosis.

When Janek finished school he was over fourteen and he soon started work on a casual basis, doing odd jobs. But he loved horses and his ambition was to be in sole charge of a pair and to be in full-time employment as an estate worker. He had to wait for about two years by which time he learned all the important field-work and could handle horses like an expert. He looked after his pair as if they were his own; he groomed them, fed them, talked to them, and would steal for them. Soon his pair out-shone the rest and occasionally was elevated to pull the second coach, they were that good.

I was making good progress at school and my end-of-year marks were moving up. I had plenty of encouragement from our teacher and at home. My brothers were checking my homework, helping with early difficulties, and repeatedly telling me to work hard. Father always showed keen interest in my progress by listening rather than talking. It was difficult for him to do otherwise as he could not read nor write, but his mental arithmetic was excellent. Mother's eyesight started deteriorating, and having no glasses, she could only read with difficulty, but she carried her fat prayer book to church every Sunday just the same.

There were no books at all at our home, and nobody ever bought a newspaper except Władek when he was in town and could afford it. Fortunately our school had a small library and we could borrow one book at a time. Throughout the long winter evenings we had wonderful reading sessions, year after year. Felek and Kazik were the readers in turn, changing over after a time because of the bad light from a solitary paraffin lamp, and the rest of us listened. We read the monumental works of Henryk Sienkiewicz; we cheered, and cried, and cheered again. His trilogy, in particular, is the most widely read work in Poland and everybody is familiar with it. Generation after generation were, are, and will be brought up on it. People knew the main characters intimately and extracts, whether in Polish, Latin, or Ukrainian, are quoted and adopted as by-words. We also read Orzeszkowa and other authors. Those reading sessions had an enormous impact on me. My imagination worked overtime. I had very clear mental pictures of all the main characters which have not changed to this day. I dreamed about the siege of Częstochowa and the sword duel of Pan Wołodyjowski and Bohun. We were all gripped by the story and although the heroes came from social and economic strata far above us, there also many people like us, ordinary working and poor people who in time of national crisis rose, to a man, throughout the country and fought like lions. It gave us a warm feeling inside, and I suppose this is how a sense of belonging to a nation is born, from which stem other things like patriotism, honour, and duty.

The first book I borrowed from my school was about a princess locked up in a castle, a brave rescue by a knight, and similar childish stuff. I was not impressed, having listened to Sienkiewicz, and I asked for something more interesting. Uncle Tom's Cabin was alright, I was then in the fourth form.

There were nice things to look forward to in every season. In summer I wore no shoes and my mother would kick hers off when she felt like it. It was no hardship; I would shed my winter boots as soon as I could. It was fun to paddle in ponds and streams, and in pools of water after heavy rains, in spite of obvious hazards.

Big woods extending for miles were within twenty minutes walk from our doorstep. They belonged to the squire of the next village. We used to pick wild strawberries there, lots and lots of them. And there were also cherry trees, right on the edge. Boys would climb them like monkeys and I was one of them. I would bring home several pounds of cherries and there would be cherry flans, *pierogi* stuffed with cherries, and cherry this and cherry that, and my father would make cherry vodka for Christmas.

I was probably six years old when I swam the length and the width of the big pond. This was a test, and after that I was allowed to swim without supervision. No child had been known to drown there, as we were all good swimmers.

On hot summer evenings horses would be brought to the big pond for a drink and a swim. It was great fun to catch the tail of a swimming horse and be pulled for some twenty yards. Some horses hate swimming, they panic and try to jump out of the water, they snarl and protest and their eyes blaze with fright and fury. Others would enter deep water quietly and swim without any fuss. Riding a horse bare-back into deep water was quite exciting - step by step, deeper and deeper, until only the horse's and rider's heads stuck out of the water and then, losing the ground from under its hooves, the horse would launch itself forward and paddle furiously with all four legs, moving very fast indeed, until it could feel solid ground again.

Harvest was, of course, a very busy time. The corn was cut by a "Made in England" machine which had the name "Deering" painted in several places and which was pulled by four horses. As the horses pulled the machine, the driver would engage a gear which would result in rapid movement of the cutting knives located in front of the platform on which the corn stalks would fall. Four rotating arms would then push the cut corn from the platform and on to the ground in small neat heaps - one heap after another, around and around the harvested fields. The heaps of corn-stalks were sheaved immediately by a couple of dozen or more casually employed women and girls from the village. They would also stack the sheaves in lots of thirty in such a way that when the last one was put on top vertically it would protect the ears from rain. These small stooks would be moved by carts under cover as soon as possible, or transferred to a convenient point near a road and built into huge stacks the size of a large house, covered with a thick layer of straw shaped like a roof and held in position by tree branches tied at the top point and hanging down on both sides. The driver of the harvester could only control the rear pair of horses, but he had to watch the machine as well. The real control of the four was in the hands of a small boy, the lighter the better, who was riding on the front left horse. The boy and the driver had to understand each other well to achieve smooth working of the harvester.

For three consecutive harvests I was the boy leading the four. It was a full-time job for about three weeks and I was paid boy's wages in real money. I did not have a proper saddle but rode on a sack of hay strapped to my mount, and a couple of stirrups dangling from a leather piece thrown over the sack. I enjoyed the job immensely, in spite of being saddle-sore every evening. We stayed in the fields for a one hour lunch-break, having brought our own food and drinking water.

There was a young girl who would swap jobs with me for a while, to everybody's great amusement. She would ride like a man in her skirt, showing a lot of leg, and shout and laugh and joke with everybody around the field, while I tried hard to make about fifteen sheaves and stack them before she would appear again. I could not do it all by myself and usually the two girls, one on each end of my stretch, would help. At the end of the day, tired as we all were, the girls would bunch together and sing on the way home - beautiful Ukrainian songs.

Autumn meant gathering wild mushrooms, picking apples, the potato harvest, and endless potato-stalk fires in which potatoes were baked. I can almost smell the smoke from those fires to this day, and feel the taste of delicious hot baked potatoes. Our cottage would acquire a winter overcoat in the form of a one foot layer of straw, tightly packed from the ground to the roof, and held in position by vertical posts. And there would be a family winter shopping expedition to town for winter wear and boots, and lost buttons and things.

The migration of birds was quite spectacular. Storks would assemble in their hundreds on the shallow pond near the flour-mill and the adjacent meadows and for several days they would hold a conference and debate, and decide the important issues facing them. It was not a simple matter for the stork population in Northern Europe to evacuate itself to Africa. There were three established routes: one through the Balkans and Turkey, the second through Italy and Sicily, and the third through France and Spain. Then there was the election of group leaders, and what to do with the old and infirm. We would watch our group from a distance. Neither child nor adult would disturb them. The stork is a respected bird and if a pair builds a nest on top of a house and raises a family it also brings luck to the people of the house. Often an old cartwheel would be placed on top of a roof to provide an ideal base for a stork's nest, and a pair in search of a good site would gladly accept the invitation.

That it was a debate I had no doubt. They would stand on their thin legs in water a few inches deep, throw their heads back, beaks pointing to the sky, and make a frightful racket as if they were arguing furiously about something. Then they would relax, plod around a bit, catch a little frog or two, and start arguing again. The pond and meadows were excellent feeding grounds and it was obvious that they were also building up their strength before the long flight ahead of them. On the appointed day they would rise in their hundreds, circle the pond, gain height and take position in their respective 'V' formations. The first formation with the group leader at its head would set course south and other formations would place themselves behind, to the left and to the right of the first one, and away they would go. People would stop, look up, and watch; children would wave, shout "good-bye" and "see you next year". A few storks left behind would continue feeding, seemingly unconcerned, pretending that all was well. But all was not well, their end was approaching fast, they must have known it, and seemed to accept their fate with dignity; they commanded respect, not pity.

Cranes, too, would be moving south at about the same time. Their 'V' formations were much longer and they sang as they flew. It was a simple, sad, and continuous two-tone cry, followed by a short pause as if to punctuate the movement of their wings.

In winter we all wore high boots - boys, girls, mothers, fathers, everybody. The heels of boots had a metal rim on the outside and it was those rims that we skated on the frozen big pond before it was covered with many layers of snow. How was that done? Well, you had to take a few fast steps forward, or better still a run, angle your right boot, and put your weight on the right edge of the metal rim; the left foot would follow almost simultaneously, accept its share of body weight also on the right side of the rim but trailing behind a bit. With clear ice you could cover fifty yards in a straight line or a right curve. With left leg forward you could make a curve or a circle to the left, on the left edge of the rims of course. If you were skilled you could change the leading leg without stopping the movement. I spent hours with my friends doing just that. There were a few homemade skates about, consisting of an iron bit mounted on a piece of wood whose cross-section was in the form of a triangle. They would have to be tied on with strings to boots - a very wobbly and unsatisfactory affair.

Christmas was the highlight of winter. We always had a Christmas tree. The earliest one I remember was rather uninspiring and a poorly dressed thing with lots of homemade paper chains. Then, one year, it was all changed by a unanimous decision to spend money and buy things which would last from year to year and be the envy of the neighbourhood. Everybody contributed and Felek walked twelve kilometres to the nearest town and back over snow-covered roads on a clear but frosty day. Mother was worried that it was too far and too cold, but nothing would stop him. He brought back a sackful of wonders - coloured glass balls of different shapes and sizes, silver and gold glittering strings, an angel, small candles and holders, sparklers, sweets wrapped up in fancy coloured paper, and other bits and pieces. I could not believe my eyes, we were all delighted with his purchases, and when the tree was dressed it was truly magnificent.

Christmas Eve is THE day of the season in Poland. When the first star appeared shining bright in the sky our family would assemble by the Christmas tree, all in their Sunday best, and Father would break *opłatek* - a thin white bread wafer - with Mother and the five of us in order of seniority, wish each one of us well and give us a hug. Mother would do the same and so would the rest of us until everybody had broken the wafer and hugged everybody else. It was a brief, solemn moment, overflowing with emotion and there were tears in Mother's eyes when she smiled and kissed us all in turn.

The traditional meal which followed was not the elaborate affair which one reads about in magazines. Ours was an economy version, but we did start with *barszcz*, and we did follow with fish - salted herring though, not carp (the pond would be frozen) - and there were other tasty things to follow, until finally *kutia* would arrive. To make *kutia* you take wheat grains, allowing a handful per head, boil it in a little water until cooked, pound some poppy seeds and sugar with a pestle and mortar into a sticky mess, stir in a bit of butter, honey and cream, to achieve a consistency of mud, then mix it well with the wheat grains, taste it, correct the sweetness with honey and serve it cold. It looks terrible, a sort of pale mauve sludge, but it tastes really nice, if peculiar. Anyhow, it is different from anything you are likely to have tasted before in your life.

Kutia was a magic dish in so far that were you to throw a spoonful of it at the ceiling and if the wheat grains stuck to it, it would mean that the next cereal harvest would be good, and if not - expect disaster! To ensure a good harvest one should be liberal with the honey. Only once did we all have a go, to our mother's horror, and the whole ceiling had to be repainted. From then on we drew lots to decide who was to perform this prophetic ritual.

Vodka was drunk throughout the evening in minute glasses, always bottoms up, and after *kutia* father would treat us to his cherry vodka, which was the last course of our splendid meal.

There were never any Christmas presents at our home for anybody. Nobody expected any, and nobody was the worse for it; we were very happy without them.

Shortly before eleven p.m. two brothers would leave for a while and return with a pair and sledge well packed with straw, and straw bales to sit on. We would dress warmly, pile on and proceed to church for Midnight Mass, singing carols and picking up friends who were braving the elements on foot. I will never forget our family Christmas.

Easter was the real beginning of spring. Roll on Easter, people would say in winter, and everybody was longing for a bit of warmth in the sun. A few weeks before Easter all families would start making *Pisanki*. First you boil some eggs and let them cool. Then make a little tool, if you have not already got one, consisting of a conical tube with a fine hole at the narrow end and tied with thin wire to a wooden handle. Heat the tool and pour some molten wax into it and with it draw any design you fancy onto the egg surface. There were some beautiful traditional designs passed on from generation to generation. The wax would harden when cold and the eggs would be put into a vessel containing dye. The simplest and most popular dye was made out of the red outer skins of onions which were first boiled in water, left standing for a few days and strained. After a week or so the egg shells would absorb the warm red-brown colour, and they would be plunged into very hot water when the wax would dissolve and - hey presto! - the *Pisanki* were ready, a white design on a red background. You could have several colours by the same method, but that was a job for experts.

Pisanki would be admired, swapped, cracked, and eaten, and saved as models for the next year. Some were blessed in church and on Easter Sunday one or two were peeled and cut into small pieces on a plate. I remember Father holding the plate and wishing us all a happy Easter and each of us taking a piece of egg and eating it. It was not as solemn a ritual as on Christmas Eve with *opłatek*, but nice and warm none the less, bringing the family together again and generating a sense of unity and good will.

Our school-teacher showed us how to make a doll out of two whole egg shells which were joined together and stood upright, one on top of another. The top shell was painted as a face and the bottom as a body. I thought I would like to make one. I made two small holes on the opposite sides of each egg on the long axis, blew out the contents and thus acquired two empty shells. Then I melted some lead on the kitchen stove, put a small funnel into the hole of one egg shell and asked Father to hold it and cover the bottom hole with his finger, which he did. He was talking to a friend and hardly paid any attention to what I was doing. I then fetched the molten lead and poured it into the funnel and on to his finger. He yelled, the egg shell hit the ceiling, and he plunged his finger into cold water, looking quite bewildered. I was not very popular that evening.

It was customary, and therefore permitted, to throw a bucket of cold water over your neighbour on Easter Sunday morning provided he, or she, was not wearing Sunday best. You could use a jug, a saucepan, a bottle - anything went. Everybody was on guard, and everybody was trying to do the same thing. The result was that all ended soaking wet and swore revenge for next year. The story went that the squire's lot, and their guests, would sprinkle the ladies with eau de cologne, but the squire would pour buckets of water on the male populace just as we did.

A day before Whitsun week-end a horse and cart full of freshly cut, long, leafy branches would arrive and we would make holes in the ground outside the house, stick them firmly in, and create an instant garden of Eden for the next few days. This was done, I think, to honour the spring.

In spring storks, cranes, wild geese, and swallows would return again, and how nice it was to see them back. New life would explode everywhere, in the fields, meadows, and woods, by lakes and streams. Masses of marsh marigolds would encircle the shallow pond, and dramatic skies with fantastic clouds chasing one another would add to the enchantment and beauty of the season.

The School in Hrubieszów

It is strange how fate can arrange events and channel the lives of people in the most unexpected directions. It never entered anybody's head that my life would be any different from that of my brothers. After four years at our village school I would probably join a bigger school in the next village for another two years and that would be that as far as general education then went. I might have been apprenticed to a carpenter, which I would have liked, or a smithy, a shoe-maker, or a tailor - all four being available close to home. Alternatively, I could have taken any unskilled job on the estate to begin with, and learned something useful as I went along, like Janek. But this was not what fate had in store for me.

It happened that a young and very attractive girl graduate from Lwów university, Pani Stasia, was employed as my last governess, for Dziunia, the nonngest child of Mr Białkowski. She was excellent at her job and did Dziunia a power of good. She was lively, friendly, direct, and had a good sense of humour. She never treated anyone in a subordinate position as a lesser mortal, quite the contrary, she showed great interest in people, their families and children. She soon became well acquainted with all of us and particularly liked my parents and Władek. I was noticed with some interest: "A schoolboy - good - which form? Starting the fourth next year - I see. Do you like your school? Yes? That's unusual, boys do not like school much." Then we started playing a game. Whenever we met within shouting distance, she would yell at the top of her voice – "7 x 5?" and I would shout back "35" while playing with other boys or running, or whatever. Having given a wrong answer a few times and heard her reaction: "Wrong! Pull your socks up!" I sweated blood and learned my tables to perfection.

Pani Stasia examined my annual school reports, talked to my teacher and, by the time my final school report arrived, she had it all worked out and was ready for action. But before she made a move she persuaded the teacher to call a meeting of parents of the last form, which had never been done before. My father went and, as I heard later, they were all told that the 4th form did quite well on the whole and that we should seek more knowledge on our own and read as much as possible. But that there was 1 girl and 1 boy who showed promise and their parents should make every effort to send them to the gimnazjum (grammar school) in Hrubieszów, our district town. I was the boy. My parents and brothers were pleased but nobody took the suggestion seriously. After all, it would cost the earth, last eight years, and who could look that far ahead? What about the entrance examination? Formalities? Paper-work? Nobody knew where or when to begin even if the family decided to go ahead.

A few days later Pani Stasia made her first move. She talked to Władek and told him that she knew the teacher's views, agreed with him wholeheartedly, and suggested a meeting with the family to discuss it all. The meeting took place one evening and she offered to give me private tuition for one year and prepare me for the entrance examination to third form, which I might fail, but would certainly be accepted for the second; she had no doubt about it. What about the cost? She knew what everybody was earning and had it all worked out. Everybody who earned would have to contribute his share for about three years but when in the sixth, seventh, and eighth form I should be able to earn some money myself by giving private lessons to younger pupils; she had no doubt about that either. She was so positive that they agreed, very cautiously at first, and asked about her work – "How can we repay you?" She was ready for that too: "Oh! that's easy", she said, "As long as he works hard, makes good progress, and you are all nice to me, that is all the reward I want".

I had one year of the best tuition with the nicest tutor I could wish for there was a lot of homework everyday and more for weekends. I still had time to play with my pals, but not as much as before. There were no summer holidays free of school for me that year, but I did not mind at all. I worked hard and really enjoyed it. There was something new every day and she knew how to get the most out of me and keep me fully stretched. But I had some dark thoughts too. I wondered where all this would lead me to. I did not like the thought of living away from home, amongst strangers, not knowing a soul. I would miss my parents and my brothers terribly. Would I not rather be a good carpenter? What would I do after I matriculated? On the other hand, there was the excitement of the unknown, and the urge to go on. I was curious, I wanted to look and see what was beyond the horizon.

We started learning the German language from the word *go*, and the basis of German grammar was firmly drummed into my head for ever. The only expensive book we bought was a world atlas - fascinating! I loved geography - it was like going on a long journey, further and further around the world.

The year simply flew by in no time at all. I hardly noticed what was going on around me, but there were some important changes. The field-work overseer became ill and died. Various duties were rearranged and the squire, estate manager, and my father absorbed the additional work between them. Not surprisingly the manager fell in love with Pani Stasia hook, line, and sinker. At first she was just friendly towards him and no more than that, but his ardour and devotion began to make an impression on her slowly but surely. I noticed that he was getting in our way more and more frequently and my lessons were cut short occasionally - he was becoming a nuisance. (He won in the end. Pani Stasia fell in love, and decided to marry him against the advice of her family. They stayed on the estate for about a year and then moved to Hrubieszów.)

My father's new duties brought him even closer to the people in the village. He had to go there more often to call for casual workers - women mostly - which was particularly important in summer and autumn. Neither he nor my brothers had any enemies in the village, quite the contrary, we had several friends there. It was unfortunate for the relationship between Poles and Ukrainians that some anti-Polish agitators at that time were starting their dirty work among the Ukrainian-speaking villagers. The history of relations between ethnic Poles and the Ukrainian minority is very sad and at times downright tragic and bloody. There are many old wounds and old scores to settle on both sides. During the period of Poland's partition Austrians played a cynical game by inciting and encouraging friction which often led to arson and murder. The Soviet Union did the same in 1940, particularly in and around the city of Lwów.

The only unpleasant local incident I remember occurred on a certain Sunday evening one summer when my three brothers and four of their friends walked to the village shop and stopped near the village green where an open-air dance was about to start. They had a brief chat with some girls they knew, proceeded to make their purchases and on the way home passed the green without stopping this time. When they were about a hundred yards away from the green a crowd of young men brandishing sticks surged forward with shouts and yells in pursuit of the seven-strong party. My brothers and their friends assessed the odds correctly and retreated at a gallop towards our home, being chased by some twenty to twenty-five well armed, blood-thirsty young fellows. This went on for some five hundred yards more until the 'magnificent seven' retreated inside, bolted the main door, grabbed anything which would serve as a weapon and took up posts in the hall and by the windows in readiness to repel the invaders should they try to break in. When the pursuing lot reached our front door they milled around shouting, swearing, laughing, and banging on the door with sticks, inviting the seven to come out and fight. At that moment my father walked in on the scene coming back from the stables. He had a sound walking stick with him, which would not do him much good had they turned on him, but they did not. He shouted at them in Ukrainian to be quiet, and when the noise subsided he asked them why they were there, what was it all about, and getting some answers from the inside and hardly any from the outside. He ordered them to 'get the hell' out of our yard or take the consequences with the police. He knew some of them by name and promised them a chat with their fathers. To every-body's surprise the warriors retreated sheepishly. I watched it all from a distance as I arrived at the scene shortly before Father. A bottle of vodka was opened and Father's bloodless victory was celebrated in style. Mother was not there which was just as well, because she would probably have flown at them with a frying pan and inflicted serious injury on somebody. Władek was away, to his regret. He had some ideas on how they could have accepted the battle against overwhelming odds and still won, but I do not remember the intended stratagem.

My four brothers were a force to be reckoned with. They were hardly ever engaged in a brawl or a real fight. On one occasion though, when their friend was attacked outside a house where a dance was held, and called for help, two brothers jumped through a window and two ran through the door and managed to beat off the villains. Some blows were exchanged, and bruises were in evidence, but no bones were broken. Their prompt action met with general approval and, having inspected their bruises, Mother was quite satisfied that they had acted properly and no harm was done.

Władek married Victoria and their baby girl was born at a proper time. They lived in a one room cottage on the other side of ours. We all made a great fuss of the baby and Victoria was very proud of her beautiful little daughter.

Pani Stasia arranged everything regarding the entrance examination, which was competitive, and Władek found accommodation for me with the school janitor for the next school year. The examination was held in July and it all went as Pani Stasia had predicted. I did not quite make it for the third form but they were glad to accept me for the second, starting on 1st September 1929. There was jubilation at home and I basked in glory for the whole month of August.

I was kitted out, everything brand new, expensive, and slightly too big to make it last longer. The uniform was navy blue with a stock collar jacket. A few years later the design was changed and we had to wear black ties and white shirts. Similarly with caps - at first it was a handsome four corner cap and later a round navy cap of the same design as the famous Marshal Piłsudski cap called *Maciejówka*, which he wore during the First World War and until the end of his life.

Within the first ten minutes in my new school I had a traumatic experience which left a scar. I found my classroom and sat quietly in the corner on the last bench near a window. Several boys and girls who knew each other chatted, laughed, and moved about. Then a schoolmaster came in, asked us to sit down, and said that he would now read the register and would the one whose name was read stand up and say "present". He would not require us to stand up again - just this once so that we might get acquainted quicker. All went well until my name was read and

I stood up and said "present". To my amazement everybody looked at me and laughed; even the master had a smile on his face. I went scarlet realising that it was my name they were laughing at. Nobody had laughed at my name at the village school, but they laughed here. I was shocked, angry, and resentful. I stared back at the laughing faces; I felt my eyes getting moist and tried desperately not to cry but I failed and a few tears rolled down my cheeks. The heads turned away, the laughter ceased and for a moment there was a dead silence, and only the master and I were standing and looking at each other. "Sit down" he said. I sat down, gazing straight ahead at nothing in particular.

"It is not the name that makes a man, but the other way around, remember that all of you", he said, and went on reading the register. I thought hard about what he said, made some resolutions, and was ready for the next time whenever it would come.

I do not know the origins of our family name but I have heard that it was a practice of some Austrian civil servants when issuing identity papers to people who had none, or had lost them, and could not read, to invent names for their own amusement. This might have been the case with us, or not, but it could have been as our name sounds like the name for a bedbug. Jews from Eastern Europe settling down in England, and in Leeds in particular, before the first World War had similar experiences because they could not spell.

Nobody laughed again when my name was read and gradually it simply meant me, the boy in the corner, the last on the bench, and nothing else. The whole school heard of our first roll call of course, but it did not matter really to anybody except me - I never forgot that first day.

The following two months were extremely difficult. I shared a small room with an older boy who was a bully. I suffered his antics until I could stand it no longer and we had a fight. It was a draw, at least I thought so, and he behaved decently ever afterwards. I was very lonely, my heart was not in my work, and I thought of home a lot. People would smile and exchange a few words but I could not respond, it was too soon, I could not trust anybody.

The school day comprised of five one hour periods from 0800 to 1300 hours, six days a week, except Saturdays, when the last period ended at midday. There was a break of ten minutes between periods with an extended one of twenty minutes starting at 11 o'clock, to give us time for refreshment. People ate whatever they brought to school with them. Some would run along the main street to a very nice Polish equivalent of a French charcuterie, owned by Mr Krasnopolski, where they would cut a fresh roll in half and fill it with delicious ham, pâté, smoked sausage, or whatever you asked for. The janitor's family fed me well and I had a snack for elevenses like everybody else - I was never hungry. Some time later the Parent's Committee set up a milk stall on the school premises where one could buy a glass of milk. I was given some tickets for free milk but after I used a few I threw the rest away - I did not want any milk unless I could pay for it like everybody else.

There were three consecutive days free of school on that first autumn, from Saturday to Monday. I asked the janitor for permission to go home if I could find a lift to Wereszyn and he agreed. I went to the market on Friday afternoon and talked to several men with horses and carts and found one who lived in Witków, some three kilometres from my home. I offered him 1 shilling for the lift which he accepted, But I had to wait for hours until he was ready to leave. We arrived at his farm late, it was pitch dark, and he and his wife insisted that I should stay the night, which I was glad to do. They were very kind, gave me some supper and a glass of milk, and bread for breakfast the next morning.

I was so pleased to be home again. My parents and brothers welcomed me warmly but they were surprised at my unexpected appearance and questioned me about school, quarters, and food; was everything alright?

"Yes, yes, everything is fine, really fine; lessons are no problem, I can cope, there is nothing to worry about, all is well, really," - I tried my best to assure them. Mother put an end to it by saying that they all missed me very much and were glad I could come, and perhaps I missed them too a bit, which is as it should be. I had two wonderful days at home and intended to walk twenty-one kilometres to Hrubieszów on Monday, hoping to catch a lift part of the way. But father would not hear of it and in the end Janek drove me back. Back at school I thought about my visit home with mixed feelings - Janek should have been working on the estate instead of driving me back… it must have been embarrassing for Father to ask the squire for horses needed somewhere else… I should have walked back… I should have stayed at my digs instead of dashing home like mad… it was a bit childish really… I must not do it again.

Our *gymnasjum* was named after Stanisław Staszic - a local celebrity and scientist who did important work for the country and the region in his time. The building had two floors and had the shape of a capital letter 'L'. The main entrance was situated on the short leg facing the pavement and the main street. To the right of the school gate and along the edge of the pavement ran a high fence for about seventy yards. To the left stood the Catholic church and on the opposite side of the main street, but a bit farther, was the Orthodox church with its onion-like domes pointing to the sky. The *gymnasjum* and the Catholic church were very good neighbours, but the two churches were only on nodding terms.

On the ground floor were six classrooms, secretary's office, janitor's office, boys' and girls' cloakrooms, store rooms, etc., and on the first floor were two more classrooms, assembly room, staff rooms, Head's office, library, and the Head's flat. All rooms were heated by tiled, coal-burning slow combustion stoves, which were lit early every morning for about six months of the year. Underneath the ground floor were several cellars used mostly for storing coal. At the back of the school was a fair sized mud yard with fences on the left and right and two more buildings on the opposite side. They were right on the edge of a very steep river bank. The smaller of the two buildings consisted of a janitor's flat and some store-rooms, and the bigger had a carpentry workshop, French language classroom, physics and chemistry laboratory, dental and medical room, and single quarters for one master. The boys' lavatories were in a far right corner of the yard, but the girls had theirs indoors.

The tuition was free. The school provided a lending library, ink, and chalk for blackboards. Everybody had to buy text-books, exercise books, pencils, pens, water-colours, brushes, drawing paper, etc. At the beginning of each school year one could buy second-hand text-books from chaps or girls who moved up a class. Everybody did this and we looked after our books as they were our capital investment. To support the school a parents' organisation was formed a few years before my arrival, which decided to build an extension and provide a fully equipped gymnasium. This was a colossal project which necessitated a compulsory levy of two hundred zloty a year for every one of us. Pani Stasia had it reduced by half for me after lengthy arguments and a means test.

The gym project was completed about one year after I joined the school, and immediately another was started - a sports field, running track, changing rooms, and stores, and diving board. The field was by the river and the shortest access to it was by a footbridge built for free by the sappers of our cavalry regiment. This was a great asset and a joy to all.

Hrubieszów was the seat of local government; it had administration offices, a court, police H.Q., hospital, two dental surgeries, one pharmacy, a large primary school, a girls' secondary vocational school, boys' secondary engineering school, our grammar-type school, coal power station, main railway station, one hotel, one cinema, one tennis court, a Jewish Synagogue and their teaching and social establishment, a para-military organisation called *Strzelec* (riflemen), a gymnastic organisation called *Sokół* (Falcon) and one gentlemen's club. The 2nd Mounted Riflemen Regiment had its barracks about one and a half kilometres outside the town.

The town was built on an island formed by two branches of the Huczwa river - a fair sized tributary of the river Bug. To get to the heart of the town one had to cross one of the three bridges, but the town over-spilled considerably to the west and north west, where the ground was higher. Adjacent to the river on three sides and facing the island were lovely meadows and beyond them splendid oak woods in one place, conifers in another, and four villages within a five kilometres radius, as well as some individual houses dotted here and there. The population was over 10,000 I think, and probably 50% Jewish. Most of the shops and warehouses were owned by Jews and they also dominated certain trades such as tailors and shoe-makers. Other fields were pretty well mixed - there were non-Jewish and Jewish doctors, dentists, lawyers, photographers, etc. Jews were well organised as a community, they had intelligent leaders, and looked after their own with compassion and generosity. Most of them practised their religion but socialists were drifting away from the orthodox believers. The socialist organisation was called Bund and they had ideological connections with the Polish Socialist Party (PPS). Bund had its own weekly paper in Polish which I read with interest, by courtesy of a pretty girl. Their two outstanding leaders - Adler was one of them - were executed by the Soviet invaders in 1939 or 40.

Religion was treated very seriously at our school. A Catholic priest - Father Tarkowski - was on the staff and a story went around that he was a cavalry officer before he became a holy man. That probably explains why his Mass never lasted more that half an hour, and sermons were another five minutes only - short and to the point, no waffling. His about turn at the altar, followed by "Dominus vobiscum", was executed with parade ground precision and it was great to watch. He was a good man and respected by Christians and non-Christians alike, and we did not think that it was his idea to have a roll-call before Mass every Sunday - orders from above more likely. He taught us scripture, history of the church, ethics, as well as something about other Christian churches, Mahomet and Buddha. When a form had a religion period Catholics, being in a majority, would stay in the classroom, whilst Jews would proceed to another room for a chat with a rabbi, and the Orthodox lot would do the same with their holy man.

Our masters were upright, hard-working and under-paid men and women and I remember most of them with affection and respect. We were required to address them formally by the title "Professor"; the term "teacher" applied to schools of lower status.

Polish language and literature were taught by Dr Felicja Szczepańska - a four foot nothing mother of a small child. She was marvellous. She had complete control all the time and could make all the class participate in a discussion with ease. She opened my eyes to the greatness of Polish prose and poetry and it is thanks to her that I acquired an insatiable desire to read.

Professor Dubik was a history master - short, dark, with a big moustache and a hunch-back, very demanding, hard but fair, and a very good teacher. You had to swot facts and dates, yes, but you also had to relate, compare, analyse and consider neighbours in the east, west, south and north. One of his questions in the last year was Polish-German relations from Mieszko I - well, that was a thousand years of history. He would listen, fire a question or two, then ask somebody else to continue, and we could spend two periods like that. Everybody had to be ready to carry on if asked, hoping to do reasonably well.

Lucjan Świdziński - our form master - taught mathematics. He was about fifty years old, tall, with dark hair, well built, moustache, patient, and persevering. He would not move forward until he thought that even the dimmest amongst us understood what he was about. He was a dedicated and politically active social democrat. Occasionally he would steal five minutes of his period to talk to us on some important aspect of current affairs. I saw him, once, speaking at an open-air political meeting, so I stopped and listened with great interest until a policeman told me firmly to push off. I tried to argue that I had the right to listen but he was much bigger than me.

I do not remember the name of a jovial, fattish, middle-aged master of Latin and ancient history. On entering his classroom he would shout at the top of his voice: "Salve pueros!" and we would roar back in our thin voices "Salve Magister!" Smiles on all faces - a good beginning to any period. I loved mythology and ancient history but it took me two years out of five to enjoy Latin.

Professor Jopyk was the German language master. Not an inspiring personality but a good, conscientious teacher. I owe a lot to him as he started me as a private tutor to youngsters of reasonably well-off parents, whose German he wanted to see improved. He did this for my last three years - thank you, Professor Jopyk!

Physics and Chemistry were rather poorly taught by Professor Baruś. The man could not explain things clearly, but everything was in text-books so it did not matter. Nature and Geography were dropped somewhere before the 6th form. Philosophy in the last form was by way of an introduction only with no examinations and no real work was required.

PT was most enjoyable. I was not good at anything in particular but had a go at whatever was on.

In the eighth form we all took the matriculation examination, which was the requirement for university courses. The better the marks, the better chance of getting in, as the numbers of places were limited. I took Polish literature, German, History and Maths. Everybody had to take four subjects but you could take French instead of German, and Physics instead of Maths. Our school was a 'humanistic' type, but there was also a 'classical' type with compulsory Greek and Latin final examinations, and 'Mathematical cum natural sciences' type where Latin was not required.

My marks at the end of the second form were low, mostly 'pass'. The end of the third form was a bit better. But it was only in the fourth form that I started to feel confident and began to compete with the cream of the class, realising though that I still had a lot of catching up to do. Then, to my utter surprise I was elected for one year as the form's head boy by an overwhelming majority of my class-mates. I had to chair the form's regular meetings under the patronage of the form master, who was there to advise on procedural matters. The object was to learn how to run, in a democratic way, our own affairs, such as they were. This brought me into contact with seven other elected head boys, and with the Headmaster who appeared to treat us very seriously. I did my stint without making any great blunders, nor did I distinguish myself in any way either, nevertheless I noticed that I acquired a little prestige which was rather nice. And yet I felt that there were so many things that most of the boys and girls knew which I did not, saw which I did not see; they had been to places I had never heard of before. I did not belong to their world, but I had already left my own behind and there was no way back. I had to move ahead, I had a lot more learning to do than most of the class.

At the end of the fourth form my marks moved up and I had one 'very good!', some 'good', and some 'satisfactory'. It was a reasonable mix and I was satisfied and so was Pani Stasia. She and her husband had just moved to a bigger flat and offered me digs should I wish to change. They agreed to have the same payment in cash and in kind as the janitor and it was all arranged for the start of the fifth form. I stayed with them one year but Pani Stasia and her husband had a serious marital problem. I found it distressing and had to move to other digs. I was very fond of them both, they were the link with my past, and supported me until the day I left. Eventually they solved their problem very well, raised a family, and lived reasonably contented lives.

Our school gave a pantomime of a sort after Christmas when I was in the fifth form. There were lots of animals in it and I was the bear, wearing a fur coat inside out and a mask made in the school workshop. I was moving about on all fours making friendly noises, when somebody threw a sweet in a fancy wrapper at me. I stood up, unwrapped the sweet, put it in my mouth and roared with delight, clapping my paws and jumping up and down. This brought a shower of sweets and approving noises from the audience. From then on I was in every school play and loved it.

In the last two months of the fifth form I earned some money for helping a small boy with his homework at the request of his mother. It was enough for a short scout camp during summer holidays, but I changed my mind and instead took a teaching job during August. I earned fifty zloty, enough to buy a school uniform winter coat which I did not have. It lasted for three years and I was very pleased with it.

In the sixth form I began to earn real money being recommended to parents as a suitable tutor by two masters. First it was a girl with a German language problem. Then two more girls who needed help with homework - all three being in the second form. I told my parents that I would provide my own clothing and shoes in future. They were glad that Pani Stasia's predictions were correct. During that year I bought a pair of black shoes, shirts, white detachable collars, which I was taking to the laundry run by nuns for washing and starching, underwear, a warm scarf, gloves, socks, and whatever else I needed and could afford. At the end of the year I still had enough money saved to pay my way for a two week scout camp near Gdynia, on the Baltic coast. This time nothing would change my mind - I went.

The Scout movement was very popular in Poland and our school was proud of its group which was about fifty strong. I was a patrol leader for a while but gave it up as soon as I started giving private lessons and became the group secretary and diary keeper.

We arrived at Gdynia first thing in the morning. I was still dozing in my seat when I heard somebody shouting "The sea! Look! The sea!" I jumped to the window and there it was - an incredible expanse of water as far as the eye could see. I gazed at it in wonderment, full of awe, amazed, and struck by its vastness, its powerful presence, laying there quietly and glittering in the rising sun. "So this is what the sea looks like" - I thought - marvellous! just marvellous! I could not think of a better word.

We made our camp in a clearing of fine old pine woods within one kilometre of the sea and about seven kilometres from Gdynia. General supervision, supplies and money were handled by our P.T. master. The running of the camp cooking and training was the business of the council of elders with the group leader in the chair. My job was to keep the detail diary – "make it a readable thing, not just facts and figures and remember Pani Szczepańska will have a look at it" - were the final words of my chief. I had a completely free hand and was excused all duties and exercises. After breakfast all patrols, except the one on camp duties, would disappear on their various Red Indian war games, or whatever, while I would aim for the beach - we had glorious weather all the time. I attended most of the debriefings of patrols and patrol leaders and knew well what was going on. The P.T. master was taking photographs on my request and the diary began to grow nicely with a bit of embroidery here and there. My aim was to impress Pani Szczepańska first and foremost, and I think I succeeded.

We soon struck an acquaintance with girl scouts who were billeted in a school nearby under the watchful eyes of many school mistresses. They invited us to their camp fire which was a great success. We reciprocated and again it was fun - we had good story-tellers, mimics, and of course we all sung to our hearts content. When the singing was over little Zosia was asked to say 'Our Father' while we all listened silently, flames flickering in the gentle breeze, and the night closing in on us rapidly. Then came the finale: *'Idzie Noc'* (the night is coming) sung quietly at first, then hummed quieter and quieter until the sound was no more. From that moment no loud talking was permitted and all should disperse to their tents. We whispered farewells to the girls, winked at the pretty ones, waved for as long as we could see them and that was that - the end of another lovely day.

There were other scouts camping in the area and a combined camp fire was arranged for about six groups. When we all sung together we must have been heard in heaven - there was joy, good will, and friendship ringing in our voices, and no evil spirits could have possibly touched us at such a time - later perhaps, but not at a camp fire.

Our school had no boarding facilities. 'Digs' in private houses, although checked and approved by a master, were often below adequate standards. Accordingly the parents committee acquired two old houses and after some conversions and extensions provided proper facilities for about twenty-five boys and fifteen girls, including kitchen, dining room, showers, wash-rooms, and a flat for Professor Baruś and his wife, whose job was to look after the boarders. As soon as I started the seventh form he talked to me and said that the boarding house was full and that he needed somebody who would live-in and act as head of the boys' house, helping him supervise the younger lot in particular and see that the rules were observed. He thought of me and suggested that I might like to take the job in exchange for free board and lodging. I jumped at the offer and moved in next day. I sent a letter home with the good news. All that they still had to contribute was a hundred zloty a year payable in two instalments, which I could not meet on my own yet, not the first instalment anyhow. I reduced my private lessons to the most profitable two and decided to spend more time on my own work, bearing in mind that in less than two years I would be taking the final examination.

It was a great year. Right at the beginning of it I told a sweet Jewish girl that I loved her, and she told me that she loved me too, and we promised to love each other for ever. It was all very innocent like most school romances in my days, but we did not miss an opportunity to fall into each other's arms whenever there was one. It was fashionable for Jewish girls to fall for a Goy, announce at once that it was all hopeless, and on alternate days to be blissfully happy and utterly miserable; but "What could one do? Such was life!" they would whisper, rolling their beautiful eyes and trying hard to impersonate their ancient sisters in Greek tragedies. Jewish boys did not like it, but they knew that in the end the girls would be marrying them, not us, and as every girl must have her Goy, it was better for them to have one sooner than later and get it out of their systems.

Some of the girls were called at school, and at home, by their Christian names, like Maryśka, a diminutive of Mary, and Helka, a diminutive of Helena. The former was a beautiful daughter of Mr Grynszpan, a dentist, and they emigrated to Mexico before the war. The latter was the one who promised to love me for ever, but recognised the hopelessness of it all before I did. She married a Goy while deported to a labour camp in the Soviet Union. Her husband was a half-Colonel in the Polish army when they left the country and emigrated to Australia. They have a son and a daughter and somehow I am sure they are a happy family.

All together there were four Jewish girls and three boys in my form. Of the three boys one, Chaim Rojter, was a talented violinist, a nice chap and my rival. Hersz Regel was a good, hard-working all-rounder and definitely one of the gang. His elder sister was the belle of the town. Horowicz was an outstanding mathematician, very capable, very poor, and an active communist. He noticed that I was reading the Bund's weekly paper which Helka was lending me regularly, and thought that I was ripe for something stronger, bearing in mind that I was one of the proletariat like himself. We arranged to meet every Sunday after Church and study some serious author to begin with and see how we got on. The first time we met he took me to a semi-derelict house where we climbed some stairs up, and then down, through a darkish passage, and ended eventually in a room with a table and a few chairs and nothing else. The place looked grim and its only window was high, near the ceiling. I had no idea where I was. He produced "The Political Economy" by Bukharin, and we dug into it with gusto. We never went to the same place again but used a porch in a nice house instead.

It was not too bad at first, in spite of some reservations I tried to express mildly but was overruled, until we came to specifics. Far too materialistic, I thought, and everything pre-planned, nothing can go wrong, just follow the line and your leader. Individuals did not seem to matter, people were tools of some supreme creed whose aim was to bring about heaven on earth, for there was no heaven possible anywhere else. The trouble was that people had to use force and be beastly to one another to create this heaven on earth, and to continue using force to perpetuate its existence. We began to differ. The crunch came when at a certain point Bukharin ridiculed the concept of soul and attacked all religions. What is this 'soul'? Is it located in any particular part of the body and, if so, which? If it is in every particle of the human body what would happen to it if someone lost a leg or an arm? Would we also lose a proportion of our soul? and so on, and so on. I had had enough. I said that man had believed in the supernatural since the beginning of time, whereas atheism had become a state religion only since the Soviet Revolution. And would they succeed even if they closed all churches, imprisoned all priests and outlawed religious practices? If their arguments are so sound why not try to convince people and let them choose freely? This was how Christian religion started and grew in spite of every conceivable opposition. The Romans could not kill the faith of a handful of Christians, and what about Jews and Jehovah? And you and your soul? Have you not got one? I would have no more of it and we agreed to differ fundamentally on Bukharin. I promised not to talk about it to anybody and kept to my word. The communist party was outlawed in Poland at that time. As for Bukharin, Robert Conquest described what sort of a man he really was in his book "The Great Terror", and how Stalin, his master, played with his life like a cat with a mouse until he had him executed.

On the evening of 12th May 1935 Marshal Piłsudski died at the age of sixty-seven. The whole nation went into mourning. Although expected, his death shocked the people. A wave of sorrow, grief, uncertainty and fear swept the country. What now? Who was to guide the nation in these dangerous times? With Hitler in the west, and Stalin in the east, Poland was again in a precarious position - between the two proverbial grinding stones. We needed a man of vision, a statesman with qualities required at a critical time at the helm of the nation's affairs. People will argue for a long time to come as to which way Poland's destiny might have moved had the great Marshal retained his intellectual and physical powers for another ten years. Had it been so, and whatever might have followed, I for one, would have been convinced that the wisest course was chosen and the best possible effort made. As it happened lesser men were at the helm, but their patriotism, sincerity, and devotion to the cause cannot be questioned; each one of them, politicians and generals alike, tried their best for Poland - what else could one ask of them?

I think it was in the first term of the seventh form that we discussed the possibility of having a shop on the school premises selling pens, pencils, exercise books, etc. The form master liked the idea and said: "What you really ought to do is to have a co-operative shop. If everybody buys at least one share you would have the capital and general support, and it would be a useful experience". An organising committee was elected there and then and given one week to think about it and draft Articles of Association for discussion with the master. Three of us worked hard and produced a one page effort which we thought was not too bad. Lucek (we called him by his first name behind his back) looked at it and said: "Yes, you have managed to point your thoughts in the right direction and if we combine your draft with my notes we might end up with a proper job". He then unfolded several pages covered with his neat hand-writing and point by point, reading and explaining, opened our eyes as to how involved the whole thing was and how important it was to safeguard share-holder's rights and interests. Next, a meeting of the whole school was held where everything was explained and everybody was invited to buy shares. The Articles of the Association were displayed on the School main notice-board for all to see. It was a resounding success. The shareholder's meeting elected the management and the audit board and passed the Articles. We were off, and business was booming, until a few months later when several Jewish boys and girls came to me with their share certificates and asked for their money back. "Changed my mind" was the stock answer to my questions. When one of my pals came to do likewise I refused and demanded an explanation:

"If you want the truth, all Jews will withdraw their support unless you change your business methods!" -

"What is wrong with our methods? What are you talking about?" -

"You buy only in Christian shops and nothing at all in Jewish shops. You should buy at both on a pro rata basis" -

"We tried, but were given a better discount in Christian shops. This is good business, is it not?" -

"Yes, but you should have told the Jewish shops to give you the same discount and they would have!" -

"O.K., we will try again if you take those shares and sell them back to the former holders, agreed?" -

"Agreed!"

There were no more problems, but there was a lesson to be learned there - Lucek was right.

I had two relatively minor health problems in school, and it is because of the way they were tackled that I think it might be worth mentioning them. Early in the fourth form I had some sort of infection in my right thumb, which became inflamed, swollen, and painful. The janitor took me to the school doctor who looked at it and told me that he would have to open it and that I was to come to the hospital at three pm. I went and he was ready for me in a small treatment room where he was attended by a big, strong man. The doctor said that he would hold my arm and hand to make his work easier. The fellow stood with his back to me, put my right arm under his right arm, gripped my forearm and hand, placed it on the table and held it firmly there. My nose was touching his back just above his waist and I could see nothing at all. Then, suddenly,

I felt an excruciating pain. I yelled, kicked, and pulled at my arm, all to no avail. The doctor made a couple of deep incisions, let the blood run for a while, put a dressing inside, bandaged my thumb, and only then was I released from the iron grip. He told me to come back in three days to have the dressing changed and everything should now be alright. I was in a state of semi-shock when I walked out of that room. Three days later a nurse unwrapped the bandage, stuck together with blood, and eventually only the dressing inside the thumb was left. She fiddled with the bits which stuck out, distracted my attention and with one sharp movement jerked it out. I yelled, blood poured out, and I was ready to hit her. She bandaged the thumb and told me to come again in three days. I never went, the thumb became septic and when my brother Władek saw it three weeks later he took me to a well known Jewish doctor who was very gentle and explained everything he was doing. I saw him three times and the thumb cost the family twenty-five zloty - more than a pair of good shoes.

In the seventh form I had a bad toothache. Our school dentist was a very attractive, tall young lady who had just joined a dental set-up in our town. She examined my tooth and decided that it must come out. "It will hurt, but I am sure you can take it" - she said sweetly - the viper! "Open your mouth wide, grip the sides of the chair and hold it firmly, keep your eyes shut…, yes… that's right" - then she yanked my tooth with a twist hoping to get it out with one mighty pull, but it refused to budge. She tried it again quickly and broke the tooth. I felt as if my head was coming apart, the pain was terrible and there was still the root to be removed somehow. I did not make a sound but my forehead was dripping with perspiration. I rinsed my mouth, spitting blood, and we both had a rest. She was sorry it did not come out at the first go but she must get the root out. She did it eventually. It was hell, but when it was all over I was surprised to see her more distressed than I was. She went very pale, drank a glass of water and sat down. We looked at one another, half smiling, and I murmured -

"We have won!" - She stood up, put her arm around my shoulder and said -

"Thank you! Go home, lie down and rest a bit, I will square it up for you".

She was soft and tender and I thought I could kiss her now, if it was not for my bleeding tooth.

In the last term of the seventh form we were advised of the availability of paramilitary summer camps - everything 'on the house'. I opted for a gliding camp near the source of the river Wisła, in the hills of south western Poland, together with a classmate of mine, Bolek Rządkowski. We were issued with khaki-drill uniforms and a railway warrant and away we went. It was a long journey with changes at Przemyśl and Kraków where we had a few hours to explore and were glad of it. Przemyśl was rather drab, sprawling in a disorderly fashion, and it had not yet recovered from the hammering it had during the First World War. What I saw of Krakow, and it was very little, I thought beautiful, and I promised myself to come back one day and walk every street of it. I wanted to see the resting place of our great Kings and Marshal Piłsudski, Wawel, Kościuszko Mount, the Cathedral, University, and all the wonders of this most Polish of Polish cities. It was some fifty years before I could fulfil this promise. And by then Lwów, and Wilno, the two bastions of Polish culture in the eastern parts, were part of the Soviet Union.

The gliding camp was under canvas, efficiently run by the military, with plenty of good food. There must have been a hundred of us from all parts of the country. We were divided into groups of about ten with an instructor in charge who was also the mother and father and a friend to his lot. At least that was the intention.

Our instructor was a warrant officer in a smart uniform. I think he was a retired Polish Air Force pilot. He lined us up in a single file and gave us a short lecture on psychology, which went something like this: "You might be surprised if I begin with psychology. As it happens I know something about it. You see, by looking at your physical appearance, I can tell which of you will finish the course and who will fail. There are four physical types of humans: Picnic, Choleric, x and y (I forget the last two). Cholerics never make it, some Picnics do, some don't, and the other two types are O.K. Now let me look at you." - He walked in silence up and down our file, scrutinising everybody from head to foot, and back several times, then stopped, and continued – "You! and you!" - he said, pointing his finger at two chaps, one of them being Bolek, my mate, - "are Cholerics. You will never make it, but try, do your best, I will do my best, and let us hope I am wrong. Mind you, I have never been wrong before and I will eat my hat if you prove me wrong, but let us not pre-judge events. Right, this is your glider called *Wrona* (Crow), and we shall now begin learning how to fly the thing, and by the time I finish with you, birds will be watching you with amazement!" They were, he was right.

The *Wrona* was a peculiar flying machine. It was built entirely of wood, canvas, glue, and a few screws. Its design could not have been simpler. A rectangular wing with two ailerons was joined in the middle at 90° to one end of a long main spar. At the other end was the tail unit. From the tail ran another main spar below, and at a sharp angle to the first spar, but in the same vertical plane. The bottom spar extended forward beyond the leading edge of the wing, and perched on it was the pilot's seat, joy-stick, and rudder bars. The two main spars were joined by secondary spars. The construction was very strong, cheap, and it was easy to change broken parts and repair it. There was no cabin, trousers would flap in flight, and you would see the ground between your feet - like flying a broomstick.

The first lesson was on how to make short jumps and not to bend the contraption in the process. For that we used muscle power alone and this is how it was done: the tail end of the glider was fixed by a quick-release catch to a strong metal post driven hard into the ground, The pilot-to-be fastened his belt, took the joy-stick into his right hand, his legs resting on the rudder control, whilst somebody else lifted one end of the wing from the resting position on the ground and held the wing parallel to the ground. Right in the nose of the bottom main spar was a hook. A long elastic rope would be laid on the ground forming the letter 'V' with the sharp point near the hook. When the rope was attached to the hook, three chaps at each end of the rope ran at the command "GO!" and pulled the elastic rope. On the command: "OFF!" a chap sitting by the tail released the catch and the glider would be catapulted into the air and land having made a short jump. The trick at this stage was to hold all controls in neutral position and let the glider do its own flying and landing. These short jumps were carried out on flat ground. A slight movement of the joy-stick resulted in a rapid climb or descent, ending in either a stall and heavy thump on the ground, or a few fast and hard bounces which were called 'kangaroos'. The two 'Cholerics', as expected, were masters in these spectacular manoeuvres. As we progressed, so we moved up the mountain slope higher and higher until we reached the top, employing horse power to pull the glider up. Straight flights were then followed by turns, circles, and spirals to the left and right, and always landing at a pre-selected field.

Having done all this we moved up to a better glider, *Salamandra* (Salamander). The two 'Cholerics' by that time were safely home, glad to escape alive from their instructor. They had got as far as three-quarters up the mountain. One day they had both landed on top of young conifers inflicting serious injury to their gliders but none to themselves. Our instructor was triumphant:

"What did I tell you? Wasn't I right? If only my bosses had more sense and kept Cholerics away from gliders we would save ourselves a lot of trouble, but no, nobody listens to me." It was difficult for us to tell him that 'Cholerics' in other groups were doing quite well and that only his 'Cholerics' always failed.

The *Salamandra* was a different bird altogether. It had an open cabin protecting the pilot's body as far as his shoulders. Its construction was similar to the *Wrona's* with an improved wing design and consequently better performance. After a few familiarisation flights we entered an exciting phase - soaring above and along the ridge. The take-off was the well-proven muscle power straight into the wind - a middling breeze was ideal - all hands running down the slope and pulling like hell. The glider would immediately rise some fifty feet above the ridge pointing windward, then a gentle elongated figure '8' was flown between the central line of the ridge and the windward slope. Once the central line was crossed the glider would be sucked down and had to force-land down-wind with unpleasant consequences. With a good breeze one could carry on soaring, always turning into the wind, for as long as good conditions prevailed. This was fun and we did it in turn gradually increasing the soaring time from five to thirty minutes, gaining the international pilots 'C' category at the end. The badge was the size of a tuppence piece, dark blue with three silver flying birds on it.

A separate course ran at the same time for the third year officer cadets of the Polish Air Force College, who were to be commissioned soon as fully trained pilots. They had already completed their operational conversion courses on combat aircraft and it was interesting to note that they broke a number of gliders into smithereens by flying and landing too fast. I liked the look of those young men and thought that should I join the forces I would try for the Air Force.

There was not much summer holiday left when I returned home proudly wearing my badge. I brought some photographs and some postcards with me which were greatly admired.

Soon I was back at school in my last year, found a couple of private tuition jobs, and was all set for serious work. Then quite out of the blue, Władek Skrobiszewski - a class mate - asked me whether I would like to move to their house and work with him for our finals in exchange for board and lodging. He would like that as he needed some help and would I think it over. I considered it carefully and decided to accept. There were two reasons for it; firstly I would be forced to do a great deal more work because I would have to make sure that he is up to scratch. Secondly, living in a doctor's house with Władek, his parents and two elder sisters, one married to Lt Kwiatkowski and a practising lawyer, would be an experience. I thought that something might rub off on me in the way of social graces, anyhow I would not lose anything except a bit of camaraderie in the boarding house. I moved in and we started work in earnest. I had some catching up to do in mathematics myself, which I had neglected for the past two years, and as the day of reckoning was approaching fast I arranged six two hour sessions with Wacek Smaga, a first class chap, to pull me up to a reasonable standard, on condition that I paid him the going rate. Time was money and I would not have it for free so Wacek accepted the cash reluctantly in the end. This was a confidential arrangement and paid good dividends in the finals. My written work was no problem and the oral at the black-board was plain sailing too. Lucek could not believe his eyes and talked to me afterwards: "What happened? You seemed to know more than I thought you did". So I told him about the six secret sessions which made him laugh and murmur something as he walked away fiddling with his moustache.

There were a number of bright spots in that otherwise hard year. A travelling company gave a performance of "Halka" by Moniuszko, my first opera and the most memorable one. No other opera, whether in France or England, ever made as deep an impression on me as "Halka".

A soprano and a tenor of high repute were invited by the school and gave us a wonderful evening, talking about music and singing great solos and duets. The gym was packed with all of us and as many parents, friends, and neighbours as could be squeezed in. One of the soprano songs was called "*Endele Mendele*" - a charming and very tender love story between two Jewish youngsters. It captivated the audience and the whole school, and mamas and papas sang and hummed it for weeks afterwards.

Our school play was a success once more and I enjoyed my part again. I particularly liked the rehearsals, the build up of excitement and even the last minute disasters.

And then came the event of the year - 'Studniówka' - for men only. It was a tradition for chaps to have a solid drinking session a hundred days before finals. Kazik Wróblewski organised this unforgettable event. His father was manager of a landed estate about twelve kilometres from Hrubieszów. They had a comfortable house with plenty of room and were willing hosts. They prepared everything, greeted us on arrival and then disappeared for the night to their friends. A cavalry NCO who was the fiancé to their daughter, took over and conducted everything with military precision.

We arrived early in the evening prepared to stay the night. A couple of large rooms were set up as dormitories with straw-filled palliases and blankets, and there was a bucket or two in strategic positions. Our host announced that we must be cold after our journey and would we follow him, We ended up in a room where, on a table, stood seventeen small glasses filled with vodka, and some snacks. He opened the proceedings with a toast to our success in a hundred days and we reciprocated with a toast to him and his beautiful fiancée. While he was busying himself with glasses and drinks for supper, we talked and joked and sung, Chaim played his violin, and it was very jolly. We had never been as close to one another as this before. I thought this was a truly happy gathering.

An excellent cold supper was prepared for us. Jewish chaps declared that to-day was not a kosher meat day, and they were scoffing smoked pork loin with gusto and various types of pork sausages and other non-kosher meats with the rest of us. Toasts, speeches, and jokes followed, and more toasts and more speeches, and after the supper was over, we were ready for soul-searching discussions and sorting the world out in general. My rival Chaim and I opened up our bleeding hearts and talked of our love for Helka. We concluded that women cannot be trusted and that our policy should be 'safety in numbers'. But neither of us knew what to do when a girl gets under your skin. We swore eternal friendship, Helka or no Helka. And so it went until well after midnight by which time we were all more or less drunk and collapsed on our palliases. Next morning we were revived with hot, strong coffee and despatched home in a couple of horse-drawn carts. That was a night, that was.

Time was running out fast and I had to decide what to do next, after my finals. I was reasonably confident that my grades would be good enough for a university degree course. I would have dearly loved to read Polish language and literature, for pleasure more than anything else, but I knew that was not possible, short of a miracle. My two eldest brothers were married, Kazik's health was causing concern, I could not accept any more sacrifices from my parents and Janek, and so I said good-bye to my university dream and decided to apply for admission to the Polish Air Force College. There would be no need for any assistance from home at all and after three years

I would earn a good salary as a pilot officer and be able to do something nice for my parents at last. I chose the Air Force because I enjoyed the gliding and thought that power flying would be even more exhilarating. The Air Force was something relatively new, there was a feeling of adventure and romance about it, and I was drawn to it. I discussed my plans at Easter with the family and was glad that nobody seriously tried to talk to me out of it. Mother had some reservations but she said that she really did not know anything about it and it would be better if I made up my own mind. Władek was all for the cavalry, of course, and when I tried to convince him that the Air Force was the Cavalry of the future, he said: "Yes, yes, but what about horses and swords?"

I must admit that I had always rated the cavalry very highly. Their esprit de corps was great. Men were smart, well behaved, and proud of their regiment. The local regiment had close links with the town and people loved to see their horsemen riding. When the regiment returned from a month of manoeuvres in the field great excitement would sweep the town. It was customary for ladies to ride out, meet them and bring them back home; they rode to town in front and the regiment behind them looking spick and span having spent their last day in shaking off the month-old dust and sprucing up themselves and their mounts for the occasion. People lined the streets, waved, shouted greetings, and threw flowers at them. It was always a very warm homecoming.

Once I went to their 'at home' display for the town people on an enormous training ground near the barracks. We saw spectacular individual horsemanship, then sword-work at full gallop with hazel sticks being cut left and right, and then lances picking up small rings on both sides of the run, also at a gallop. But the most impressive thing was the final parade of the whole regiment - one thousand horsemen! After they had passed the spectators at a walking pace, they changed into a slow trot riding in a wide circle, then fast trot, and passed us again at full gallop thundering like blazes, both men and horses so obviously loving it - it was marvellous!

Władek Skrobiszewski and I paddled his kayak about four kilometres downstream one summer day to see the regiment crossing the river, which was wide and deep at that point. Squadron after squadron in column of twos entered the water and swam across - hundreds of them. Most of the horses and riders did well but some horses were frightened, reared, and men found themselves in deep water with their horses gone. Those who could swim swam, but those who could not were in trouble. Some managed to catch the tails of other horses and were pulled across, others needed help. There was one heavy boat downstream in the middle of the river for emergencies, but it was a clumsy thing and could not move fast. And this is where our kayak came in. We dashed to a chap who had swallowed a bucket of water by then, extended one end of a paddle to him and pulled him to the tail of the kayak so that he had something to hold onto and delivered him, coughing and spluttering, to the bank. We worked hard like this for ages. When it was all over the Colonel himself thanked us and we shared some food and hot black coffee with the cavalry.

In 1939 the Polish Army had eighteen cavalry regiments. They all fought with distinction and the nation was proud of them. There were some stories in the west about our cavalry charging at German tanks with swords and lances. It was not like that at all.

The exams came and were over quickly. The subject of my Polish paper was "The Jewish question in the works of Eliza Orzeszkowa". The German paper was odd: "Give the causes of the First World War", unfair we thought, this was history in a foreign language, not on really. My question for oral history was a stinker – "Social reforms in sixteenth century Poland". Fortunately I wrote an essay on this in the seventh form and still remembered most of it. Maths was easy.

I was very glad that Władek also passed; his parents were very pleased and I felt I had earned my year's board and lodging.

A school ball was arranged for the following week-end with the regimental band to play for us. The ball was opened by a short, fat, and elderly school doctor - (yes, the one who operated on my thumb) - who was the best mazurka dancer in town. He and one of our nimble-footed pretty girls were leading at least a dozen pairs of mazurka fanatics, moving fast with intricate steps, jumps and whirls, to the delight of everybody. Were you to choose a dance that would interpret Poles you could do no better than choose a mazurka.

They played waltzes, polkas, *obereks*, tangos, and we danced and danced. Girls of our form wore 'civvies' for the first time in school and tried to look frightfully grown up. Helka wore something blue - she looked good in it and she knew it, the little devil. Lucek danced with Perla a lot. He was sweet on her in a fatherly way and she was flattered. Kazik Wróblewski was the dance leader and he surpassed himself with what we called 'waltz manoeuvres'. It was a great ball - the best! We felt so grown up and eager to get to grips with life; we should not have hurried - clouds were gathering in the west and in the east.

Soon after our ball I said farewell to my class-mates, eleven girls and sixteen chaps. We had spent seven enjoyable years together, the last two of which were particularly good. I had become more confident and I was no longer a burden on my family, earning enough for my needs and more. I even bought Helka a manicure set for her birthday, which was sheer extravagance but made her love me a little more for a while. All this was behind us now and we were spreading our wings and flying away from our nests.

I was called for my medical at the Air Force Medical Establishment in Warsaw, and for the entrance examination at the Air Force College School in Dęblin. I had no problems with either. On the way back from Dęblin I stopped at Kazimierz-upon-Wisła and called on Helka who was at a Socialist Youth Summer Camp nearby. We walked to this beautiful town, had tea, I kissed her good-bye and left. It was a sad meeting, we did not talk much, we both knew that this was the end of our sweet romance, no matter how hard we pretended that it was not. Such is life, dammit!

The results of my examinations came very quickly, I was accepted and advised that joining instructions would follow.

A few days later I met our Headmaster by chance in town and he stopped me:

"I was meaning to talk to you" he said, "Have you made any plans? What are you going to do?"

I told him that I had been accepted by the Air Force College and that it was all settled.

"Oh good!" he said,"Good. I was wondering whether you would like to go to university.

I thought I could persuade the town elders to provide a scholarship, but there is no need for it now, is there? Well, good luck!" and he was gone.

A miracle would have been possible after all, if only the old buzzard had thought of it a bit sooner. On the other hand I was not sure that I would have liked to depend on the town elders too much.

I went to the public library and borrowed an armful of books for my summer reading. I had walked in previous summers, a couple of times, to the library and back, a distance of twenty-one kilometres and four hours each way, but not this time. Apart from Polish authors, the library had a lot of foreigners as well. I remember reading Galsworthy (yes, the "Forsyte Saga"), Byron, Tagore, Rolland, Maupassant, and of course the Russians. I was not yet ready for Dostoyevsky, nor for Balzac for that matter.

The joining instructions arrived in good time and I was ordered to report to a camp near Różan, not far from Warsaw, where entrants to all Officer Cadet Schools were to receive basic military training. There were several hundred of us, all mixed up, all looking alike in our khaki drill and heavy boots. At first it was drill, drill, drill, and nothing but drill, individual, in sections and platoons, eyes right and eyes front, then the same thing with rifles, which we could dismantle and assemble blindfold. Next, came the light machine-gun, heavy machine-gun, light mortar, and range. The last stage was attack and defence, the latter included digging a hole in the ground, better known as the 'grave'. For the grand finale we attacked, as a battalion, with everything blazing away with blanks, things exploding, smoke and fire, hurrah! And all hell let loose. We had to beat real soldiers who were in defensive positions and, of course, we did.

It went on like this from 1st September to Christmas 1936. We never left the garrison area, there was nowhere to go, we were in the middle of a forest.

Our instructors must have been sentenced to this purgatory for some serious crimes. I doubt whether any of them liked the job and the location, but they worked well and were driving us hard, trying to break some of our civilian ways and knock us into military shape. At the end of the day everybody was tired; we ate like horses and slept like logs. When I left for Christmas I was thinner, stronger, and fitter. They fitted us out with reasonable going-out uniforms and we could hardly wait to get the hell out of there and go home.

Our instructors-come-section leaders were regular army NCOs - good chaps, but simple, and they often mixed up the use of longer words such as conservation with conversation with amusing results, particularly if they were referring to boots. They had their standard jokes and mannerisms when inspecting our quarters and turning our bedding upside down because beds were not made up to their standard. But none of it really mattered and in the end I forgave our section tormentor for all his sins as we shook hands on parting.

The bed next to mine was occupied by a cavalry officer cadet whose name was Kirgładze. His ancestors were Crimean Tartars - Mohammedans - who settled in the Wilno region some centuries ago. It was fitting that he joined the cavalry for Tartars were great horsemen.

Once, after 'lights out' somebody came rushing out of the ablutions and bumped into the Orderly Officer who had come to check that all was well. He did not think it was, alerted the platoon, rifles and all, and took us for an hour's walk along the forest lanes. He became our pet hate until somebody else's crimes surpassed his.

Christmas at home was as warm and loving as ever, but I was aware of how really humble our home was and I felt, with sadness, that my parents deserved something better for all their work, for raising five sons with all the care and love they could muster, and firmness when needed. They did not grumble, they were considerate and cheerful. Were they content with their lot? If they were not, they certainly never showed it. I do not suppose they had time to think about themselves. It was the family, the future of every son which mattered, and as the family grew in numbers, with daughters-in-law and grand-children, they drew strength from the close relationship and joy from the little ones.

Kazik did not look too good. He had seen a couple of doctors, tried their medicines, but there was nor real improvement. He still worked most of the time. Nobody talked about it but Mother noticed my concern and said, one day: "Don't worry, we will do what we can".

On reporting to Dęblin a new life began. The origins of the Air Force College, also known as 'The School of Eaglets', go back to 1925 when the 'Air Force Officer's School' was formed in Grudziądz in northern Poland. In 1927 the school was transferred to Dęblin, where its home was first in the truly splendid palace, formerly the seat of the Jabłonowski family. It is a vast two storey building of excellent proportions, with basements along its front and cellars at the back. The front entrance looked like a portal of a Greek Temple, with four high columns adorned with noble Doric heads. The grounds, although considerably reduced, were very beautiful, with a small lake and fine trees, shrubs and lawns. The place grew to meet the future needs of the

Polish Air force, and when I reported there in January 1937 it was called then The Air Force Training Centre Dęblin (CWL Dęblin).

The primary task of the CWL was to run the Air Force College. Secondly, a one year navigator's course was run for volunteer junior officers from the other services, better known among the flying fraternity as Abyssinians. And thirdly, to train reserve officer cadets as pilots and navigators.

It was a modern training centre with first class instructional, technical, supply, domestic, and sport facilities. It had a master airfield with large, up-to-date hangars and workshops, and three or four satellite airfields in the area. There were also married quarters for officers and other ranks, sick quarters, with a small ward and nursing staff, and a cinema.

The single storey accommodation area had several dormitories and wide corridors which joined a main corridor at ninety degrees leading to the main entrance, dining room, gymnasium, and the Commandant's office. There were eight beds in a dormitory with proper mattresses and bedding. In addition, every cadet had a wardrobe, a small bedside locker and a stool. In the middle of the room stood a large table with some chairs around it. In the corridor there were stands for rifles allocated to individual cadets and signed for.

Our entry, the twelfth, was the last one to complete the full three year course before the war. At first, we were organised as one squadron, commanded by Capt. Józef Ostrowski, whom we quite naturally called *tata* ('Dad') Ostrowski, and sub-divided into four platoons commanded by lieutenants. The tallest cadets were in the first platoon and the shortest in the fourth. I was in the third, our officer i/c was Second Lt Wolański, and Wacław Grandys was our senior cadet. The Commandant of the CWL was Col. Stefan Sznuk.

We had a nice welcome. The third year cadet pilots took each one of us up in the two-seater open-cockpit PWS-26 trainer, the first powered aircraft I had ever flown in. I was impressed. It was a good way to start the course, but then we had several months of solid ground school ahead of us before we could even get anywhere near an aircraft again. Most of the flying was done in the summer months and most of the ground school in winter.

Several subjects were taught in ground school, some of which were covered in one or two terms and others went on and on for ages. We were learning about aircraft engines, instruments, map reading and projections, navigation, theory of flight, meteorology, ballistics, weapons and bombs, Morse, armed forces organisation, history of wars, and foreign languages. In the gymnasium we had compulsory boxing, fencing, and dancing during one term - which was quite funny as we had to change sexes several times during a lesson.

The squadron and platoons had senior cadets deputising for the respective officers. After breakfast the squadron paraded by platoons in two ranks and the squadron cadet reported to the Orderly Officer stating numbers present, sick, etc., the officer taking the morning parade then shouted a greeting at us, and we shouted the greeting back at him. It went like this:

Czołem podchorążowie!
Czołem panie poruczniku!!
(czoło is forehead, but czołem means hullo! or farewell!;
podchorążowie are officer cadets and porucznik is lieutenant)

It was a good greeting in the best military tradition and was meant to show mutual respect. Next, we would form a column of fours and march about one kilometre to the ground school, the squadron cadet leading. The Orderly Officer on the pavement inevitably shouted an order: "Squadron will sing" - and we burst into one of many fine songs we knew. Later on we discovered that the tango was a really good marching tune, if you added a bit of edge to it, and as the tango had swept the world by then, we were singing 'Habanera', 'Why have you forgotten me?', 'Don't cry little one' - all very sloppy but nice. But there was nothing to beat the First World War songs and they remained our favourites.

If an officer did something beastly to us we sang one particular song about a cad who had a golden horn and a hat made of feathers, he lost the lot and the only thing he had left was a rope (to hang himself). The message was loud and clear and the reaction swift – "Stop! Another song!" We would then either comply, or remain silent, or sing the cad and golden horn song again. The last two were desperate measures and used only when we had to make a stand, even if it meant an extra hour of drill in our own time.

My seven room mates were from all parts of the country and from various social strata; it was an interesting mix.

Janusz Marciniak came from Lublin, a county town in the middle of Poland. He was a body-building fanatic and was very proud of his muscles and enormously expanded chest. We called him 'bellows'! A lively, temperamental, and aggressive chap. He was a very good friend most of the time, but fell out with everybody in turn, had a row, and then became best of pals again very soon. Good fun, amusing and infuriating, always ready for a practical joke and a laugh. Good old Janusz!

Zygmunt Drybański was a man from the west, the Poznań region. They are solid, sound, common sense people over there and he was all that and more. He had a dry sense of humour, did not waste words, a realist with stubbornness and perseverance and a fine, aggressive basketball player.

Antoni Dzięgielewski was educated in Równo, a large garrison town in the east. Thin as a beanstalk, intelligent, gentle and quiet, and a bit of a dreamer but he could dig his heels in and be determined if he chose to do so. A thoroughly nice chap. He was not interested in sport, he preferred to read a book.

Mieczysław Babiański lived in the Wilno region, in the north-eastern corner of Poland. Lively, polite, a smooth talker and a pleasant companion but a bit of a snob. He came from a well-to-do family, judging from his enormous monthly allowance.

Roman Suwalski came from the lake district in the northern part of the country. Upper middle class, like Babiański, and a close friend of his. He had excellent manners, quiet, and somewhat reserved, a ladies' man.

Mieczysław Waszkiewicz was also from the Wilno region. A sound and reliable fellow with an enquiring mind and a lot of horse sense, a good debater.

Tadeusz Owczarski came from Warsaw. Intelligent, restless, and with a warm personality. Not a pusher, rather too modest for his own good, always courteous and considerate. Misjudged by some as a lightweight. A very likeable chap indeed.

As for myself, well, it would be up to one of the seven to retaliate, but only two could do that now - one in England and one in Warsaw. Of the rest, one was killed in an accident in France and four died in the air flying from England. They will stay in my memory to the end of my days.

I had no problem with my surname. A few discreet smiles here and there, as to be expected at first, but I was quite used to that. There were no other problems either. I knew that I would be broke for three years but I was prepared for that. In fact, I had a few bob saved for a rainy day. The cadet's weekly pay was equivalent to a shilling and a few pence, enough for shoe polish and toothpaste. Most of the chaps had either a monthly allowance from home or an occasional windfall of cash from somewhere. I had none. I can honestly say I did not feel deprived of anything nor was I envious of anyone. On the contrary, I developed some sort of false pride in being completely independent and completely broke. This soon became obvious when my room mates noticed that I was not treating myself to a cup of tea and a doughnut at elevenses, and they understood why I could not accept a cuppa from anybody. The initial ice was broken very quickly and good relations were established all around.

The ground school for all those months until Easter and beyond, until we started flying, was a hard slog enlivened by bouts of drill, kit inspections, rifle cleaning, cross-country running, and gym. We did not play rugby or cricket. Basketball was played in the gym and in the open air, and so was netball. The latter is not at all as sissy a game as some people think, if you play it our way. We kicked a football now and then but nobody took much interest in it. The sporting accent was on athletics, gym exercises and the two games mentioned before.

Regrettably there was no canteen, games room, or a club room with radio or newspapers and periodicals, but each platoon had a large study room in the basement where we had compulsory homework periods. It was a Spartan set-up.

Our dining room was vast, the size of the gymnasium and, in fact on top of it. It could accommodate all three years with a lot of room to spare. When the Orderly Officer sat, we sat, on long benches on both sides of very long tables. The senior entry sat on chairs at the top table with the Orderly Officer in the middle of them, who had to take all meals with us. The food was good by my standards and there was plenty of it. In the first year we were marched in column of twos to the dining room but were allowed to walk out individually once the Orderly Officer, followed by the senior entry, followed by the second year entry, had left. We did not have to pick up our spoons on command - it was not really as bad as it might sound to civilians.

Movement along the corridors of the main building was sometimes difficult and full of sudden stops and starts, depending on how many senior cadets we met. The rule was that if you saw one of them approaching from the opposite direction you had to stop, turn ninety degrees with your back to the wall, and stand smartly to attention whilst he was passing you. I thought this was a bit too much and always carried out the manoeuvre in an exaggerated fashion with a cheeky grin on my face. The seniors were a bit embarrassed by this adulation and never pulled you up if you forgot to do it, or made a joke about it.

Easter came and I went home for a week. It was so nice to see them all again and be welcomed so warmly. There was pride in my mother's eyes when she looked at me in my smart uniform, no longer a boy but a flier-to-be. We talked, laughed, drank some vodka, and in no time at all I had to go back. Mother quickly wiped away a tear, I kissed her hands, hugged everybody, and was away in the familiar cart and pair. Janek let me drive all the way to the station.

Soon after Easter we started flying from a satellite grass airfield called Zajezierze which was on the western side of the river Wisła. We travelled there standing in big open lorries. The journey took about twenty minutes each way and we returned for lunch. We wore overalls, leather helmets, and goggles. The aircraft was the RWD-8, a very light monoplane, two-seater open cockpit trainer, powered by a 110 hp PZInż. Junior; its maximum speed was 170 km/h, cruising speed 140 km/h, range 435 km, and ceiling 4,200 metres. Before we went up, however, we had to learn all there was to know about parachutes and how to pack them. Every cadet had his own parachute, looked after it, kept it in his locker and packed and re-packed it himself under supervision. We also had to make one jump, to be convinced I suppose, that it worked, but we jumped with two parachutes... just in case. We went up in an old three engine Fokker bomber to 800 metres and down we came - it worked for everybody!

Our platoon was divided into four groups with a flying instructor in charge of each one under overall command of Lt Wolański. Every morning four aircraft piloted by four instructors, with four cadets as passengers, flew from Dęblin master airfield to Zajezierze where the rest of us were already there. And soon each group began buzzing in its own sector of the sky in the vicinity of the airfield.

At first we learned to fly straight and level at a constant speed with nose on the horizon, then dive gently, and level off, climb and level off, level turns, diving and climbing turns, and all the time learning how to take off and getting the feel of the aircraft on approach and landing. After that, came circuits and bumps (repeated take offs and landings) and, at last, the first three solo circuits, each with a landing, hopefully, on point, which meant that the aircraft should end its landing run by the mobile flying control post. We were taught not to use power on approach unless it was necessary, nor on the landing run until the aircraft came to a halt. There were no brakes. Movement control was by means of one white and one red flag - white for taxi, take off, land, and red for stop, over-shoot, keep away. There was the usual wind-sock on the edge of the airfield and a white letter 'T' near the flying control post.

Our platoon instructors were all NCOs and on the whole they were a good bunch, some better at the job than others but all were very competent pilots. My instructor was Cpl. Kasprzyk.

My first three solo circuits were probably the best I ever made on a RWD-8, the aircraft stopped dead by the control post each time; I never managed it quite so accurately again. From then on we changed seats with the instructors, whose job it was to be our guardian angel, whilst we practised map-reading and short navigational triangles, until we were allowed to do all this by ourselves. Next came the first solo cross-country from Dęblin to Okęcie (Warsaw) and finally the big triangle: Dęblin - Rakowice (Kraków) - Skniłów (Lwów) - Dęblin - refuelling at the end of each leg. Over fifty chaps did not complete the initial flying course and opted for training as navigators during the remaining two years in Dęblin.

The last part of the first year programme was again the army. This was a hardy annual and quite interesting in its concept. A battalion of seasoned infantry troops was put under canvas and mixed with the first year officer cadets from all services. All junior posts were filled with the third year chaps of the Infantry Officer Cadet School to give them practice in command. The set-up was in effect a special regiment designed to give us some understanding of what makes the ordinary soldier tick, how he lives in the field, how he eats, how he behaves, thinks, talks, swears, and how tough he is. This had nothing to do with being a pilot but it was certainly important for learning what being an officer was about. It is in the knowing and understanding of your men, and vice versa, so essential for developing mutual trust and respect, where the key to successful command lies.

I was full of admiration for the infantry senior cadets, their competence, leadership and compassion for lame ducks. I felt that were I a footslogger, which fortunately I was not, I could trust and follow any of them, all credit to Komorowo - their home.

The soldiers did not really like the idea of being mixed up with us. It was all for our benefit and there was nothing in it for them, except more work and more sweat but, orders were orders.

It was a glorious summer, the sun was shining all of that month and it was hot. The lanes in the pine forest were sandy and dusty. We went through similar things as at Różan and a great deal more. After a week of sharing dust, brown bread and black coffee, and having sweated gallons in joint efforts, we were all on first name terms; the spirit of comradeship was growing very nicely.

The last three days were a final test of our endurance. We marched from dawn to dusk with full battle gear, carrying all that a soldier needs on our backs. 'Omnia mea mecum porto' was the saying of the Roman legions; well, we were as good as the best of them.

The Company Commanders, regular army officers, rode on horses, the rest marched. We stuck to sandy forest lanes, secondary dusty mud roads, column after column, weaving along like giant snakes. Field kitchens and supplies were moving ahead and preparing meals at appointed places; they used horse-power. Each company had a large cart and a pair for casualties. Anyone who did not look after his feet properly ended up with blisters and unable to walk. This could not happen to a good footslogger who knew his business. However some cadets failed in this respect and ended up in the cart, but such was the spirit amongst the marching fraternity that nobody asked for a ride unless ordered. I remember chaps limping and those next to them carrying their rifles and it would often be a simple soldier doing it. The feet were examined and treated and the culprit was on his feet as soon as possible. It was an offence to neglect one's feet, and quite rightly so.

At the end of the first and second marching days we spent the night in a village, sleeping in sheds and lofts on straw and hay. It did not really matter on what or where. As soon as the evening meal was over and feet were washed everybody was ready for bed. The day was breaking when we were woken up. By the time I had rolled my blanket, washed and shaved, sorted and packed the gear, the sun was over the horizon and the coffee was steaming in the kitchen. Breakfast was quickly over, we were briefed where we were going, reminded about foot-care, and away we went. There was a five minute break every hour and a longer one in the mid-morning and afternoon, with one hour for lunch. I noticed that old soldiers never wasted any energy and spent every break in a horizontal position. It was very hot and the water in metal bottles was soon warm, but it was the same for everybody.

On the third day we arrived in the late afternoon at a large meadow on the edge of the woods where we were to be addressed by a General. Again it was hot and not a breath of wind. We formed three sides of a square in two ranks and waited. In those conditions it is easier to march than to stand, and we hoped that we would not stand too long. Some twenty minutes later he arrived. "Attention! Slope, present, shoulder and order arms" were executed with reasonable precision but I noticed that a couple of weaklings flaked away and were lying motionless. The management was prepared for this, and they were removed swiftly by the medics. I do not remember what the General was rambling on about, but I prayed that he would be brief. Unfortunately he was not, until a few more chaps decided to lie down rather abruptly, which he noticed, and finished with a joke, and that was that "Dismiss!" at last.

King Carol of Rumania was about to arrive on an official visit to Poland. We had about three days to shake off the dust, change into our best blues and assemble in Warsaw for a march past. A few seconds after "Eyes right!" I saw the King at close quarters looking quite splendid in his uniform. We returned to Dęblin the same day and that was the end of the first year.

The summer holiday was at home again. There had been some changes there. Władek had become the manager of the flour-mill but nobody used such terms over there, he was just told what to do and he did it. Janek had moved to Władek's place, and my father virtually ran the estate with the squire, both working very hard. The two of them had a conference every evening, a smoke, and often a glass of vodka. There was a bond between them which I never quite understood.

I managed to get a lift into town and heard some news about my school friends. Brilliant Ciesielczuk, Dyl, Krowiński, Regel and Rojter were at the university, Bohun at the Mining Academy, Krzyszkowski and Wróblewski worked locally. Of the girls, Melchertówna married a young doctor, Staśka Kozielewicz, a good mathematician, joined a teaching academy, Cybulska was at the university and so were Doroszewska and Helka. Perla was engaged to a prosperous Jewish businessman. There was friction at the Warsaw University between Polish students, members of the ND party (National Democrat), and Jewish students. Helka had a rough time and gave up her law studies and joined a very prestigious school of nursing where her sister was. I stayed an hour or so in the town and, having borrowed some books from the library again, I was on my way home.

It was a quiet summer. I spent my time reading, swimming in the lake, and wandering in the fields and woods. Once I saw a wild boar leading five little ones into the woods. It was quite a sight, particularly as I had never seen wild boar before. I chopped mountains of fire-wood for Mother, carried lunch for my father into the fields, and tried to make myself as useful as I could.

Kazik's health was up and down. He was not too bad and we had hopes that he might recover fully in the months to come. Summer, being a very busy time on the land, kept my family, friends and neighbours, hard at work six days a week, and it was mostly on Sundays when there was time to talk and enjoy their company. I was getting quite restless towards the end of my leave and, without admitting it to myself, I was ready to go back to Dęblin.

Our entry was reorganised at the start of the second year into two squadrons. Capt. 'Tata' Ostrowski remained with us as the Commanding Officer of the pilot's squadron and somebody else took over command of the navigator's squadron, with two officers as platoon commanders, all three of them being navigators. The over-all command over the two squadrons was given to Capt. Pietraszkiewicz, a fighter pilot and a newcomer from the Warsaw lot, who was soon promoted to the rank of Major.

The ranks of pilots and navigators were boosted by the injection of a number of chaps from the Air Force Reserve Officer Cadets School My good friend Staszek Andrzejewski was one of the pilots who joined us. The navigators moved out to separate accommodation. Tadzio Owczarski was one of them and left our room.

We began conversion to the PWS-26, an open-cockpit, two seater, fully aerobatic bi-plane trainer. This entailed learning about the aircraft and engine performance, the usual handling exercises, solo flights, map-reading, navigation, instrument flying, and some formation flying.

Aerobatics were reserved for the summer term. Bad weather messed up some of our flying days and we did not get very far before Christmas.

Two days before our one week Christmas holiday began we had a fine flying day with a gentle breeze blowing straight from Siberia. It was very cold with the temperature well below zero. Cpl. Kasprzyk was allocated an aircraft with a collapsible canvas hood over the pupil's seat. He told me to get into it and said: "There will be a lot of frost-bitten noses to-day if people are not careful. We are lucky. You will fly on instruments with the hood over you and I shall hide my head in the cockpit. All I want you to do is to fly ten minutes on three different headings I tell you to steer and that should bring us back to the airfield - a small triangle, that's all".

After we landed he took up another chap, and so it went until lunch time. It was evident by then that a large number of cadets had frost-bitten noses, as well as a few cheeks and foreheads. The flying was stopped and doctors and nurses were busy dealing with the disaster. The treatment was to apply some sort of dark brown sticky paste on the affected parts and leave it there for a few days. As bandages were not used the chaps looked as if they had just put on war-paint and were about to attack the management for their misery, they were furious. Think of it - Christmas at home - meeting friends and girl-friends in this state! They really had their holiday ruined, but the tales that went around about various reactions, when we all returned to Dęblin again, kept us laughing for days.

In January we began preparation for a skiing course of about three weeks duration in the Carpathian Mountains near Zakopane. This was an annual event for the second and third year cadets. We were fitted out with skiing clothing, boots, and skis, and were on our way. An advance party sorted out accommodation in several chalets which included lofts. It was a very Spartan set-up. We were packed in like sardines, but the food was reasonable and nobody cared anyhow, it was an adventure! Some of our officers who could ski acted as instructors. We were split into groups, starting on very gentle slopes and worked our way higher and higher. There were no drag lifts, it was hard work every morning until lunch, but we were free afterwards.

To liven things up a bit we built a little ski jump with tightly packed snow - enough for hops of three or four yards. We could hardly stay upright and could just about manage plough turns, but jump we did, often landing one on top of another with shouts, moans and groans, skis flying in all directions and the onlookers killing themselves with laughter. How was it that nobody sustained a serious injury will remain a mystery. "God is kind to fools", somebody said, and I would agree with that.

We were not far from Zakopane and, of course, we had to go to the top of the peak called Kasprowy Wierch. The winter Olympics were held at Zakopane that year and the place was full of competitors and visitors. We arrived at the top by cable car and disembarked in front of a fine terminal station with café, bar, and restaurant. Somebody spotted General Wieniawa-Długoszowski, a cavalry man, well known in the forces for very good, and not so good, reasons. He became Polish Ambassador to Italy and a good friend of Count Ciano, the Italian Foreign Minister, who was persuaded to keep the overland escape route to France in 1939 open for as long as possible. Apparently the General was fifty and still skiing like a demon. But the real demons were girls, down-hill competitors practising their runs. We stood amazed, watching them going at high speed straight down the steepest slope and weaving their way below until they disappeared amongst the trees.

After coffee and a short break we were instructed to follow the leader and not to try anything silly. As we were zigzagging down the slope at a snail's pace one chap could not stand it any more and, having just been passed by a beautiful vision, he peeled off with a shout: "If the girls can do it, so can I!", and followed her. Needless to say he was picked up a bit lower down below with a broken leg. Leon Jaugsch finished his skiing course in style.

A few days later we went to see the ski jumping competition, which was something quite spectacular. These young men from many countries, hurling themselves into the air, had a great deal of courage as well as skill, but I would prefer to fly on a broom-stick instead of skis. We cheered the Polish competitors loudest and willed them to win but they did not quite make it. It was a great day.

From another visit to Zakopane I remember a small wooden church with many Saints and religious scenes painted on the walls. They all wore traditional highlander's dress and their facial expressions were very cheerful. It was a lovely church, you felt welcomed on entering and left the place smiling.

The rest of the winter was mostly ground school. Whatever little flying we did - once a week if we were lucky - was from a hard frozen surface with a bit of snow on top. Once I was a passenger in a PWS-26, in a formation of four aircraft flown by instructors to Zajezierze. One of the aircraft touched our tail plane with its wing and damaged it. My instructor reduced power and glided down dead ahead, our aircraft vibrating and shaking horribly. We force-landed in a rough field ending with our nose on the ground and the tail sticking up in the air. The propeller was broken, the under-carriage damaged, and the whole crate bent, but the two of us were in one piece, if a bit shaken. I did not realise the seriousness of the situation until he told me that he could hardly control her in descent and was unable to bank or turn. The other aircraft suffered only a minor scratch and had no difficulty in flying.

Shortly afterwards another misfortune befell me, I was given a bloody nose in a boxing bout. It was all the fault of our PT Instructor, who was an ex-middleweight boxing champion of Poland, incidentally. He paired us without any rhyme or reason and said: "Box on one whistle and stop on two". I protested at having to box with a chap a head taller than I but he smiled and said to my opponent: "Don't kill him!". I suggested to Jurek Goldhaar that we should pretend and not throw real punches. He agreed, and we danced about putting up a good show until he suddenly lowered his guard when distracted by something, and I accidentally hit him on the jaw. I immediately apologised but he would not listen to reason and went for me. I had to defend myself and it became a rather bloody and one-sided battle until two whistles. That put me off boxing for life, not that I ever liked it anyhow.

Another boxing incident took place soon after, when the same PT Instructor wanted to demonstrate some punches and selected Włodek Miksa as his partner. Włodek pleaded that he was 'too young to die' but to no avail. First, he had to hold his gloves out and catch the demonstration punches. Then the PT Instructor said that the two of them would box for a while and use these punches for all to see. He assured Włodek that he would not be hurt and they started stalking one another, Włodek retreating, the other advancing and throwing punches, until he landed a hefty one on Włodek's jaw. The PT Instructor then turned his head momentarily and started saying something, when furious Włodek, who was a good boxer, retaliated and hit him hard. The Instructor's head jerked in surprise and he went for him but Włodek retreated at a gallop to the door and beyond, winning the race and saving his life.

I liked fencing. There was no need for brutal force, it was skill, quick reactions, anticipation, and speed in attack and defence, which mattered. At least that was what I thought until I was again paired with Janusz Marciniak. Someone was acting as a referee and awarding hits to one side or another and to my surprise I was winning. It was the other way around on all our previous encounters, but not this time. After a brief break, general fencing was ordered and we faced each other again, this time without a referee. Janusz did not like losing and after a few of the usual thrusts and counters he suddenly hit me on my shoulder from above as if he was using a sword; the end of his épée bent over and inflicted a painful blow on my unprotected back. I retaliated in the same manner, and later we both admired each other's red marks on our backs. There were no hard feelings, you could not be cross with Janusz for long.

We had an excellent basketball team with Salski, Miksa, Drybański and others, which was a treat to watch. Wacek Gąsowski was one of the best runners for the four hundred meters and eight hundred meters in the country and he was later coaching a relay team which came first in the nationwide championships.

At last Easter came and the long-awaited break. I was worried about Kazik all that winter and with good reason. He had tuberculosis and was dying slowly. My parents and Janek did all they could, as Mother said they would. Every penny they earned, plus proceeds from the sale of some livestock, went on doctors and medicines. There was hardly any hope for him now, he was losing weight and becoming weaker. It was the saddest Easter ever and I left home with a heavy heart, hoping against hope that he might still recover.

The last term was a mixture of flying and ground school, and the main part of the flying programme was aerobatics. The instructor demonstrated how it should be done, then we tried it with him until he was satisfied, then we had to do the same thing solo, and start again on another aerobatics figure. We were diving, stalling, looping, rolling, spinning, and generally disturbing the birds over a large area of the sky. My instructor was Cpl. Bronisław Malinowski. He was a first rate pilot and could demonstrate any manoeuvre very well but he had difficulties in communicating and explaining clearly the reasons for errors and how to correct them. Consequently my slow and fast rolls were ending all over the sky.

The Commanding Officer of our entry, Capt. Pietraszkiewicz, was very fond of Latin quotations and had a lot of them painted in large letters in our corridors. These pearls of wisdom screamed at us from every corner. Aesthetically, it was not an improvement, anyhow I did not want to read 'Si vis pacem para bellum' as soon as I left my room.

There was one dish on our menu which was repeated very frequently for supper and one summer day we decided not to eat the accursed kasza. The Orderly Officer came to every table and asked the same question:

"Why are you not eating the kasza?", to which everybody replied: "Not hungry, Sir".

He then ordered an alert in full kit with rifles and took us for a two hour march, interspersed with air raids, gas alerts, running and crawling under fences, etc. When we returned eventually to camp he informed us that kasza was still on the tables for anybody whose appetite had improved. We loved him for this and from then on whenever he ordered – "Squadron will sing!" we responded with the 'Golden horn' song for a long time.

It was while I was at home on my summer leave that Kazik died. He was in a very bad state, terribly weak and very thin. It happened suddenly one morning when Father was home. My parents and I were standing near his bed, talking, when Kazik started coughing, then made some gesture with his hands and Father lifted him, thinking he wanted to be helped to a chair, but his legs would not hold him. I tried to help, Mother threw a rug on the floor and we laid him on his back. Kazik stopped coughing, he was looking at us with his eyes wide open, and then a strange sound came out of him, his body stiffened, jerked, and he lay there quite still and silent. Kazik was dead. I heard my Father's quiet lament: "My son, my son!". Tears were rolling down his cheeks, Mother was crying quietly, and so was I.

We buried him next day, close to the grave of Władek's baby daughter, his first child, who had died of diphtheria. The long-lasting physical and mental ordeal for my parents was over. It was mother more than anybody else who had watched him dying slowly and nursed him during the last six months of his life when he became progressively weaker and helpless. Although expected, Kazik's death was a shock for us all and deep sadness descended upon the family for a long time. I kept myself busy, trying to help Mother around the house and garden, and talking to her frequently. Not that I wanted her to forget Kazik, but to lessen her grief if I could, I saw her wiping away her tears too often.

The autumn of 1938 was the start of my final year in Dęblin. We were aware of the growing German might and Hitler's territorial expansion. With that cloud over our heads we commenced work again. By the end of the second term we were to complete the ground school programme including final examinations, and finish flying training on the PWS-26. The last term was to be devoted solely to conversion to first line aircraft and operational training either on fighters, light bombers, or heavy bombers. We were promoted to the rank of Sgt Cadet at the beginning of the first term and Flt Sgt Cadet at the end of the second term. Work, and life in general, progressed on the same lines as in the previous year, with the break for Christmas, followed by skiing in the eastern range of the Carpathians. I was glad to see my parents at peace and quite themselves again, caring for the living as always, and no doubt remembering the dead. We had our beautiful Christmas tree again and enjoyed the festive season in the closeness of the family circle as in the previous years.

Early in the first term *Tata* Ostrowski called me to his office and discussed my surname with me, pointing out that I would be at a disadvantage in my future unit. It would be desirable from every point of view if I changed it. What did I think about it? I agreed, but said I did not know how to go about it, and if it involved money, which I was certain it would, I had none and would require a loan. He said he would take care of everything and that I should decide on a name in two or three weeks.

I went to my room and announced:

"Fellows! I am going to change my bloody name, so think hard of something suitable for a warrior of my calibre. A princely sum of five zlotys will be paid to the winner out of my first salary; you have one week".

Great enthusiasm all around and more and more people joined in the name game. I had a most amusing week with some outrageous suggestions.

In the end I chose the name myself. I was looking at a large map of Poland one day and spotted the name of a village deep in the country called Kornice. I associated it with the land and fields, liked the sound of it and immediately thought of Kornicki. My friends were disappointed, but approved of my choice, declared me a winner and we celebrated with tea and doughnuts. Dęblin was teetotal for cadets.

Tata Ostrowski was as good as his word. I was issued with a railway warrant to my district town of Hrubieszów, signed some papers, and back the same day. It was as easy as that. My new name was promulgated in Orders and I became Kornicki. I have never heard of anybody else called that but if I have chosen somebody else's family name I hope I will be forgiven. For my part, I promise not to disgrace it.

The events leading to war in 1939 followed one another in quick succession. On 24th January 1939 Ribbentrop came to Poland, repeating Hitler's claim to Gdańsk and demanded agreement for the construction of a motorway across the Polish corridor to Gdańsk for the free use by Germans. He also sounded out Col. Beck, our Foreign Minister, as to whether Poland would remain neutral, in the event of war between Germany and France. He left with a decisive "NO" on all points.

On 1st March Britain and France announced their guarantee of territorial integrity of Poland, and that they would come to the assistance of Poland in the event of German aggression.

The Czechoslovakian President, Dr Hacha, arrived in Berlin by air and during the night of 14th to 15th March signed a document of surrender to Germany, with a large number of aircraft and a very rich arsenal. He said: "The Nation will curse me even though I have saved it from terrible suffering"

On 28th April Hitler denounced the ten year Non-aggression Pact with Poland.

On 5th May Col. Beck replied, ending with the words that "peace at any price is not our way and that the nation values its honour too". He was convinced at last that war was inevitable. His speech gained him nation-wide support, including that of his political enemies.

On the 23rd August the Soviet and German Ambassadors signed the agreement between the two countries which also included the partition of Poland between them (in violation of the Polish-Soviet Non-aggression Pact, expiring on the 31st December 1945). This was the result of very secret negotiations while, at the same time, Stalin was shamming support for Britain and France and held official and well publicised talks with delegations from both countries.

On 25th August the Polish-British Treaty was signed guaranteeing Poland the status quo, that is independence within the existing frontiers in the west, east, south, and north. On the basis of this agreement, consistent with and in the interests of the British policy in Europe, Poland did gain the right to claim that Britain should declare war not only on Germany but also on the Soviet Union, or any other neighbouring country, in the event of any of them trying to appropriate part of Poland's territory. Article eight declared that the agreement shall remain in force for five years. The agreement was in force at the time of the fateful and contrary decision at Teheran, and Churchill's speech on 22nd February 1944 was in effect, a repudiation of that agreement.

On 1st September Hitler attacked Poland and on 17th September Stalin's troops entered Poland without any declaration of war and in violation of the Non-aggression Pact.

It is against the background of this build up to war that the twelfth entry of Dęblin cadets were working hard during their third and final year. We were eager to get to the operational aircraft as soon as possible, which seemed more important than the examinations, some of which were of little consequence anyhow.

Towards the end of the second term an odd thing happened, I was failed in ballistics. The examination was at the blackboard. I was asked several questions which required rough diagrams and some mathematics. I had no difficulties and thought all was going well, when to my surprise, I heard our ballistic chief, a Captain, saying: "Enough! Sit down, you have failed".

I thought he was joking and asked him what marks he had given me, expecting a good pass, but he said four out of ten. I asked to be excused, found Lt Wolański, Officer in charge of my Platoon, told him what had happened and formally requested that I might be re-examined by a board of officers. I maintained that I knew the subject, would prove it, and did not accept the failure marks. He said that he would see about it and sent me back to the lecture room. We then had a short break and re-assembled for the second period. The ballistic master started by saying that I had complained of being unfairly failed and, as an exception, he had agreed to re-examine me so that there would be no doubt about my marks. I noted that Lt Wolański was sitting at the back row.

Again I was at the black-board and answered all his questions, my platoon friends watching and listening with obvious interest.

"Well, that will do." he said. "I must admit I have made an error, and you will be pleased to hear that you have passed"

"What marks have I gained, sir?" I asked.

"Six." he said.

"I would be obliged if you would continue with more questions, sir. Six is not enough, I know the subject better than that."

He thought for a while and then said: "I will give you one blackboard problem, if you solve it you will get eight, but if you don't I will fail you. Agreed?"

"Agreed" I said.

It was a text-book example with all working stages and solution. He checked the black-board against the book and when I arrived at the same solution to the first decimal point, he conceded defeat and gave me eight with good grace and a friendly chat. Marks were important for overall placing which included flying, and the better the placing, the better the chance of a posting to the regiment of your choice. It was also recorded on personal documents and had a bearing on the career prospects of young officers.

It was at this stage that a final split of pilots for operational training took place. At the beginning of the final term prospective fighter pilots departed to a satellite airfield, Ułęż, heavy bombers to the bomber base at Małaszewicze, and light bombers remained at home.

I went to Ułęż. My new instructor was Lt Janusz Żurakowski - a brilliant pilot, excellent instructor and a self-taught aeronautical boffin. All his outstanding qualities were well proven during the war and afterwards, when he became a test pilot of the highest repute in Britain and Canada.

I was lucky to be in his group. He checked us on the PWS-26 and soon straightened out my slow and fast rolls and polished up everything else. He often resorted to pen and paper, drawing diagrams, distribution of forces in a given evolution, and proving a point mathematically. He knew a great deal more about the theory of flight than any of us.

The operational conversion and training was carried out on the P.7, a single-seater open-cockpit fighter aircraft with a maximum speed of 205 mph.

The aircraft looked like a bird and you felt like a bird flying it. The first solo flights proved too much for a couple of cadets who, having bent their machines somewhat, left us and joined the light bomber crowd. There was not much clear vision on landing and a great deal of caution was essential if accidents were to be avoided. After take-off, landing, and handling exercises, we began aerobatics. The group watched and listened to the instructor's comments, as each of us took off in turn and did the same thing in a defined air sector close to the airfield. He kept us hard at it until every item of the programme was executed to his satisfaction. The next stage was formation flying and dog-fights with the aid of the British made 'Fairchild' camera guns. Then came gunnery, which comprised air to ground, and air to air, firing practice. Once, when firing at a drag target head on and from above, I approached at too small an angle and my tail wheel collided with it and tore it off. I was not very popular with Capt. Królikowski, the gunnery officer, after this performance.

On completion of training in July we were informed of our postings to various regiments and fighter squadrons, and given fourteen days leave prior to reporting to our units.

Whilst in Dęblin cadets were entitled to flying pay, which was held back and used for the purchase of an entire new wardrobe including two uniforms, shirts, socks, etc. The balance left was paid to us at the end of the last term. I bought myself a wrist-watch and still went home with more money than I had ever had before.

I was posted to the Third Fighter Wing of the Sixth Air Force Regiment in Lwów. The wing had two squadrons, Nos. 161 and 162, equipped with the P.11 and P.7 respectively. Altogether seven cadet fighter pilots were posted to Lwów; to No. 161 Squadron went W. Choms, E. Kramarski, A. Malarowski*, P. Ruszel, and to No. 162 A. Dzięgielewski, R. Łopacki, and me.

---

* Malarowski had passed out with the highest place from the 12th entry at Dęblin; the author was placed third. *Ed.*

PART II - 1939 - 1945
THE WAR

2

I arrived home proudly wearing my pilot's wings, glad to leave Deblin and three very lean years behind me at last, and looking forward to two weeks of complete relaxation. Mother inspected, and greatly admired, every item of my new wardrobe; my brothers tried on my splendid black leather coat, and everybody wanted to know everything at once. I bought some vodka to celebrate the occasion and we had a lovely family party, including two sisters-in-law and a little nephew.

Towards the end of the first week of my leave I received a telegram: "Report to your unit immediately". Whilst I was packing, somebody else was organising transport to the station and somebody else still was taking messages to all members of the family who promptly gathered to say "Good-bye". We were in a sombre mood, saying little and thinking a lot. I shuddered at the thought of my three brothers getting their mobilisation orders and leaving their wives and our ageing parents alone, and hoped that it would never come to that. I said my farewells as quickly and as cheerfully as I could, blaming the re-call on probable manoeuvres or something of that sort, but I did not think anybody believed me.

That was the last time I saw my father and it was many years before I saw my mother and brothers again.

I reported to Colonel Prauss, the commanding Officer of No. 6 Air Force Regiment, to Major Stanisław Morawski, the Commanding Officer of III/6 Dywizjon (Wing), and to Lieutenant Bernard Groszewski, the Commanding Officer of No. 162 Squadron, who showed me around and introduced me to everybody. Toni Dzięgielewski and Ryszard Łopacki had already arrived and I was pleased to see them again.

There was no accommodation in the Officer's Mess. All officers lived out under private arrangements and, as we could not afford it on our cadet's pay, which also included flying pay, we were given free quarters in one wing of a barrack block - the three of us sharing a large dormitory. The four cadets of 161 Squadron had similar accommodation to ours. In all other respects we were members of the Officer's Mess except that we did not pay for our meals. Special transport to and from the city of Lwów was arranged for the service personnel of all ranks.

No. 161 Squadron was equipped with P.11 aircraft, whereas my squadron - No. 162 - had the P.7. This was a disappointment as the P.7 was inferior to P.11 in every respect and was overdue for phasing out. I hoped that we might be re-equipped very soon.

Four P.11s of No. 161 Squadron had been deployed since March on a landing field near the Polish/Soviet border, co-operating closely with the Border Defence Corps, and changing personnel once a month. They stayed there until the 24th August, Air Force mobilisation day. The rest of the squadron departed in the middle of August to the Lubitów range near Sarny where they lived under canvas and were engaged on air-to-air and air-to-ground firing practice. No. 162 Squadron stayed at Skniłów and I stayed with it. I thought that extensive combat training would be organised for us in both squadrons, and indeed it was so in No. 161, but No. 162 was rather slow and haphazard about it. We had one big exercise for close cover of light bombers and one for interception. The rest were dog-fights and formation flying, but regretfully no air-to-air firing. There were about twice as many pilots as aircraft and the queue for flying was too long.

A few days after my arrival I was ordered to work with the squadron SNCO who ran the Orderly Room and all administration. I was to learn all that, deputise for him during his absence on leave or other duties and to take morning parade of our airmen.

"What about flying?" I asked

"You will do your fair share, we will call you when your turn comes" was my Commanding Officer's reply. I did not like that, and deserted my administration chief whenever I could.

Every working day began with a regimental parade, weather permitting. My job was to assemble the squadron ground crews, march them to the parade ground and report to the commanding Officer. Next, the officers fell in, Wing commanders took over and reported to the Parade Adjutant, and then the Parade Commander would take over the lot and order "*Do Modlitwy!*" (Prepare for prayer!) We would then remove our headgear and sing a beautiful hymn:

> "When the morning light is breaking
> All the earth and all the sea
> And all the earthly living creatures
> Praise you Lord and sing to Thee
> And the man beyond all measure
> Blessed by many gifts from heaven
> Whom You made and saved for ever
> Why should he not pray and praise You"

The hymn is usually sung in Polish churches at the very beginning of the service and everybody knows it, even agnostics. The Polish text of "*Kiedy Ranne Wstają Zorze*" is truly beautiful.

One good thing about my administration job was that I learned a few things about our men and their problems. There was one randy fellow, I remember, who was constantly in trouble with women. He boasted to me how he had managed to seduce several of them, promising each one the earth, until one of them wrote a complaining letter to the Colonel. The fellow did not know what to do and asked my advice. I replied that, by his standards, I was as innocent as a newborn baby, but that he could start with an apology and stop telling lies in future. He was quite indignant at my naïve suggestion and told me that I had a lot to learn about women, I agreed! He ended up in the cooler for fourteen days.

Wednesday afternoons were occupied with sports activities and we spent most of them swimming in a marvellous Olympic size pool on the outskirts of the city. The pool had three spring boards and a diving tower. There was a large area of grass and young trees planted at random around it. All my diving in the past had been done from trees into the river Huczwa in my schooldays, but this was different. Sgt Pilot Domagała, a good swimmer and diver, took me under his wing and worked me up through the various spring boards to the tower. It was a long way down but I could not back down and dived time and time again until I was reasonably proficient, and in the end enjoyed showing off to the faint-hearted warriors. Domagała had a very attractive and charming wife and she often joined him at the pool, bringing delicious sandwiches with her. (When the war came he left her behind in Poland, fought bravely in England, and lives here now. I do not know what happened to her.)

I did not know the city of Lwów at all but Edek Kramarski from 161 Squadron did and he organised a couple of excellent parties in popular restaurants which we cadets could afford. He knew some nice girls, who knew more nice girls, and a party of 8 or 10 could be arranged at short notice. On the last occasion we stayed on long after everybody else had gone. We bought the orchestra one small vodka each and promised more after we were commissioned. They played for us for ages while we sang and danced and enjoyed to the full our last night out ever in Lwów. [Lwów - the lion's city - a faithful Polish city, taken by the Soviet Union, but not from the hearts of Poles.]

One evening I had a useful conversation with Lt Zadroziński, who happened to be the Orderly Officer of the day. I asked him about the lives of young officers, their interests, off-duty activities, leisure, careers, and asked if anyone did any further studies in particular. He spoke quite freely and confirmed my impression that there was a lot of free time that could be put to good use. About further studies - yes, it was possible, a few chaps were doing extra-mural university courses and he could get me more information if I was really interested. I was, in one year's time, after I had settled down as an officer. He agreed that it would be a good time to start but warned me about certain drawbacks. Generally speaking, these studies were not popular with Squadron COs, and brother officers would not like it either. There was a degree of petty jealousy about it and being excused duties would not endear me to anybody. However, the top brass was in favour, if one was really serious about it. I was greatly cheered by this and decided to make enquiries in the forthcoming autumn, with a view to starting a course in the following academic year. I thought that my first year in Lwów should be a fun year and I was looking forward to it.

On the 24th August mobilisation orders were received by the Commanding Officer of III/6 Wing and I was sent in a P.7 to 161 Squadron on their range airfield with written orders to return to base immediately. The Wing became fully operational on 25th August, and on the afternoon of the 26th, the ground crew, vehicles and equipment, were loaded on a special train under the command of second Lt Kazimierz Dreń, the Wing Technical Officer, and left for the station Lublinek, near Łódź, and then by road to a landing field near the village of Widzew, arriving on 27th August.

On the 30th August I had a date with a sweet red-haired girl and was allowed to leave the camp for a couple of hours, just long enough to say "Hullo" and "Good-bye". We met in the garden adjacent to a restaurant and after I had told her I could not stay for longer than half an hour, she asked me to meet her parents and brothers who were sitting at a table nearby. They were nice people, wished me well, and we all hoped to meet again soon. We never did, and I never saw Lwów again.

On the morning of 31st August the III/6 Wing moved to the alert airfield, Basiówka near the home base, and in the afternoon we flew to Dęblin where we refuelled, and then on to Widzew.

A fair sized oat field was set up as our airfield. The oats were already harvested and only the stubble was left, as well as some stooks which were used for camouflaging aircraft. On the southern side there was a lane lined with poplars, leading to a very fine manor house owned by Mr Herse, a German; and on the western edge of the field there was a deep ditch with a hedge of wild roses, blackthorn, and weeds. The poplars provided useful cover for the aircraft and the ditch was a natural shelter in case of enemy air-raids. Mr Herse was a landowner of considerable wealth, and close to his manor house were several estate buildings and sheds. The III/6 Wing Headquarters and pilots were accommodated in the manor house and the rest of the personnel in other buildings.

Our arrival at Widzew was marred by an accident - second Lt Rębalski damaged his P.11 on landing, which reduced the number of aircraft in 161 Squadron to 9. The damaged aircraft was immediately sent by road for repairs to the PZL workshops in Okęcie, Warsaw.

We were part of the 'Łódź' Army Air Force which consisted of:

- ⊙ No. 32 Reconnaissance Squadron
- ⊙ No. III/6 Fighter Wing (161 and 162 Squadrons)
- ⊙ No. 63 and 66 Observation Squadrons (Army Co-operation)
- ⊙ No. 10 Liaison Platoon (communication flight) at the disposal of the Army chief signals officer
- ⊙ Air Force Service Units:
- ⊙ No. 7 Airfield Company comprising:
- ⊙ Nos. 61, 62 and 63 Airfield guard platoons
- ⊙ Nos. 6 and 62 Airfield platoons (construction etc.)
- ⊙ No. 61 Meteorological station
- ⊙ No. 6 radio communication section
- ⊙ No. 2 Mobile Air Stores Park was in the process of mobilisation by the 2nd Air Force Regiment in Krakow. It did not arrive at its destination.

(The above units operated under the command of Col. pilot Wacław Iwaszkiewicz whose headquarters were at Julianów, near Łódź.)

The 'Łódź' army came into being in March 1939 under the command of General Div. Juliusz Rómmel. It was deployed defensively in the area of the anticipated main thrust of Hitler's forces, and on 1st September 1939 comprised:

- ⊙ Nos. 2, 10, 28, and 30 Infantry divisions (one division was about to complete detraining and was not in position)
- ⊙ The Wołyń Cavalry Brigade
- ⊙ The Borderland (Kresowa) Cavalry Brigade (one cavalry brigade was detraining and not in position)
- ⊙ A number of National Defence battalions

The 'Łódź' Army operational area was covered by an air observation network, all posts being connected directly to the Centre in Łódź, where reports were collated, plotted, and reported to III/6 Wing H.Q. and to other units and commands as required.

The Łódź Army (Gen. Rómmel) together with the 'Krakow' Army (Gen. Szyling), 'Karpaty' Army (Gen. Fabrycy) and Reserves (Gen. Dąb-Biernacki) formed the Army group 'South'. Facing it was the German Army Group 'South' under overall command of Gen. Rundstedt, and consisting of No. 10 Army (Gen. Reichenau), No. 8 Army (Gen. Blaskowitz) and No. 14 Army (Gen. List).

In the early hours of 1st September the 8th and 10th German armies attacked the defence line held by the Polish Łódź Army, with the support of four Air Armies (*Luftflotten*) of No. 4 Air Army (Gen. Lohr), both in the battle zone and behind the Polish forces, where the main targets were lines of communication.

It was in this situation that my squadron - 162 - equipped with the out-dated P.7, without radios, entered the war. The action began at about 0500 hours when a Dornier 17 appeared on a recce mission in the Łódź area, and a readiness section of 161 squadron led by Lt Trzebiński took off and intercepted him. After a brief exchange of fire the Dornier disengaged and, being considerably faster, flew west.

In the first two days I was scrambled twice. On the first occasion I tried to intercept an enemy aircraft but it was much faster and I could not get anywhere near it. In the second occasion I fired a short burst but my gun jammed. I struggled to re-load it and then manoeuvred myself into an attacking position somehow. I intended to make a half roll and dive towards the tail of the enemy aircraft. While I was upside down my straps failed to hold me and I literally fell out, opened my parachute and landed near a village. Either the quick release lock was faulty or I opened it during the re-loading struggle. I cannot say with any certainty which was the real cause of this unfortunate accident. I was driven to Widzew in an army vehicle and to my shame I had to report the loss of my aircraft. It was an avoidable loss and I must accept the blame for it.

I think it was about noon on the 2nd of September when I was sent to the Observation Network Centre in Łódź to act as liaison officer with the Wing Headquarters. My job was to sift and scrutinise information available and advise of only the larger enemy formations, which could be intercepted from our base. Prior to that, the Centre was passing on too many details, some of which were of little use.

The onslaught of the German Air force and the two armies on the Łódź Army sector was overpowering, in spite of the fierce resistance of our troops. The odds were against us and our ground forces had to retreat in stages until they were ordered to fall back to the river Wisła. In the air the Luftwaffe had complete superiority. The reports of their actions were pouring in from dawn to dusk. It was impossible for the III/6 Wing to have any serious impact on the German air offensive, I knew that when I was passing reports to them of large and medium sized raids.

I returned to base on the evening of 4th September and found out how bad things really were with us. On the afternoon of 2nd September a fierce battle took place in the base area between seven of our aircraft and twenty plus Me-110s[*]. Second Lieutenant Dzwonek, already wounded and returning to base joined the battle, was shot down and parachuted. Cadet Piotr Ruszel was shot down and killed in the morning, and Cadet Edward Kramarski met the same fate later on.

On 3rd September the Wing operated from ambush fields, and from the main base. On 4th September three P.7s returned to Widzew for refuelling and re-arming after a sortie from their ambush field when a German Do-17 appeared overhead. The readiness section - Lt Jeziorowski and 2nd Lt Zadroziński - took off and almost immediately were attacked by nine Me-109s. In this unequal fight Jeziorowski was wounded, attempted to land, was hit again, set on fire, and crashed to his death. Zadroziński, wounded in the leg, and with his engine damaged, managed to land on an adjacent field and leave the aircraft before it was shot up and burned. The three helpless P.7s were hit on the ground and set on fire, and so were another two P.7s, damaged in previous fights and parked near a straw stook. By the end of the day the III/6 Wing had five serviceable aircraft left, and no replacements.

On 5th September all ambush fields were closed, ground crews brought back, and the wing was ordered to move next day to Drwalew, near Grójec. The advance party left at 21.00 hours to set up a landing strip and receive the aircraft next morning.

On 6th September, very early in the morning, the main party of men, including a number of pilots and equipment, left Widzew by road, while the rear party saw the five remaining aircraft off to the new airfield, some time later. A few men were staying behind to repair one RWD-8, a communication aircraft.

I flew to Drwalew where we parked and camouflaged our aircraft on the edge of the woods, and were instructed to stay put and await the arrival of our men and vehicles. A few hours later three enemy aircraft appeared at a distance bombing and firing at something. 2nd Lt Główczyński

---

[*] Throughout these memoirs the Author has used designations for German aircraft as used by allied airmen at the time, such as "Me-110", "FW-190", etc. instead of Bf 110, Fw 190, etc. *Ed.*

decided to go after them and so did Sgt Prętkiewicz and Cpl. Urbańczyk. My P.7 would not start, it coughed and spluttered and would not go and, in the end, I was ordered out. Główczyński and the two NCOs shot down three German aircraft - Henschels, I think.

I was then instructed to proceed with a driver, in a lorry to Widzew and bring back the RWD-8 whilst the men were to come back by road. Driving along we soon found out what it was the German aircraft were bombing - it was part of our road party carrying pilots and some equipment. One officer, five NCO pilots, and one driver were killed, and a few vehicles destroyed.

Our journey was very slow as everything was moving in the opposite direction. The army units were retreating, and civilians driving and on foot moved east as well. We were stopped by the Luftwaffe twice - once in a small town which was bombed, and once near Widzew where we were hiding under trees near a church while a number of Me-109s were buzzing around. My RWD-8 was ready and I was soon on my way back, flying at low level and keeping away from main roads so as not to frighten the people and troops, and not to be shot at. Everything in the air was assumed to be German, and so it was, except for our few aircraft.

On the next day, the 7th September, we were on the move again - to Malczyn airfield near Lublin, where our five combat aircraft were to be absorbed by the (Fighter) Pursuit Brigade. The woods at Drwalew contained several RWD-8s (unarmed basic trainer/communication), more than enough for the pilots without aircraft, and consequently all pilots flew to our new destination where we met remnants of fighter squadrons from the 4th and 5th Air Force Regiments.

On 8th September some of our ground crews and vehicles joined us, bringing food, fuel, and our private belongings with them. Malczyn was just a field without services and supplies and so on the next day we moved again, joining the badly depleted IV Wing (Warsaw) at Radawiec Wielki - nearer Lublin. From then on we had no proper backing and supplies and were always short of fuel. Part of our ground crews were trying to catch up with us since Widzew and did not succeed until the 15th September. Attempts at the reorganisation of remnants of various wings were made with frequent changes of airfields and the ever-present fuel problem. On 10th September we moved to Młynów near Łuck, landing at dusk, and on the next day we moved back to Jabłonna, near Lublin, again. I was sent some twenty miles away on a motor-cycle with side-car to sniff out whether there was any German penetration in our direction, while other chaps drove to Lublin aircraft factory in search of petrol. They were successful, and so was I; there were no Germans to be heard of or seen by anybody within my route.

I think it was on the 12th September that I was sent to deliver some important papers to General Headquarters located in the south eastern part of Poland in the RWD-8. I landed close to a splendid palace on a stud farm where about a hundred horses were grazing on one side of the field. I delivered the papers and when taking off I noticed, to my horror, the horses running across my path. It was too late to abort and I prayed that I might gain enough speed to become airborne in time. I did, missing them by inches, and looking into their wild eyes, almost eyeball to eyeball. It was a terrifying experience for me and for the horses.

At one time I travelled with Major Morawski, our Wing Commanding Officer, in his staff car through Hrubieszów where we stopped for supper. I met my history master for a brief chat, then I called on Mr Gregier who knew my family and left some money with him for my father. We then proceeded farther east towards our airfield. It was a terrible journey, our driver was so tired that he was falling asleep and so we stopped until daybreak for a much needed rest.

Our final move in Poland was to Liliatyn, where remnants of all fighter units and their ground crews were to concentrate. It seemed that everybody else who had something to fly was aiming for it as well. I flew there in the RWD-8 and was surprised to see quite a lot of them camouflaged on the edge of the woods already. Our ground crew brought some fuel with them and on 16th September 2nd Lt Zadroziński, sent on a recce flight to the Lwów area, shot down one He-111. Similarly, on the 17th 2nd Lt Koc shot down a Do-17. These were the last two operational sorties of the III/6 Wing in Poland.

On the same day, the 17th September, all pilots were called for briefing and informed that the Red Army had crossed our border and was moving westwards. It was essential to fly to Rumania and make our way to France by whatever means; the Polish embassy in Bucharest would help. Pilots without aircraft, and ground crews, were to move by road into Rumania. Anybody who did not want to leave the country could stay behind. Forty seven aircraft, P.11s and P.7s, took off shortly after the briefing and landed at Cernauti airfield in Rumania at about 1600 hours, as well as a number of other aircraft. My RWD-8 was gone by the time I returned from briefing, borrowed by an enterprising pilot in a hurry, and I joined my three squadron friends who were travelling in an almost new Opel acquired or requisitioned somehow by Cadet Łopacki; the other passengers were: Lt Wisniewski, cadet Dzięgielewski, and myself., All cadets of my entry were commissioned in the field with effect from 1st September 1939, so the three of us were now 2nd Lieutenants.

We started towards the border town of Zaleszczyki, trapped in a long column of vehicles of all kinds, mostly military but some civilians as well. Ryszard Łopacki was driving, nobody felt like talking much. My thoughts were sombre and confused and I was shocked by the Soviet treachery; the Germans from one side and the Soviet Union from the other, crushing us again as they did before. I felt deeply about the injustice of it all and firmly believed that those two evil regimes had to be resisted. I agreed with the thinking behind the order to evacuate to Rumania; that our allies might yet discharge their obligations to Poland and that some of us must go there, be seen by them, and fight by their side. Our progress was very slow. Soon after nightfall we met several vehicles moving in the opposite direction to us, people were shouting that the Red Army was only a few miles ahead of us and that the road to Zaleszczyki was in their hands.

"Turn back, and aim for the border bridge at Kuty" was their advice.

It was long after midnight when we joined the long queue of stationary vehicles before the bridge. We waited there until the early hours of the morning, fell asleep, and did not hear somebody unscrewing our spare wheel from the back of the car. Another driver's need was obviously greater than ours; fortunately our tyres never caused us any problem in the journey ahead. At last, the vehicles in front of us began moving slowly and we followed until we crossed the bridge. We were in Rumania.

RUMANIA

There was a sense of relief when we entered Rumania. A great deal of thinking and wrestling with one's soul and conscience had gone into the past hours and I felt exhausted. Now, a sort of macabre adventure was beginning, where time was of the utmost importance. We had to move fast and get out of Rumania somehow before the old order fell. There was a strong Fascist organisation called the Iron Guard which co-operated with the Germans, and it looked as if the 'master race' would be moving into the Balkans pretty soon.

We talked about our situation and concluded that our immediate priority was to obtain some local currency, the lei. We had been paid a lot of money before leaving Poland and I had the equivalent of about four months' 2nd Lieutenant's salary in my pocket. We understood that the banks would change a limited amount and with that pressing thought we proceeded towards a sizeable town. The road led through two villages. In the first one some good-hearted women were offering mugs of milk. We stopped and drank greedily. We were hungry. Food had been scarce in the last few days as the Ukrainian villages around Liliatyn airfield had refused to sell any provisions to our foraging parties. There was a great deal of anti-Polish agitation and hostile action going on at that time, led by nationalist elements financed and organised by Germans since years before the war.

Our kind milk provider spoke some Ukrainian and I thought it would be a good idea to start a dictionary of useful Rumanian words and phrases there and then, as the only foreign language we had between us was German and my broken Ukrainian. *Milk* was the first word, followed by *bread*, *bank*, *money*, etc. We gained some thirty useful words before we left. In the next village we were offered some apples by another kind soul, a Jewish woman this time, who had just arrived with a bucketful of them. She, too, spoke some Ukrainian and again I took advantage of it and added several new words to my dictionary, including *apples*, *ham*, *sausages*, *butter*, and numbers and phrases such as *how far to...?*, *which way to...?*, etc. Our next stop was at the bank where we were allowed to change about a hundred zloty each, which was ample for our immediate needs. We bought a lot of bread, butter, smoked sausages and ham, and had a feast in the car.

It was early afternoon when we reached the river Prut. The weather was warm and the sun was shining on a peaceful landscape as if nothing had happened and all was well with the world. We stopped by the river in a secluded spot, bathed naked, washed, shaved, and feeling much refreshed, continued our journey south. The road left the river Prut and ran along the beautiful valley of the river Seret. We spent the first night uncomfortably in the car, having turned off the main road and stopped amongst a few trees and out of sight. Everyone was tired and slept soundly until the morning light woke us up. We had enough food for the whole day and made an early start hoping to reach Focsani by the evening. We arrived at the outskirts of the town shortly before sunset and turned off the main road into a lane leading to a prosperous looking farm. Nobody there spoke German or Ukrainian and so, with the aid of my dictionary, I started my first conversation of sorts in Rumanian. "Yes, it was all right for us to stay over-night. We could sleep in the barn". The farmer, his wife, and two daughters - Maricela and Sofica - were very friendly and invited us into their house. We wore uniform and they knew we were Poles and what was happening to our country. We used sign language extensively and we understood that they were concerned about their future, the Iron

Guard and Germans were oft repeated words. The farmer wished he had a gun for their protection and we gave him a cumbersome Vis revolver, keeping our own Walter guns. He was very pleased and thanked us profusely, but his wife and daughters were a bit afraid of the terrible tool, and after a brief and agitated conversation, he disappeared with it - probably to hide it safely somewhere. The two girls were about seventeen or eighteen years of age, students at a local academy, both very attractive. Their mother offered us some food and wine and we stayed with them until the farmer took us to the barn where there was a lot of hay on one side. His daughters brought blankets and Toni and I escorted them back to the house, where we stood outside for a while, trying to communicate with words and gestures, making little progress but enjoying it. In desperation I threw my arms wide open and Maricela stepped forward with a sweet smile having misunderstood my intentions, and we embraced freely and tenderly. Toni and Sofica followed our example and so ended our second day on Rumanian soil.

After breakfast next morning the girls walked with us to the nearest bank where we changed more Polish currency, and then we intended walking to the centre of the city to shop for a few essential items, but the girls gestured with some urgency that we ought to go back. When we failed to understand why, they took us around the corner of one street and pointed towards a square where, to our horror, we saw five men hanging on high gallows. We walked back to the farm shocked by the barbarity of the public execution, which had apparently taken place the previous day. Their crime was some kind of politically motivated violence and their bodies were to hang there for a day as a warning to others.

Before our departure Maricela gave me her address and two photographs, one of herself with a dog, and one with Sofica. I promised to write from France, which I did, and she replied in the spring of 1940. The whole family gave us a warm send off with a lot of *drum bums. Drum bum* - pronounced 'droom boom' - were the first two words of a very popular song which had swept the country, as I later found out, and meant 'good journey'.

Within an hour of leaving Focsani we arrived at a main road junction and were directed by the military to proceed to Tulcea, where all Poles were to assemble in a provisional holding camp. I did not like that at all, camps are easy to get into but usually difficult to get out of. However, we had no choice and proceeded as ordered. There was a road block on the outskirts of the town and as soon as we crossed it we stopped to look around and stretch our legs. There were several quite big houses nearby and not a sign of any formal camp. It would be a good idea to stop here and investigate rather than go any further. A young Roumanian 2nd Lt, speaking German, came to us and we told him that we would like to stop in this area, could pay for cheap accommodation, and could he possibly help us? Once he knew we could pay there was no problem, he arranged everything quickly and offered to look after our interests, but he would also like us to help him, if we could. He had seen several Polish army motor-cycles in town and asked us to assist him in procuring one. We promised to try.

On the next day I explored Tulcea, which was filling up daily with odd looking civilian 'tourists', and men in khaki and blue uniforms. It was a small town lying close to the Danube delta with the usual eating and drinking places and a number of shops. From geography lessons I vaguely remembered that the delta was a unique area in Europe as a natural wild-life reserve, created by God with birds, fish, and rare plants in mind. But I did not know that to protect them from man He had sprinkled mosquitoes around and armed them with malaria. It was not a healthy place to stay for long.

In the evening our protector called on us and we talked about a motor-cycle again and about a useful contact we had made with an army chap who might be able to help him. But our main concern was that of leaving for Bucharest as soon as possible. He insisted that we could not do it travelling in uniform. The area east of the Danube was a semi-military zone with frequent checks on main roads and they would turn us back to Tulcea unless we wore civilian clothes and had a good, plausible story. He told us that in Galati, a large town on the west side of the river Danube, a tailor would make new suits for us in a few days; he then proceeded to tell us how to go about it. It was all very simple. He let us pass through the road block and we drove to a farm on our side of the Danube, opposite Galati; we gave a note to the farmer, leaving our car with him, and set off with a boatman in a small motor boat across the river which was enormously wide. A few minutes later we were intercepted by the river police who sent us back with clear and firm instructions:

"No crossing, back to Tulcea!"

Half an hour later we started off again and were almost touching the opposite bank when the river police appeared right on top of us. After disembarking they escorted us to the police station nearby where we waited whilst one of them made a couple of telephone calls. Then three soldiers with rifles and bayonets arrived and marched us some distance through the main street of the town. People were turning their heads and looking at us in surprise; some waved in a friendly manner, others just stared, while we tried to appear unconcerned about this pantomime. Eventually we arrived at the Police Headquarters where a German-speaking senior officer greeted us politely and asked what we were up to. I told him truthfully our story which he accepted, giving us a pass for the river police and suggesting a good tailor who would do the job quicker if we told him that the policeman had sent us to him. He was on our side and disliked Germans, he wished us well, and we parted on the best of terms.

A few days later we repeated the expedition and bought shirts, ties, pullovers, etc., and on our return to Tulcea a great transformation took place. We discarded our almost new uniforms, giving them to our friendly Rumanian officer, and introduced him to a Polish army officer who might be helpful about the motor-cycle, and arranged an early departure for Bucharest next morning.

There were no problems with leaving Tulcea but a couple of hours later Rysiek Łopacki - our driver - took a wrong turning in a very large village and we found ourselves in a narrow lane with one wheel in a ditch. The four of us could not push the car back on to the hard road by ourselves and, seeing several men approaching, we asked them to help us. A tall, bearded fellow of some authority nodded his head and organised more muscle power. The car was soon on the main road facing in the right direction, we got inside with the intention of driving off but the men, at least a dozen of them, stood right in front off the car. The bearded chap indicated that we were to stay put whilst he telephoned. We did not like that at all and as soon as he disappeared Rysiek started the engine to loud protestations, and began reversing. They reacted immediately and some of them ran to the back of the car leaving an opening in front wide enough to get through without injuring anybody. Rysiek saw that, slammed on the brakes, swiftly engaged first gear and shot forward leaving the shouting locals behind. Ten minutes later we saw a single policeman standing in the middle of the road waving us down to stop. He was on his own, he had no revolver in his hand, only a whip of some kind, so we decided not to waste any time on him either. Rysiek opened his window, brought the car almost to a halt, the policeman came to his side and Rysiek accelerated leaving him behind.

Our map indicated a sizeable town about ten miles ahead of us. We had to drive through it as there was no other road to by-pass it, and it occurred to us there might be a reception committee waiting for us - and there was. The road was closed by a lorry parked across it and there was a crowd of people and police waiting for us. We stopped, got out of the car and the senior police officer offered us his German, or his wife's French, in order to find out what we were up to. I used my limited German to tell him that we had business with the Polish embassy in Bucharest and were anxious to get there as quickly as possible. Our intentions were peaceful, we were not breaking any laws as far as we knew. Rumania and Poland had a treaty of friendship and we understood that we would be allowed to pass through his country to France and could count on some assistance, within the spirit of the treaty

"May we please be allowed to leave?" He listened politely and asked:

"Why didn't you stop in the village as you were requested to do?"

"We don't speak Rumanian and did not understand what those men wanted of us" I said. "Their attitude was far from friendly, we did not feel safe surrounded by a crowd of fierce looking villagers."

"All right" he said, "But what about my policeman? You did not stop for him either, why?"

"Similar problem" I replied. "How could we communicate with him? We thought that our best course was to drive to this town and explain ourselves to somebody in authority. We are glad to be able to do so to you, but judging by this road-block, we must be in disgrace. We apologise for the trouble we have caused, but we did not do anything wrong, nor have we committed any crime, and are asking your permission to let us proceed."

He advised us not to ignore the police in future and said that he would give us a police escort until we reached the next district Headquarters, where another policeman would take over and escort us to Bucharest. I thanked him for being so understanding and helpful and we all became friends again. He introduced his wife and we chatted for a while until a giant of a policeman reported for the escort duty. We parted on the best of terms, but we now had a different kind of problem. Our escort filled half of the back seat and Toni and I were squashed to one side. The Opel was a small four seater and there was hardly any room for him. To make matters worse his breath smelt of garlic. This was what hell must be like, I thought, and began thinking of how to get rid of him without creating an international incident.

We suffered for over an hour, then crossed the Danube and entered a small town. Rysiek stopped and we all got out to stretch our legs; Toni and I were half-paralysed. We had already agreed that we would lose our policeman at the first opportunity and this seemed to be as good an opportunity as any. I gave him some money and sent him in search of wine, bread, and sausages, and as soon as he disappeared into the next street we jumped into the car and drove off. It was also agreed that if we were stopped and had to explain the reason for ditching our friendly policeman we would blame the garlic and try to make a joke of it. Fortunately nobody chased us and we reached the suburbs of Bucharest unhindered, stopping at a small, modest hotel with a pleasant garden and veranda. Food and wine were available at reasonable prices and we spent some time sitting in the garden watching the locals and listening to a solo violinist playing gypsy music.

It was a long walk to the Polish Embassy next morning but we found it without difficulty, being directed by our compatriots who were everywhere. I was interviewed by an official who took down my particulars and said that the Air Force had priority for despatch to France and that they were making arrangements to send us by land or sea as soon as possible. I had to join a queue outside the Embassy, have my photograph taken and return with two prints in order to have the passport completed and issued. All this was done by the next day. It was a provisional document on a large sheet of white paper with a photograph and the usual particulars, stamps, and signatures. The entry made under the heading 'occupation' read 'student'.

The Embassy was a final point for thousands of service people as well as civilians, men, women, and children. More and more were arriving in Bucharest daily and our Embassy staff worked on relentlessly day and night. They were well informed, intelligent and enterprising people; scheming, wheeling and dealing, bribing, and doing everything they could to get everybody out of Rumania before the Germans took the country over.

With the brand new passports in our pockets we did the usual round of the embassies to get transit visas to France and had no difficulties except with a Rumanian exit visa - they were not giving any. While we discussed our problem over coffee, and wondering how much money we might need to bribe them, a Polish-speaking waitress, who was obviously listening to our conversation, spoke to us and suggested a meeting with her friend, who had a friend in the right place, to solve our problem - for money, of course. We met them both the same evening but nothing came of it and it was soon apparent, after a few minutes of conversation, that they were confidence tricksters and were only interested in our money and how to extract it from us.

In the centre of Bucharest there is a beautiful park called Cismidziu with fine trees, shrubs, a lake and ducks. I spent a lot of time there whilst awaiting events. On one occasion I met, by pure chance, Mrs Markowa and her daughter Maryśka who went to the same school as I, in Hrubieszów, but was my junior by several years; I gave her private German lessons at one time. Mr Marek was the head of the district administration, an important man with an official car and a chauffeur. He sent his family to Rumania but he remained in Poland and never left the country. The mother and daughter made their way to England in 1940 or '41 via French North Africa. I met the mother once in the Polish Red Cross around Grosvenor Square - the building was offered to the Poles by its generous owner.

Rysiek Łopacki sold the car which had brought us to Bucharest without telling us of his intention to do so. The car must have been given to him by somebody in Poland, and was his to sell, nobody questioned that. He decided to invest the money in jewellery and acquired a ring with a fair-sized diamond, which he wore on his finger. I hope the stone was real, but I would not have trusted crafty Rumanians without some expert advice.

As we no longer had any transport we moved to a hotel nearer the embassy. I carried most of my belongings in a Dęblin-issue, black leather brief-case which I still possess, we travelled light in those days. All in all, we spent about ten days in Bucharest. I liked the city and would have enjoyed a holiday there under normal circumstances.

At last we were instructed to proceed by rail to the Black Sea port of Balcic, close to the Bulgarian border, and there to await arrival of a ship. There was a fast train to Constanta, and a slow one, or a bus to Balcic. We had heard of certain checks by the military in an area east of the Danube, both on trains and on the roads, and some thought that a train to Cernavoda - a large town on the eastern bank of the Danube - and a taxi to Balcic, might be a good idea. It would be in the interests of the taxi driver to deliver his passengers to their destination and he would, no doubt, cope much better with any military checks than any of us. Rysiek decided to travel by train all the way, whilst the three of us opted for the second alternative, and left the train at Cernavoda. There were several taxis by the station and I selected one which looked in good shape and started negotiating a deal. The driver insisted on part advance payment and had to be satisfied that we could pay the rest later, before we departed. It was a quiet drive through a very rural countryside. We experienced two military checks without our being bothered at all as our driver managed to talk, joke, and laugh his way through each of them.

On arrival at Balcic, an attractive sea-side resort with a fine bay sheltered on three sides by high ground, we paid our driver and suggested he could earn a bonus if he could find us accommodation, preferably with a family. He said he would fix it in no time at all and left us waiting in the car. He returned quite quickly with a hefty policeman by his side and said that the policeman would be glad to accommodate us and his wife would cook meals for us if required. This was better than we could have hoped for. It would certainly be safe to stay there, the lawman would, no doubt, look after his paying-guests for as long as they could pay. It was a fine house with a patio over-looking the bay, standing on the northern slope, and quite close to the centre of this attractive town. We had a large dormitory with three beds and settled down happily, having paid one week's rent in advance, which was surprisingly cheap.

The town was gradually filling up with air force men, arriving daily from Bucharest in small batches. A group of senior officers ran the show with an embassy man, and a word was passed around telling us to sit quietly, behave, and cause no problems with the police; further instructions would be given in due course.

It was early October, the weather was fine and the sea still warm. I swam and walked a lot, the coast was beautiful, particularly to the north of the town. Our domestic arrangements worked admirably. Our hostess was a nice Bulgarian woman and I could communicate with her after a fashion, using a mixture of Polish, Ukrainian, and Rumanian words, while she spoke slowly in Bulgarian. She was a good cook, fed us well and cheaply, and we lived there en-pension. Her husband was a likeable rogue, a womaniser, and too fond of drink. It was difficult to refuse his invitations to rough drinking places where we paid for all drinks, sipping one glass to his three.

One day *Tata* Ostrowski appeared in a large café, our usual meeting place, and we jumped to attention and greeted him warmly and noisily. He was pleased to see us but told us that as we all wore civilian clothes, we should try to behave like civilians.

"You know, like you did before you went to Dęblin, look a bit untidy and sloppy, don't march but walk about nonchalantly. If I had a bit of time I would soon make good civilians of you!" he said, smiling.

It was nice to have him around. He was a symbol of sanity in the mad world around us, and a reminder of a secure and orderly life which was now no more.

Our ship, 'Patris', arrived one day and moored some distance from the shore. Next morning several Rumanian Home Office officials set up shop to hear our requests for exit visas. It was a chancy business, you either got one, or you did not, depending on the whim of the official working with an interpreter. They would look at you, ask a question or two and stamp the passport with an exit visa, or say:

"You were in the forces, visa refused" and then retain your passport. I had heard that money might help, but not always. Perhaps there was some minimum decided upon below which they would not respond, but nobody knew the form exactly.

"What is your occupation?" I was asked. I swore that I was a student and was to be called up for national service next year but they did not believe me.

"Visa refused" was the verdict. I showed the interpreter all the money I had left, he smiled, and told me to keep it, and send the next chap in.

It was on the second day at dusk when the embarkation began. A final check of passports and exit visas was made on the quay by torchlight and the holders of proper documents were sent to the ship by a large motor boat. The boat returned to the quay and took the next load, and so on. Our people had a small, but fast, motor-boat which ferried passports with exit visas from the ship for distribution among chaps such as myself who had no exit visas and no passports, whilst we waited in a dark area some distance from the quay. Eventually I was given somebody's passport, told to memorise all particulars and proceed to the quay for embarkation. There was a lot to remember: name, date of birth, colour of eyes, occupation, etc., all in about fifteen minutes. I went, with my brief case and a small parcel, to the check point where two men stood with torches, flashed a light on my face and on the passport, asked my name and date of birth and I was moved on to the boat. Five minutes later I was on the ship, handing my passport over to the chap who was collecting them for despatch to the shore again.

I had heard it said that the 'Patris' had been a passenger boat designed for Mediterranean cruises, carrying about three hundred and fifty people. I do not know exactly how many of us boarded her in the end but estimates varied from just under one thousand to about one thousand two hundred. The fact was that we were packed in like sardines and people were sprawling everywhere, in cabins, corridors, decks, and even in life-boats.

The night was warm, the sea calm, and the sky glittering with stars, as we left Balcic bay. I found myself a corner on the open deck and sat down watching the lights on shore fading away until I could see them no more. I lay down with my Dęblin brief case for a pillow, closed my eyes, and tried to sleep, but I could not. I felt as if my brain was being bombarded with mixed up visions of my family, with smoke rising from burning villages and towns as far as the eye could see, smashed and burned aeroplanes, smouldering lorries and carts, dead horses, and that never-to-be-forgotten hospital in Łódź, full of wounded and dying men - lying everywhere on beds and on the floor, in rooms and in corridors, some moaning in agony, others lieing silently with their eyes closed or wide open, waiting and hoping.

I must have fallen asleep in the end and when I awoke the dawn was breaking. There was complete silence on deck except for the monotonous throbbing of the ship's engines. I watched the sun rising in the cloudless sky with the promise of a fine day and felt calmer, all was not lost yet.

Our Black Sea and Mediterranean cruise was no picnic, but there was food and water and we were all fit and sound physically and therefore capable of taking up arms again. Our spirit and morale, however, was badly bruised and it was essential for every individual to sort himself out, repair the damage, and regain a degree of equilibrium. As for a sense of purpose and comprehension of our duty, there could be no doubt.

The sea journey was a good opportunity to revitalise our inner forces, take a positive stance, and start looking ahead with hope. We talked, exchanged news and views, argued, and even cursed in anger, or secretly wiped away a tear for a friend when all brakes failed. It was an exhausting and seemingly never-ending mind and soul-searching process which was, at the same time, a source of strength.

We sailed in daylight through the straits of Bosporus. The golden tips of minarets shone brightly on the Turkish side and welcomed us to the narrow water. Ships, ferries, yachts, and boats of all description were everywhere going about their business, while the 'Patris' pushed its way through and occasionally hooted some mad dinghy sailors out of the way. Fine villas, terraced gardens, mosques and forts were coming and going out of sight as I stood on the deck watching the Turkish coast - it was all so new and different from anything I had ever seen before.

We went through the Sea of Marmara and the Dardanelles, when the weather started to deteriorate. Passing through the Aegean Sea all I could see were the dark shadows of beautiful Greek islands. A fierce storm raged for a day and a night with ferocity rarely encountered in those waters - it was hell. I remember getting out on deck at night when I could not stand the stench of people being sick any more. The boat was pitching and rolling at incredible angles, a few crates became loose and were sliding from side to side, the wind was howling with tremendous force, and it was pitch dark. I laid on the deck for a while, holding on to something, until my eyes became accustomed to the darkness and then I crawled around the superstructure where I found a safe corner out of the wind, with a pile of ropes entangled around something. I sat there for hours in relative comfort, breathing in wonderfully fresh air.

Heavy rain at dawn forced me inside. I joined Toni who was looking green and announced he was about to die and did not wish to speak to anybody. Pan Jan was in an equally sorry state and Rysiek staggered away in search of the Purser and the latest news on the weather. He and the Purser became pals in spite of the fact that the Greek did not speak Polish and Rysiek spoke nothing but Polish.

Toni was lying next to a door which was always closed, but I noticed a minute gap which made me think that it was not locked and tried to open the door. To my surprise I was making progress by moving the door to and fro and when the gap became larger I saw cushions inside to the height of four feet. I whispered to Toni and Pan Jan about my discovery and the three of us pushed the door hard and created a gap wide enough for me to pull one cushion out, then another one, and another - dozens of them were soon flying around to the delight of our neighbours. Eventually I squeezed myself inside - I was in a bathroom. I threw out more cushions until only those in the bath-tub and one layer on the floor were left. Toni and Pan Jan joined me and the three of us ceremoniously staked a claim and took possession of the bathroom as our private apartment. We decided there and then that one of us must always stay inside as there was no key to the door and there were numerous pirates on board.

Rysiek joined us after he had seen his Greek pal and swore that the storm was apparently so bad that the Captain and crew were standing by to abandon ship if necessary. I do not know how this dramatic information was conveyed to him in sign language, or perhaps he heard it from another 'reliable source', but if it was true few of us would survive unless, of course, the boat refused to go down without its Captain.

Gradually the wind subsided, the boiling sea simmered down, and the sun shone again for us. As we moved south the weather became warmer and the decks were crowded day and night. Two days before we reached Malta we ran out of drinking water, but there was plenty of wine on board and the Greeks suddenly decided to accept Polish zlotys, charging us the earth of course. Somebody suggested that the water problem was likely to improve once all the wine was sold, but I could not believe they would be so mean. I had quite a lot of Polish coins with numbers 10, 20, 50, or 100 on them, the highest being worth a shilling, and I tried to use them instead of valuable paper money. It worked, I 'out-Greeked' the Greeks, and recouped my losses from earlier purchases when I paid an outrageous price for a bottle of plonk.

Early one morning we reached Malta and the 'Patris' moored outside the entrance to the Grand Harbour. We took on water and provisions and more than half of the passengers were transferred to another ship in Valetta. The four of us decided to stay on 'Patris' - we were quite comfortable in our bathroom apartment, the journey to Marseilles would take only a few days, we had water and food, and we were likely to be in France before the other lot. Late in the afternoon of the same day we were on our way. Everything went well from then on, the weather continued to be fine, the sea calm and even the 'Patris' cooks excelled themselves in their efforts and produced decent meals throughout the rest of the journey. At last the coast of France appeared on the horizon and two seagulls greeted the ship noisily. Rysiek thought this was a good omen and took a photograph of them. We stood on deck watching the coast growing larger and larger until we entered the harbour. I wondered what lay ahead. France had failed us, but they would fight for themselves. I preferred to hope rather than doubt and was eager to enter the country of Poland's traditional ally, who had let us down many times in the past, but perhaps this time it would be different.

FRANCE

The citizens of Marseilles welcomed us in the harbour. A group of ladies set up shop near the quay and handed a packed meal to everybody with a smile and a word of welcome as we were walking towards a fleet of buses parked nearby. "Merci Madame" I said to an elegant matron, wishing that I understood what she had said to me. Language, a problem again, better not to speak German here, I must learn French quickly I thought, as I entered the bus.

I looked through the window at the beautiful Rhône valley as we were speeding towards Lyons. Our destination was a huge exhibition hall which was to become my home for a few months. The vast area was subdivided into accommodation sections for officers and officer cadets. Other ranks were accommodated in a dilapidated barracks at the French Air Force base at Lyon-Bron, a few miles away. The conditions were primitive. Bunk beds and straw palliases in a sort of corral, but I thought we would not be there for long so it did not matter.

The French kept away at this stage and provided only logistic support, such as it was, mainly a roof over our heads and food. We had no pay except pocket money. Time dragged on and our tempers were getting short. What are we waiting for? When will we start flying? What is happening? Do the bloody French not need pilots? What good are we to anybody sitting on our back-sides in this bloody hole? These were but a few of the questions which were asked and shouted around. But this was a difficult period, everything was in the melting pot and, although the Polish government was already formed, time was needed to honour our agreements, establish procedures, and put it all into effect.

To understand the events leading to the formation of our government in France one has to go back to the day when the Soviet Army invaded Poland. During the night of 17/18 September 1939, President Mościcki, the Polish government, and Marshal Śmigły-Rydz with part of the General Staff, crossed the border bridge over the river Czeremosz, near Kuty, and entered Rumania. They were all interned by the friendly Rumanians and unable to function in any way. President Mościcki however, acting in accordance with the constitution (Article 24), laid down his office and nominated Władysław Raczkiewicz, an experienced and universally respected politician and ex-leader of the Senate, as his successor, on recommendation of the Polish Ambassadors in Paris, London, and Rome, communicating through the Ambassador in Bucharest, R. Raczyński. The new President formed the government in Paris on 1st October 1939 composed of prominent Poles who had succeeded in getting through to France, with General Władysław Sikorski as Prime Minister and Commander in Chief, and A. Zaleski as Minister of Foreign Affairs. Thus the continuity of the only lawful Polish state authority was assured and was in the hands of men who commanded respect and enjoyed the confidence of Poles at home and abroad, and of our allies. The new Polish president and the government moved to an extra-territorial seat at Angers allocated by the French government. It had at its disposal the Polish Treasury gold which had been successfully transported to France.

The President nominated a National Council from representatives of every political opinion, which worked alongside the government, filling the role of a parliament for the duration of the war. The Council had chosen Ignacy Paderewski as leader, who inaugurated its work in a notable speech setting the Council's programme and undertaking full support for the government's declaration that post-war Poland would be a democratic state. He remained in office until his death on 29th June 1941.

Before formal agreements were signed between Polish and French governments all members of the Polish Air Force and the Anti-Aircraft Artillery were under the command and control of General Zając. All that the French did for us in that period was to provide the bare minimum of logistic support,.

The Polish-French-British Agreement of October 1939 provided for the transfer of three hundred aircrew, and two thousand technical personnel to Great Britain (for service in the RAF Volunteer Reserve). The rest were to remain in France and serve under French command.

The Polish-French Air Force agreement was concluded on 4th January 1940 and supplemented on 17th February 1940. It gave the French Air Ministry complete control with the exception of personnel matters, which of necessity had to be tackled jointly, and provided for the formation of two Fighter Squadrons and an Army Co-operation Squadron. The Polish Headquarters had the right to visit units where Poles served. In the meantime life in our corrals was not exactly what we expected. I was disturbed by allegations of misconduct directed against some senior officers. A term 'leśne dziadki' was coined, meaning literally 'old men of the woodlands' or even 'woodland gnomes', implying incompetence of senior officers, which was ridiculous. Reports were written to that effect and boards of officers were appointed to investigate. I was surprised when one such board required me to answer questions concerning the conduct of the Officer Commanding III/6 Wing, Major Morawski. It was alleged that he did not fly during the war, was this true? Why was that? What did I think about it? etc. etc. I said that had we been able to operate effectively longer and in a different manner, he would no doubt have flown himself and led the wing into battle, but we had suffered enormous losses in the first five days, there were no replacements of aircraft, pilots were queuing to fly and the younger ones could hardly get anywhere near the aircraft. We had operated in small sections mostly from ambush fields away from the main airfield and means of communication, and this was not a job for the Officer commanding a Wing whose presence was constantly required at the army air headquarters. Only an idiot could accuse him of anything improper in the circumstances. I heard no more about this but I know that one of the accusers subsequently had a safe job in England and survived the war; Major Morawski was flying bombers and was killed in action .

The wave of recriminations, accusations, hasty judgements, swept our corral suddenly and went away just as quickly. It was defeatist in its context and sounded more like enemy propaganda than anything else. A fuller picture was emerging of how the war in Poland was fought and it was becoming progressively clearer, to everybody, that the Poles had nothing to be ashamed of. The account of battles at Kutno, Hel, Westerplatte, and the defence of Warsaw spoke for themselves.

Christmas was grim that year. It was a time for fervent prayers and resolutions. My thoughts were in Poland, with my family, and with millions of Poles under German and Soviet occupation. There were some jollifications as well, sustained by wine, with songs, devil-may-care talk, laughter and tears. I had just had my 23rd birthday and was still a bit vulnerable in spite of a martial posture.

The rest of the problem was Sikorski's antagonism to the late Marshal Piłsudski and his camp, which stayed in power after the latter's death. Sikorski's conceit and pride were further fanned by his zealots settling old scores. Consequently an isolation camp was set up in Cerisay for surplus officers and officials and those whose loyalty was suspect. Later two similar camps were set up in Scotland.

Training of ground staff began at various French establishments in January. On the tenth of the same month a group of pilots, selected for the first Polish Fighter Squadron, was sent to Montpellier for a three month training course which they completed in one month. They returned to Lyons and continued further training on Morane MS.406s (CO Capt. S. Łaszkiewicz). On 26th March they were sent to various French squadrons in small groups to gain experience; they were to provide the cadre for the second Fighter squadron as soon as more pilots were ready. The training was already beginning in Lyon-Bron under the command of Major Marmier and Capt. Rougevin.

At that time the Soviet Union was fighting Finland with the intention of adding to its empire yet another Soviet Socialist Republic, as they did with Estonia, Latvia, and Lithuania. France planned to help the brave Finns and the Poles offered to form a Fighter squadron as part of the French force. This was accepted and the 'Finland Squadron' was formed and trained in Lyon-Bron. They were equipped ultimately with the Caudron CR-714 Cyclone, but never went to Finland and fought in France having been re-named '1/145 Squadron' (145 French, 1st Polish).

The fighter pilot training centre at Lyon-Bron had a capacity for forty pilots a month. Initial flying, bomber and recce training were carried out at St Etienne, Rouen, and at Blida in North Africa. Navigators, gunners, and so on were trained elsewhere. Everything was moving rather slowly, due partly to the congestion at various training establishments with long waiting lists.

I received my first pay as Second Lt in January, and in February I became a proud holder of the 'Carnet de Solde Individuel' - a pay book, which I still have. Pan Jan, Czesiek Główczyński, Toni Dzięgielewski and I, moved to a small flat in the old part of the city and started house-keeping, which was quite hilarious. We needed expert advice and guidance which was willingly provided by a lady friend of Pan Jan, who was later assisted by a lady friend of Czesiek. They helped us to shop, showed us cheap eating places, occasionally cooked a meal, and taught French for free. The flat was always full of people, friends called at all times and pandemonium reigned supreme.

There were no opportunities to make any contact with French officers and they made no effort in that direction themselves, unless they had to, they kept aloof and obviously did not think much of us. France felt safe behind her invincible Maginot Line. The men serving there were treated like heroes, they grew beards which were a distinctive mark and admired by all. Everywhere propaganda posters appeared with drawings, maps, and slogans. The one which stuck in my mind read: 'Nous vaincrons, parceque nous sommes les plus forts'. There were anti-war posters just before Hitler attacked Poland, one of them apparently proclaiming that no Frenchman wanted to die for Danzig. We were even blamed for starting World War II by not meeting Hitler's demands - look at the mess we were all in now!

The attitude of civilians to us varied from very friendly to rude, and all kept their homes tight shut to us. Both the French communists and fascists worked against us, and Lyon was full of the former lot. I was confused. One day somebody made a friendly gesture, but another day somebody else would swear at you as if to balance the sentiments. My general impression was that when it came to patriotism, fighting spirit, and honour, French women changed places with their men and wore trousers - they were twice the men than their men themselves. In the meantime, the official war communiqués reported with monotonous regularity, day after day, "rien a signaler".

Our foursome split after a while. The flat was too much of a good thing and our house-keeping too erratic for comfort. I shared a room with Pan Jan at first and worked seriously at my French, joining the Berlitz School of Languages where I laboured with four other chaps for about six weeks.

I gave up when two of them fell out and I could not afford the increased fee. I found the cinema a good place to pick up colloquial expressions and saw every film with Fernandel in it, the funny man with big ears, and the 'Prisoner of Zenda' series - ridiculous plots but simple language.

March had passed and April came and some of us were still marking time. Langhamer, Wydrowski, Dyrgałła, Jakubowski, Stabrowski and I, decided to take a week's leave. One fellow bought, or borrowed, a car and three of our party risked their lives when driving to Juan Le Pins in his very tired Citroen; the other three, including me, went by train. We found rooms in a modest hotel and had the place almost to ourselves as it was only mid April. Mimosa was in full bloom everywhere and the countryside along the coast was beautiful. We visited Cannes, Nice, and Monte Carlo, where we watched the changing of the guard at the palace of the Prince of Monaco while drinking coffee at the opposite end of the square. Our funds would not permit any of us having a flutter at the casino, but I remember a night out in Nice - it was a variety concert in aid of Poles. They were very kind and made a little fuss of us.

One day our driver took a wrong turning in Juan, went up a hill then down a steep narrow lane which joined the main road at the bottom. The brakes were not quite good enough for that particular hill and as we, willy-nilly, entered the main road, a baker's van appeared at the junction at the same time and, hooting madly, we collided with the rear of the van. The impact was quite gentle but hard enough to cause the rear door to be flung open and loaves of bread started to fly all over the place. We all got out and gathered the bread whilst the baker was shouting, swearing, and gesticulating. As luck would have it, a policeman was on the scene almost immediately. He looked around and saw that nobody was hurt, and not much damage done to either of the vehicles; turned to us and quickly asked several questions:

"Are you Poles? Who was driving? Did your brakes fail? Did you hoot? You did, good!"

He then turned to the van driver, shouted at him rapidly, would not listen to him, waved him off and, to our astonishment, the driver jumped into his seat and was gone without another word. -

"That was a bloody Italian" said the law-man, "Do you know that Mussolini is shouting that the Cote d'Azure belongs to Italy? What impertinence! But you really must do something about your brakes, it could be a French baker next time, eh? Ha, Ha!"

It was about the 15th May when I started flying training at a satellite airfield of the Lyon-Bron base. Captain Tański was the Chief Flying Instructor and his French Commanding Officer was Captain Rougevin. The airfield had minimum administrative, technical and catering facilities, and only some tents for guards and ground crews. We travelled daily from the city by buses, being picked up at several points, had lunch at the airfield and returned to Lyons in the late afternoon.

Pan Jan was posted to Blida in North Africa and Esperance, his lady friend, was very sad. I shared a room with Główczyński which she found for us, in a nice house belonging to two elderly ladies who fed us well and looked after us like mothers.

The first flight was dual check with an instructor in a light aircraft followed by a few solo flights. Then, familiarisation on a SPAD-510, a beautiful biplane fighter built shortly after the first World War, followed by a test for acrobatics. "Show us what you can do over the airfield. Here is your chance to impress the Frogs, if you know your stuff" murmured my instructor.

As I was the first from our group to start the show I had no pattern to follow and thought I would do one of the combinations we had practised in Dęblin and Ułęż. It was a series of tight vertical and horizontal figures moving slowly over the airfield in one direction, then back, and ending in a neat approach for landing. Everything went smoothly, and I thought the SPAD-510 was one of the best aircraft for aerobatics I had ever flown. Apparently I managed to impress the Frogs and was moved to the Caudron-Cyclone, a modern fighter but under-powered with an engine of only 450 hp. I was surprised at the length of the take-off run on our grass airfield and the poor rate of climb - no wonder they were to be withdrawn from operational squadrons, as the gossip had it.

One day, shortly after take-off, I had an engine failure and decided to turn back to the airfield as there were woods on three sides. I managed, but only just, having to jump over some small trees on the edge of the airfield, which caused loss of speed and consequently I landed heavily; and bent the under-carriage and propeller quite a lot. As I was getting out of the wreck in disgust, and without a scratch, Captain Rougevin was speeding in my direction with his interpreter. He was not very happy with my explanations and thought I should have done better:

"You owe the French government at least two hundred thousand Francs for repairing this thing" he said, half jokingly.

"At my rate of pay it will take a life-time, Sir!"

He delivered me to the crew room and that was the end of the matter, except for a detailed statement I had to make about it.

I completed my training on the Morane 406 shortly before France collapsed, and flew a couple of patrols in the area without encountering anything.

On the 10th of May the Germans invaded Belgium and bombed several French airfields, including Lyon-Bron where twelve Polish airmen were killed and sixteen wounded.

On 14th May the Polish Air force consisted of:

- ◉ 4 Fighter squadrons (GC 1/145 fully operational as one unit, and half of the second squadron - the Montpellier group; the rest was at various stages of training);
- ◉ 2 reconnaissance squadrons (one in training on Potez 63s and one in ground training school);
- ◉ 1 Bomber squadron formed on 24th May (ready by the middle of June, but never used);
- ◉ 59 pilots in 'Chimney Flights' - i.e. defence of industrial and strategic objectives.

I was on the airfield when the news came of the French capitulation. Armed guards were already posted by the parked aircraft and we were briefed that a train would be provided to evacuate us. There was no time to collect private belongings from our quarters in Lyons. We were not allowed to fly away in bomber trainers nor in fighter aircraft, it would be against Captain Rougevin's orders and he could not help us. We boarded the train and after four - five hours of a slow journey through the beautiful Massif Central we de-trained and were taken by buses to La Cavallerie Camp near Millau, in the department of Aveyron, where we stayed the night.

There were not many French servicemen about and four of us investigated two hangars which were padlocked but had rather flimsy walls made of corrugated iron sheets. One of the hangars was packed solid with light aircraft and we decided to return at night. The aircraft must have belonged to a flying club and private owners. There were several different types, including a beautiful Czechoslovakian motor-glider called 'Komar', but their tanks were empty. There was also a car parked in the corner which had very little fuel either. It looked in good shape and after a while two chaps who knew about cars managed to start it, We then drained every drop from the aircraft tanks and filled up the car. It started again and worked well on the aviation fuel. A decision had to be made about what to do with it and we agreed that two should travel by car and two by train to the same destination, just in case we should need it later - one never knew. We removed the door-lock, left it ready for a quick get away and went to bed.

Next morning we departed for Argeles-sur-Mer, near Port Vendres, where our two rally drivers joined us, and waited a day for embarkation orders.

There was friction and confusion between the French Navy, Army, and Air force senior officers at Port Vendres, who were contradicting one another. Apparently Admiral Darlan's orders forbad evacuation of Polish troops to Africa. This order was cancelled and two French ships and one British - 'Apapa' - evacuated two thousand two hundred men on the 23rd and 24th June. 'Apapa' sailed with one thousand men aboard on the 24th via Gibraltar to Britain.

Our group with Lt Col. Madejski in charge was re-directed by train to St Jean-de-Luz where we arrived early on the 23rd and met our two drivers some hours later. I played poker in the train for hours and won several thousand francs, lending the money back to some chaps who finished the game penniless. I never had such luck ever again.

The situation there was much better than on the Mediterranean coast. On 22nd June four British ships with an escort of one cruiser and two Canadian destroyers anchored off St Jean-de-Luz but could not start embarkation until 0400 hours on the 24th because of the very rough sea. A French General arrived with gendarmes at about 1100 hours and demanded that the embarkation must stop as it was contrary to the terms of the Franco-German armistice and that the Poles must surrender, or he would use force. But he agreed to wait, postponing the use of force until 1300 hours, by which time the embarkation of three thousand men was completed with the loss of two servicemen and one civilian by drowning. Another one thousand two hundred left through other Atlantic ports. Altogether about six thousand men of the Polish Air force were evacuated. Only one hundred and fifty pilots were flying operationally in France, losing thirteen of their own and destroying fifty-six enemy aircraft.

After the capitulation, French people, servicemen and civilian alike, appeared to be glad they were out of the war. Some cried in sorrow or in shame, others shrugged their shoulders without a word, a handful went to England with us, dressed in Polish uniforms, but everybody I came across seemed to be dead inside. This time they let themselves down more than anybody else.

I sailed to England in the 'Arandora Star'. The sea was rough and I felt sick most of the time until we reached Liverpool. According to the German radio, the ship was sunk somewhere in the Atlantic.

ENGLAND

It was a short bus ride of just over an hour from Liverpool docks to our tented camp in a fine park. A fleet of buses moved swiftly through the grey suburbs of the city and into a flat countryside, which was very green, neat, and orderly. I saw little splashes of colour in front of sound brick or stone houses under slate roofs. It looked as if prosperous and industrious people lived there, who also liked flowers and shrubs by their windows.

There must have been dozens of tents all over the park. Loose straw, palliases, and blankets were available and, together with five other fellows, I established residence under canvas adjacent to an ancient oak tree. We were soon introduced to corned beef and mash, tea with milk, jam, and odd shaped loaves of bread which were a bit gluey and tasted of nothing in particular. Luckily for us the weather was fine and we spent the next five or six days trying to regain our equilibrium, and made a first step in learning English.

"First you must know something about pronunciation" said one clever fellow who had already been introduced to the mysteries of the English language.

"Take the most frequently used little word which consists of three letters: THE. The correct pronunciation according to me is….,!!!" a peculiar noise shot out of his mouth which sounded like ZEE.

"Now you try it for the next hour or so then I will tell you how you are getting on."

I had no idea that it was possible to pronounce those three letters in so many different ways. Apart from ZEE, I also heard DEE, DY, DZE, TZE, TZY and other odd noises in between. By a majority of votes we settled for DZY, and borrowed a book which was changing tents every half hour; we copied some words and phrases and tried to learn their meaning and pronunciation. It was hard going.

On Sunday we had an open air Mass. The service started as usual with the beautiful hymn *Kiedy Ranne Wstają Zorze* and ended with *Boże Coś Polskę*. The first one being an adoration of God at the breaking of dawn, and the second a fervent supplication for freedom and the former greatness of our country. God and Poland are inseparable in the minds of most Poles - a commitment to one is a commitment to the other.

Our next move on the 2nd July 1940 was by train to the Polish Air Force base at Blackpool. It had been established some while before, with the transfer of Poles from RAF Eastchurch who were the men brought from France the previous winter to form bomber squadrons in England (three hundred air crew and two thousand ground personnel). The base was named 'No. 3 School of Technical Training Blackpool' and consisted of a Training Wing, Administration Wing, No. 2 Recruiting Board working closely with the RAF, Polish Record Office, a Holding Unit, Aircrew Selection Board, Translation and Publication Office, and a core of Medical, Chaplain, Police and Intelligence Branches. All new arrivals from France went through Blackpool, as did others from practically every corner of the globe.

I was accommodated in a boarding house together with about ten other officers. This was luxury by all previous standards, the food was good, but strange - English!

Details of recent tragic events were coming in and by then I had a reasonably clear picture of what had happened. Hitler's blitzkrieg against Belgium and Holland had begun on 10th May. Rotterdam was bombed almost to extinction. British and French attempts to stop the German advance failed in Belgium and by the 19th May General Gort, British Commander-in-Chief, was forced to retreat to the sea, whilst the Germans moved ahead and reached Boulogne, thus out-flanking the Maginot Line and isolating the British. The defeat of France was inevitable unless the French could have mounted an effective counter attack, which they never did. The British perimeter had shrunk under pressure until they assembled at Dunkirk and waited for evacuation on the beaches under heavy air attacks. Boats and craft of all sizes, six hundred in all, known as Little Ships, plus two hundred naval vessels, rescued 338,000 men, including about 120,000 French and Belgian troops who became the nucleus of the Free French Army under General de Gaulle.

On 19th June the Polish Commander-in-Chief broadcasting from London, ordered all Polish troops in France to proceed to ports, contact the British, and evacuate to England. One of our infantry divisions fighting on the French right flank was left alone by its French neighbours and refusing to surrender, fought its way to Switzerland where it was interned for the duration of the war.

On 13th May Churchill became Prime Minister and offered the people "Nothing but blood, toil, tears and sweat". To General Sikorski he said, on the 19th June "We are now united for better or worse".

The expedition to Narvik of British, French, and Polish troops, which captured the town, was withdrawn. The force comprised five French battalions, three British and four Polish (*Podhalańska* Brigade commanded by General Bohusz-Szyszko). Also the Royal Navy, including the aircraft carrier HMS *Glorious* (sunk) and three Polish destroyers ORP *Burza*, *Błyskawica*, and *Grom* (sunk). The Germans were in control of Denmark and Norway with neutral Sweden supplying them iron ore. What next?

In the meantime Blackpool was full of people on holiday coming and going week after week as if nothing had happened. The weather was warm and sunny most of the time - very un-English. I explored the town and its main attractions and was quite amazed by it all. My first visit was to the Winter Garden, where I saw an enormous organ rising from the floor with the virtuoso Dixon bashing at it, and several hundred couples dancing. It made a deep impression on me – lucky people, I thought, may you be spared the horrors of war and the humiliation of defeat. But I did not dwell on serious thoughts for too long: a girl smiled at me and I asked her to dance. She became my first English teacher for the next few days, and then another one took on the arduous work. I asked a couple of them whether I could write to them and have my letters corrected and sent back. One of them was very good at it for several months, but the other had difficulties with grammar and had to be dismissed. The best teachers were those who knew some French or German, but I met very few of them.

There was a most popular show going on throughout my time in Blackpool - an ice rink show with some twenty beautiful girls dancing on ice in splendid costumes to the music played by a fine band. Two of them lived in our boarding house and about six in the house next door. The younger ones had their mothers or aunts staying with them. They were a very nice lot, friendly and kind, distributing free tickets quite frequently. I saw the show at least four times, having paid for a ticket only once, and enjoyed it immensely every time. It was difficult to reciprocate properly as we were paid only pocket money of about one pound per week, but they did get an odd box of chocolates or a rose each now and then.

By the end of July 1940 the Polish Air Force (PAF) had 8,384 men on its strength in Britain; bitten twice but not defeated. On 5th August a new Polish/British agreement was signed whereby PAF - legally a part of the independent Polish forces - was subordinated in every respect to the RAF. Originally, the agreement envisaged the formation of four bomber, two fighter, and one army co-operation squadrons, but was soon altered and thirteen squadrons were formed in 1940 and early 1941 (four bomber, seven fighter, one night fighter, and one Army co-operation) with two more in 1943 and 1944 (one fighter recce and one artillery observation).

News of the Luftwaffe attacks on coastal airfields, radar stations, and channel ports, came as a shock to the peaceful land of England - the first stage of the Battle of Britain had begun (12 - 19th August). This was followed by attacks on fighter airfields around London, and from the 7th to 30th September on London itself by day and night. The 303 Polish fighter Squadron joined the battle on 20th August followed by 302 Squadron on the 30th August, both squadrons flying Hawker Hurricane Is. In addition fifty-three Polish pilots fought in RAF squadrons by September, and seventy-three by October.

Air Chief Marshal Dowding, C-in-C Fighter Command, had at his disposal twenty Spitfire and twenty-two Hurricane Squadrons by July, with a further eight formed after the French campaign. The effective daily strength of this force was about five hundred fighters. Across the channel the Germans concentrated about two thousand seven hundred and fifty aircraft, employing no more than fifteen hundred on any one day.

The contribution of the two Polish squadrons amounted to seven and a half per cent of the total enemy aircraft destroyed, and the individual Poles fighting with the RAF squadrons added five and a half per cent by the end of the second phase of the battle. The two squadrons lost six and eight pilots respectively and nineteen Polish pilots were lost fighting in RAF squadrons. 310 (Czech) Squadron fought with distinction at the same time and my friend of later years - Tom Vybiral - became a shining light of the Czechoslovak Air Force and eventually led the Czechoslovak Wing of two fighter squadrons. This bloody and decisive battle was won by the RAF - but only just. It was the first victory of the war against united Nazi and Communist powers and a turning point in the war.

On 18th September 307 Night Fighter Squadron was formed by Squadron Leader S. Pietraszkiewicz (ex Dęblin Commanding Officer of No. 12 Cadet entry) at RAF Station Kirton-in-Lindsey, Lincs. I was one of the pilots. The aircraft, the Defiant, had a turret with four machine-guns which could rotate 360 degrees and was operated by a gunner. The pilot had no armament and his sole role was to fly the machine. All pilots of the squadron, including the Commanding Officer, were ex-fighter pilots, and from the first day we started to talk about transferring to fighter squadrons - the Battle of Britain was still raging and London was burning. The Air Officer commanding heard of this and visited us within the first ten days. All pilots were lined up and he asked everyone the same question:

"Do you like the Defiant?" and was given the same answer

"No Sir".

By the end of the month we were all posted away and a new lot of pilots arrived to take our place.

A group of five of us reported to RAF Old Sarum on 2nd October, to be told that a mistake must have been made as they had nothing but Tiger Moth aircraft and were about to start initial flying training. We spent a week doing nothing, living in a very comfortable Officers Mess and drinking beer in the White Hart, an ancient pub in the centre of Salisbury. Władek Szczęśniewski had a small gramophone and bought his first record, which we played for hours. It had Tchaikovsky's

Capriccio Italiene on one side and the French song 'Boom! Tarara Boom!' on the other side. We also squeezed in a visit to Salisbury Cathedral.

On 9th October we reported to No. 5 Operational Training Unit at RAF Aston Down, but when they saw that we were already converted to Defiants from our pilot's Flying Log books, they posted us to 303 Polish Fighter Squadron at RAF Leconfield, near Hull, where we reported on 11th October. The Squadron had just been withdrawn from RAF Northolt in 11 Group for rest, replacement of losses, and training of new pilots. All newly formed Polish squadrons had the posts of Commanding Officer and two flight commanders duplicated for a while by RAF officers. Thus Sqn Ldr R. Kellett, Flt Lt John Kent, and Flt Lt A Forbes were duplicating Sqn Ldr W. Urbanowicz, Flt Lt Z. Henneberg, and Flt Lt B. Grzeszczak. All six were outstanding men and particularly Urbanowicz, who fought in Britain, and in the Far East with the US air force.

George Radomski and Boguś Mierzwa from the 12th Dęblin Cadet entry were already veterans of the squadron; it was nice to see them and hear about their experiences. The squadron had then about fifteen pilots under training. Four days after my arrival I was flying a Hurricane thanks to Flt Lt Henneberg, who was doing his best to keep us airborne.

Late one afternoon three low flying Heinkels dropped several bombs close to the hangers and sprayed the area with guns. It was a surprise attack, they came from the sea below radar and got away the same way. Sadly there were casualties - one dead and several wounded. The squadron started flying dusk patrols to protect the airfield.

Air Vice Marshal William Sholto Douglas, the AOC No. 11 Group, visited the squadron and decorated several pilots. Sqn Ldr Urbanowicz was replaced by Sqn Ldr Kowalczyk. Flying Officer Zadroziński became ill, it was schizophrenia - he never recovered. Czesiek Główczyński was in hospital with his hands badly burned. He recovered but not to fly, and was appointed Air Force Personal Assistant to General Sikorski. I went to see him in the squadron's American Studebaker car - a gift from the Polish government.

One evening I was sitting on my own in the quiet room of the Officer's Mess looking into the future with the help of a pack of cards when Sqn Ldr and Mrs Kellett walked in.

"What are you doing here all alone?" he asked.

"Fortune telling, sir".

"Really! How exciting" chipped in charming Mrs Kellett, "You must tell me mine, do! Please! I won't take no for an answer", and she did not.

I muddled through a routine of a kind I had learned and told her what I thought she would like to hear. She was pleased and insisted I should do the same for her husband. In his cards I unmistakably saw a lot of money coming his way very soon, but there was grief close to it. Every part of the routine pointed that way. A few days later he went away and I heard that his father had died and left him a fortune in coal mines. They both reappeared in the Mess again, telling everybody about my supernatural powers and from then on I knew no peace until the squadron moved back to Northolt on 3rd January 1941, without the Kelletts.

Northolt was engulfed in fog most of January and hardly any flying was possible. On the 20th I was posted, together with a number of other pilots, to 315 Squadron which was formed at RAF Acklington, Northumberland, under the joint command of Sqn Ldr S. Pietraszkiewicz and H. Cook. Our aircraft were Hurricanes Mk I. At the same time and place 317 Squadron was also formed on Hurricanes with Sqn Ldr S. Brzezina and M. Mount as joint commanding officers. Heavy snow fell and buried us for over a fortnight. There was very little flying in February, and on 13th March the squadron was moved to Speke, near Liverpool, as fully operational. I was in 'A' Flight commanded by Flt Lt W. Szczęśniewski and a Canadian Officer. Flt Lt Mickiewicz and an RAF officer who came from China had the 'B' Flight. We started training in earnest and did not expect the disaster which befell the squadron within a fortnight of our arrival. On 27th March I was sent urgently to assist the Air Traffic Controller who had difficulties with 'B' Flight in the air. As I recollect, it all started with a training flight above a thick layer of cloud. When the formation was about to return to base they were directed to intercept unidentified aircraft. This was done without due regard for the state of fuel and the aircraft were given various courses to steer for a considerable time. When I arrived at the tower the controller and his staff looked very worried.

"Tell them in Polish to return to base immediately, they are approximately here" he said, pointing to an area west of Southport on his map.

"All aircraft steer 090 degrees, you should reach the coast between base and Blackpool. You are cleared to go below clouds. Report fuel one by one."

Not everybody answered and those that did had little fuel left. I did not know their exact position and I do not think the controller knew it either. I thought that if they could only reach the coast they might be able to force land safely on the flat ground of the coastal area. It looked bad, and it was. Two pilots collided and perished in the sea (Flying Officer Szulkowski and Sgt Paterek), one was missing and never found (Pilot Officer O. Holden), one ditched near a ship and was saved (Flying Officer O. Woliński), and two made it, just.

Our confidence in Speke Controllers was shattered, and not without good reason. I had once asked them for clearance to go below clouds and they brought me down into a deep valley in the Welsh mountains with peaks all around me in clouds; it was a miracle I did not hit one of them. Good controllers were scarce in the early years of the war and those in the north were the least experienced. Our operational work consisted mostly of convoy patrols. Large numbers of ships were moving in and out of Liverpool harbour all the time and occasionally German planes would jump out of the clouds and in again on their solo missions, taking photographs and dropping bombs.

All pilots were trained for night flying at RAF Valley in Anglesey. I spent five days there with our Canadian Flight commander. He was surprised to see me reading an English book in the Mess one afternoon.

"How much do you understand?"

"More than half if there is action, and less than half if there is not."

"What is this one about?"

"Cowboys and horses."

"All action?"

"Yes, but one cowboy is a bit of a philosopher. Now, what does he mean by this... and that...?"

From then on he was helping me to understand cowboys and Indians. Slowly, under his guidance, I moved up the social ladder as my comprehension improved.

On 8 May 1941 Liverpool was bombed for the first time. I was in the cellar restaurant of Reeces when the bombs started falling. They were after the docks and ships but the adjacent area suffered as well. I spent the rest of the night on a sofa in somebody's house - there was no transport to Speke by then and no taxis either.

Officers of a Polish merchant ship which had sailed in a convoy from the US came to lunch in our Mess. They reciprocated with an excellent Polish meal on board their ship. The battleship King George V invited us for drinks and a conducted tour - most impressive.

Our social life was very pleasant. People were friendly and so were their daughters. There were tea dances, dinner dances, drinks in private homes, in the Adelphi Hotel, and other places, as well as the theatre. Włodek Miksa met Angela Pilkington and brought her and her sisters to our Mess dance - it was a warm June evening and everybody was smiling. The Station commander's wife had never danced so much in her life before as she did that night and we did not neglect the wives of other RAF officers either. This was a swan song before we left Speke for good.

On 14th July the squadron moved to Northolt and was re-equipped with Spitfire Mk IIs, joining 306 and 308 squadrons and thus becoming a unit of the No. 1 Polish Fighter Wing under the command of the valiant and shrewd Wing commander T. Rolski. This was the beginning of the war for 315 Squadron.

* * *

I flew my first mission over France on 23rd July 1941, as a guest of 308 Squadron by way of introduction to the shooting war. I was told to stick to my section leader come what may, keep my eyes open, watch my tail, and my neighbours, and the sky, and not to do anything silly; they would not like to lose me on my first flight.

We took off and met several other squadrons over a pre-arranged point and together with a handful of light bombers we flew to a target in the French coastal area - well over a hundred of us. Fighter squadrons positioned themselves around the bombers and above, one lot on top of another. We were over twenty thousand feet with France below us when I heard on the RT that enemy aircraft were approaching, and later there were reports of attacks and warning shouts - somebody was fighting somewhere. I thought we were moving about a bit nervously when I remembered the golden rule: never fly straight and level for any length of time - and so I too weaved behind my energetic leader, trying desperately not to collide with anybody and not to lose him. I managed, but I did not see much else except him and my immediate neighbours. Our squadron was not molested and we all came back in one piece. I landed drenched with perspiration, jumped out of my aircraft, lit a cigarette and inhaled deeply...

By the end of August I had flown a dozen times over France, mostly as one of a large force comprising a number of fighter wings whose job it was to escort and protect often not more that six Blenheims - probably the lightest bombers in the RAF. They could not do much harm, but they were challenging and their escort was throwing down a gauntlet, in effect, to come up and fight. And they did. There were a hell of a lot of Germans concentrated in packs along the coast from Amsterdam to Brest in 1941. We became best acquainted with the lot in the St Omer-Lille area and near Le Havre. Their aircraft were better than ours. The Me-109 was superior in climb, dive, and armament, but a Spitfire could out-turn a Me-109 with ease at any time. Sometimes they would attack in packs from several directions, or nibble at the edges, or dive at terrific speed through the whole formation starting from above the top wing, down to twelve thousand feet where the Blenheims would be, firing at anything which might come in sight for a split second and away. It was all terribly fast, guns blazing all around, their and ours, aircraft turning, diving, climbing, in series of individual dog-fights, people getting hurt, aircraft being holed or exploding when hit by big guns on the ground.

At other times our fighters would go out alone looking for trouble, free from the cumbersome task of protecting bombers. A surprise attack by either side would result in losses to them or to us.

In bad weather with low cloud base a section of two or four aircraft would be sent to shoot up a target across the channel, flying there all the way almost at zero feet and returning in clouds if chased - this was called a Rhubarb. We were also sent to protect Motor Torpedo Boats, reconnoitre enemy shipping and do other useful work. And so it went, day after day, on and on.

We flew twice on the 9th August and 315 Squadron had its first victory and the first losses; it shot down 'two-three-three' Me-109s (two destroyed, three probably destroyed and three damaged) but we lost F/O Czerniak and Sgt Niewiara. I knew Czerniak quite well, flew on his wing, and thought highly of him. I felt his death deeply.

The squadron gained a big success on 14th August when flying with the Northolt wing on a fighter sweep in the St Omer area. It surprised an enemy formation of about thirty Me-109s and shot down eight-one-one without a loss. A fierce engagement took place a few days later when a superior force of Me-109s attacked us. We were milling around for quite a while and fought off the opposition successfully, returning home all in one piece if somewhat shaken. There were no claims of enemy aircraft destroyed on that day but most of the guns fired.

I shall always remember a spectacular squadron take off on 16th September which ended in a disaster. We were spread over the airfield, all twelve aircraft taking off from the grass simultaneously in a north-easterly direction, with hangars and the Officers Mess on the left. Sgt Adamiak, being on the extreme left, was squeezed out of space and hit an Army post killing two men and wounding two, but he came out of it with hardly a scratch. I saw it happening and froze for a moment. Northolt wing, minus Adamiak, flew a fighter sweep around St Omer again, where we met stiff opposition. In the ensuing engagement our squadron shot down three-one-one for the loss of one of our pilots.

On 21st September our Commanding Officer, Sqn Ldr S. Pietraszkiewicz, force-landed in France and became a prisoner of war until 9th May 1945. He was succeeded by Sqn Ldr W. Szczęśniewski, Officer Commanding 'A' Flight until then.

My good friend Włodek Miksa found himself in the midst of eight Me-109s quite alone on 21st October, and had a devil of a job, and enormous luck, in extricating himself from their attention. It seemed that, in their eagerness to bring him down, they were getting in each other's way whilst he, fighting desperately for his life, fired at whatever appeared in his gun sight shooting down one-one-one. He landed utterly exhausted and unable to give a coherent account for a while.

Northolt Wing was sent alone a day or so later on a low level 'Ramrod' bomber escort mission in the Mardyck-Ostend area. There were canals everywhere and we set a petrol barge on fire, several of us having a go at it.

We lost our second Commanding Officer on 8th November. He was a fine officer and a friend. I had great respect and affection for him. I knew him from Poland when he was Commanding Officer of No. 161 Squadron before and during the September 1939 campaign. He peeled off and went down near Ostend calling over the RT "This is BRICK-BAT leader, I have no fuel" and was heard no more. Two weeks later news came that he was safe and a prisoner of war like his predecessor, not returning to the UK until 10th May 1945.

The third Commanding Officer was Sqn Ldr S. Janus. On 22nd November he led our squadron when it was ordered on a disastrous experimental mission which cost many lives. Six Hurricanes armed with little bombs were sent to attack some factories in Bourbourg, near Dunkirk; our squadron provided close escort. All six Hurricanes and five Spitfires of 315 Squadron were shot down. The other seven came back riddled with bullet holes. Flg Officers Łukaszewicz, Grzech, Grudziński, and Sgts Kosmalski and Staliński died in this ill-conceived operation. The area was saturated with anti-aircraft guns of all calibres and the light guns had a field day, to our sorrow. I never heard of Hurricanes being used in the same way again on the Western front. On that fatal day I was in readiness from dawn in 'A' Flight when briefing was ordered for this operation, with take off time set for about 1200 hours. A change of pilots would normally take place at 1230 hours and I thought our lot would fly. However the second lot came to the briefing as well and argued that they should fly, whereas we maintained that take off would be in our time and it was only fair that we should fly. The Commanding Officer decided in favour of the new lot and sent us packing for lunch. Had I flown, I would have been in exactly the same escort position as Grudziński, my best friend, God rest his soul.

My next visitation to France was on 6th December when, together with Sgts Adamiak, Kowalski, and Lipiec, we flew a Rhubarb mission to shoot up Verton distillery as the first target, and/or Berck airfield as the second. It was all low-level stuff. We discharged short bursts at a steam locomotive first and a couple of minutes later fired at the low glass tower of the distillery - the vulnerable point - as well as some windows in the adjacent buildings. As we were pulling up the light AA shells began bursting around us. I thought they would be waiting for us at Berck, the element of surprise had gone, it would be silly to attack Berck now and I started to climb towards the clouds but they were too high for comfort. I called to others that I was going down to low level again, they joined me and we returned home safely. A week later we had a pat on the shoulder from Sqn Ldr Jankiewicz, our liaison officer at Headquarters 11 Group.

Two days later Northolt Wing was parading between Berck and Le Touquet with our squadron on top. There was no sign of opposition until I suddenly saw two Me-109s attacking from above the section of four led by Benio Groszewski. I tried to warn him on the RT, turned towards them firing at a far too great a range to distract them but it was too late; we lost Benio. He was my commanding Officer in No. 162 Squadron in Lwów and throughout the war in Poland. He never joined the band of excellent fliers in German POW camps: this was his last flight and he died.

They made me Officer Commanding 'A' flight, to my great surprise. There were chaps with fine combat records whereas I could not boast anything except that I was there. It should have been anyone of at least four of my friends. However, ours was not to reason why...

On 18th December - my twenty-fifth birthday - I took part in a Fighter Sweep which turned out to be a parade high above enemy airfields, which the Luftwaffe decided to ignore and allowed me to have a peaceful and enjoyable day followed by a noisy session in the Mess bar.

Things were happening on the international scene which had great bearing on the conduct of the war. First, the Atlantic Charter signed on 14th August 1941 by Churchill and Roosevelt was a great morale booster to us all. Articles one, two, three and four declared that no territorial changes would take place without the freely expressed wishes of the people concerned, that self government and sovereign rights would be restored wherever they were taken away by force. There was to be freedom of speech, freedom of worship, freedom from want and freedom from fear. Those were fine principles worth fighting for.

Secondly, Japan attacked Pearl Harbour on 7th December 1941 and the United States declared war on the Axis powers. The whole might of the USA with its human and economic resources and advanced technology was committed. England was no longer the only power in the west fighting Hitler. The President of the USA agreed to give first priority to the war in Europe in spite of strong opposition by General Douglas McArthur, who wanted to defeat Japan first.

Thirdly, the Polish government in London signed the co-operation agreement with the Soviet Union on 4th December 1941 and consequently Polish soldiers were leaving prisons and labour camps in the Soviet Union and forming an Army with the view to fighting the common enemy. Poles, wherever they were, had a right to expect that the Soviet Union, having annulled her Treaty of 1939 with Germany, would respect the Polish/Russian frontier mutually agreed in 1921, as well as her independence and democratic constitution.

There was talk between exiled governments in London about the possible federation of East European countries, Poland and Czechoslovakia at first, and Yugoslavia and Greece joining discussions later.

On the Eastern front Kiev capitulated in September and the Germans took seven hundred thousand prisoners, but the drive to Moscow failed. They were in sight of the Kremlin on 5th December but retreated some ninety miles when the Red Army counter-attacked. Intense cold set in and 'General Winter' took a hand in the war as in 1812.

In North Africa Rommel was pushing towards Egypt, and on 15th February 1942 Singapore capitulated.

The weather clamped down just before Christmas and the conditions for operational flying were poor until March. We did as much training as was possible, practising cloud and formation flying, interceptions, cine gun attacks, night flying, low level flying, and of course taking turns in readiness duties during all the hours of daylight.

In the first two months of 1942 I flew in one fighter Sweep up and down between Le Touquet and Cap Gris-Nez, one convoy patrol, and one shipping reconnaissance between Dunkirk and Ostend.

In January I had one week's leave and explored central London - it was only fifty-five minutes by Piccadilly line from Ruislip. I walked the splendid streets of this great city with its wonderful buildings, monuments, churches, and parks, such as I had never seen before and spent a lot of time with the ducks at St James'. Then I came across the theatre land. I had heard of the Windmill and lost no time in paying a call there. It was fun and the girls were sparkling and beautiful. My next show was a matinee performance of the Desert Song, which I enjoyed enormously. I can still hum a few bars of the principal song: 'My own, let me call you my own'. It was all new to me so that I was bowled over by one thing or another every day of my leave.

Back at Northolt the Officers' Mess was crowded. Two snooker tables were constantly in use and bridge was played at several tables in the Card room. Poker was forbidden and it was played only in private quarters by the gambling elite. Money was changing hands within the same group so it did not really matter who won. The danger was, however, that an amateur could talk himself into a game and lose his shirt, remaining penniless until the end of the month. The Mess bar was a popular place and for the benefit of RAF officers, a notice was put up with the words 'English spoken' in large capital letters. They were the station administrators, accountants, suppliers, intelligence, security, airfield defence, transportation etc. We all got on well together but as we spoke Polish all the time and they insisted on speaking nothing but English I would not be surprised if they thought of Northolt as purgatory.

After dinner the largest part of the Mess population transferred itself to the friendly town of Ruislip, about a mile away. Apart from the usual range of shops, where everybody wanted coupons for most things, there were two coupon-free cinemas and the Orchard Hotel, all three enjoying our whole hearted support. The Orchard Hotel was the jewel of Ruislip. It had a good-sized bar, and a dining room where a small orchestra played every night and where you could eat and dance, or drink and dance, or just drink and watch the dancers, according to the state of your finances and luck. The proprietor and his staff were our friends. They coped admirably with our high spirits, and the low ones when fortune turned against us. They had a very efficient bush telegraph and were well informed about the affairs of Northolt wing, responding properly to events. The boss looked after his youngest and poorest customers with particular care and when he noticed a chap trying to make his half pint of beer last for ages he would discreetly send him a pint. At the end of the evening the orchestra played '*God Save the King*' followed by '*Jeszcze Polska nie zginęła*' and locals and foreigners stood to attention for both National Anthems. The Orchard Hotel played an important part in the war effort of Northolt Wing and I for one salute the proprietor and his staff for all that they did for us in those days.

March brought better weather and our squadron flew with Boston bombers as middle cover to a target at Armentières, near Lille. There were lots of German fighters in that area and some tried to get to the Bostons but were chased off. F/O Stembrowicz was in a difficult position at one time until Sgt Blok and I intervened and all was well. Bomber Command sent a word of thanks to 315 Squadron later that day.

On the next day, the 9th, we flew at twenty-five thousand feet as top cover with six Bostons far below. A few pecking attacks were made but nothing of consequence occurred. Later in March two fighter sweeps followed. The first, on the 23rd, went to Dunkirk, St Omer and Hardelot, and provoked only hesitant reaction by seven Me-109s who ran away as soon as one squadron turned on them. The second was unopposed.

* * *

On 1st April 315 Squadron left Northolt after eight months of hard work. We flew to RAF Woodvale, situated on the coast between Liverpool and Southport, for a period of rest. Our new operational task was to protect convoys in the Liverpool area and scramble a section of two against any odd raiders picked up by radar. In addition, replacements would have to be trained, old pilots given leave and the squadrons licked into good shape again for another spell at Northolt.

Włodek Miksa was Officer Commanding 'B' Flight by that time and the two of us enjoyed friendly rivalry. His social life was very busy at Angela's home not far away. He met her when we were at RAF Speke, and towards the end of the war he married her.

The airfield was separated from the local golf course by the Liverpool-Southport railway line, and immediately south of it was the friendly commuter village of Freshfield.

I was billeted with my very good friend Florek Fiedorczuk in a very large Victorian house owned by a retired colonial civil servant and his wife. They had two daughters, one married and living away, and the other training to be a nurse and visiting her parents only on rare occasions. There was a full-size snooker table in their billiard room where the old boy gave us a thrashing or two. His wife was delighted to hear that we played bridge and promptly organised a couple of sessions. Unfortunately we could never understand their bidding and neither could they understand ours. Our bridge was more like poker and bidding often went: one heart (or whatever), three no trumps, six hearts, and we either made it or not. That, of course, was bad bridge and quite rightly they gave us up.

Next door was a beautiful old cottage where the Patons and their daughter Joan lived, and further on along the lane stood an old church. Mr Paton had a brother who lived near Ormskirk with his American wife and shared his beautiful country home with his sister, Mrs Paterson, and her daughter Ailsa. The family owned and ran a factory in Liverpool which at that time was set up for production of essential war supplies. Mr Paton's parents lived in retirement in a lovely house on the edge of a lake in Grasmere, in the Lake District.

Freshfield opened its homes and hearts to us. Early one evening we were asked to join our hosts for a drink and met Joan, who smiled sweetly and invited us to her birthday party. We accepted gladly, hoping there would be more pretty girls like her and looked forward to the great day. It was a roaring success with several lively and charming girls there, some mamas and papas, about six chaps from our squadron, an odd civilian or two and a few RAF fellows. I danced with Ailsa a couple of times, when she took me by the hand and said "Come and meet mother". I met her mother, two uncles and aunts in one go, and after we fired the sacrosanct "How do you do" at each other, the inevitable question "How do you like England?" followed. I had several good answers ready and the conversation rolled on somehow in an amusing fashion, with Ailsa translating difficult bits into basic English. Her mother, an intelligent, witty, and warm-hearted lady, was in sparkling form. I left Ailsa with her relations and danced with Mama until she called her daughter to the rescue. Joan, Florek, Ailsa, and I became friends. The girls were much younger than us and we treated them gently and properly, and I am glad to say their parents trusted us.

Southport was a very pleasant town with nice hotels, cinemas, and a theatre. I remember the Carl Rosa company giving a performance of Madame Butterfly which I enjoyed very much with Florek, Joan, and Ailsa. The two of us were invited to the theatre in Liverpool to see Macbeth, which made a great impression on me. I think John Gielgud was playing the leading part.

One evening our Commanding Officer drove his service Hillman to a Southport cinema with five passengers. It was still light when we went in but quite dark when we came out. A policeman was standing by the car. He wanted to know why the car was left in the street without lights on. Having established who we were he asked the CO:

"Would you leave your car outside the cinema like this in Poland?"

"No" came the quick reply, "In Poland we ride to the cinema on horses."-

Some light hearted exchanges followed and we parted on the best of terms.

On 6th May Sqn Ldr Janus was promoted and appointed Wing Leader of the Northolt Wing. He was succeeded by Sqn Ldr Wiórkiewicz.

Towards the end of May Florek and I were given three weeks leave and ordered out of the Station. We studied the map of the UK and decided to take railway warrants to Aberdeen, stopping, perhaps, in a few places on the way there and back. Joan and her parents suggested Grasmere as a first stop and offered to book accommodation in a Temperance Hotel which was good and cheap; other hotels had bars if we were desperate for a drink. Ailsa and Joan offered to act as guides and fixed a long week-end with their grand-parents under overall supervision of Ailsa's mother. The weather was excellent and our guides led us up mountains, around lakes, and along rivers. There were some spectacular views, enjoyed all the more in good company.

On Sunday we all went to the beautiful Grasmere church and as we were walking away at the end of the service twelve Spitfires with PK letters – our squadron - dived gently on us in close formation, pulled up, changed into battle formation and went mad attacking fishes in the lake. It was a spectacular performance but we disowned them until we were sure nobody was upset. We had lunch with the grand-parents on that day and when Florek and I arrived we bowed slightly and clicked our heels.

Mr Paton senior told us this was a German custom and we ought to give it up. "Yes, sir" I said, and clicked my heels again, which made Ailsa laugh and she tried to imitate me to everybody's amusement.

We stayed in Grasmere until our money ran out. It was very pleasant there, the hotel fed us well and the elderly ladies who stayed there semi-permanently enjoyed mothering us.

Back at Woodvale we became better acquainted with the Beaufighter boys who were buzzing around at night and sleeping in the daytime, and to liven things up a bit, we arranged a joint low-level mock attack on RAF Valley in Anglesey. They invited Army Gunners to get in some practice in airfield defence and in the end it all snow-balled to a bigger show than we intended. Everything went well except that one over-eager Beaufighter was so close to a chimney that it collapsed somehow, but hardly any damage was done to the aircraft and nobody was hurt. A great spontaneous party followed in the Mess bar which sealed the friendship of the two squadrons. They went to Malta later in the year and did very well there.

The Royal Engineers were learning how to build a Bailey Bridge not far from us and asked us to interfere with their work. Six aircraft went and, flying very low, chased some of the soldiers off the bridge.

Later on Lady Jersey, our squadron mama, arrived on a visit which was planned to coincide with an inspection by General Ujejski. He brought a sackful of medals for pilots and our splendid ground staff, and we thanked him by parading in the air and on the ground.

There was a place called the Miramare in Southport, a sort of light refreshment café run by a mother and two daughters. The pretty one was called Joyce and she was also in charge of their record-player. It was a good place to pop into after the cinema. Joyce loved dancing and we all danced with her at one time or another. She was invited to our Mess dance that summer, which I almost missed being detached to Valley, and we all made a tremendous fuss of her. Joyce did not live long, she contracted tuberculosis towards the end of the war, and when I called on them she was in bed, very weak, dying. On taking leave I kissed her on her pale cheek, tears rolled from her eyes and I could hardly control mine. She was about the same age as my brother Kazik when he died of tuberculosis.

We buried Sgt Nawrocki in Freshfield Cemetery - he died in an accident - and F/O Sawiak, killed in action. Sawiak intercepted an enemy aircraft over the Irish Sea and fought a duel with it, both force-landing in Eire. He was badly wounded, died in hospital, and his body was returned to us.

Włodek Miksa chased a German aircraft into the balloon barrage at Barrow-in-Furness.

Joan had joined the WRNS and started her training at an establishment only a few miles from home. She met a handsome RN Lieutenant and there was talk of romance - Florek suffered.

A village dance was arranged for a worthy cause. We were invited and most of us went. The dance was preceded by a witty speech and an auction of some nice things which were going at quite high bids. We decided to have a go on the understanding that everyone would chip in. Our target was a wonderful fruit basket. As I was bidding higher and higher there were some confused whispers around.

"They can't afford it, bid on", "Let them have it, they want to contribute."

In the end I won, announcing that it will only take a minute to get the money from my backers, and having collected it I went to the stage, paid up, and offered the basket for auction again minus one enormous orange which I divided between our lot. I was glad they allowed us to contribute and thus feel in some measure a part of the community. The Freshfield people were truly wonderful.

On 15th August Florek Fiedorczuk was returning from air-to-ground range practice. Flying very low over the beach, he hit a concrete post and was killed instantly. The squadron lost a brilliant pilot of great promise and I lost my best friend. Joan's RN training place was only a mile away from the scene of the accident, and she soon knew who it was. The church was full of people when we assembled to pray, and to bury him. Flt Lt Olszewski, the squadron adjutant, who was old enough to be Florek's father, buried his head in his hands and wept. That started a flood of tears all round. Joan and her parents, Ailsa and her mother, and many other good people of Freshfield who knew him came to mourn a friend. His grave is close to that of Sawiak and Nawrocki in Freshfield church cemetery.

We said farewell to Woodvale and Freshfield on 5th September and left for Northolt. Ailsa gave me a St Christopher medallion and I promoted Mrs Paterson to the honorary rank of 'Aunty' and promised to keep in touch.

We flew only once to France in September escorting six Bostons and were jumped by a pack of FW-190s near Le Havre. Our squadron shot down one-one-none, but there were some losses in other squadrons. I came back with a bullet hole and damaged oil tank.

Our Commanding Officer was appointed to a staff job and Sqn Ldr Tadek Sawicz took over on 10th October. He was an excellent man for the job, and commanded loyalty, support, and respect from everyone. He improved our flying discipline and battle formation coherence, moulding us into a confident and efficient team. He led us well and I enjoyed flying with him. In pre-war days his squadron friends gave him the nick-name *Szczur*, meaning *rat*, and they still used it. Somehow it fitted him as he was short, slim and dark, but there was an affectionate ring about it when applied to him.

Out of our four flights across the channel in October, three were uneventful but one operation was something quite new. On the 9th we took part in a two Fighter Wing diversion prior to a raid by 108 USAAF Flying Fortresses on Fives, near Lille. 306 Squadron encountered opposition and Flt Lt Gill, who was with us in 1941, shot down one-one-none. The performance of the Fortresses was as follows: twenty turned back, seventeen failed to find the target, seventy-one bombed the target, one was shot down and two collided. Their gunners claimed forty-eight fighters destroyed! This was not the best of beginnings, but they soon sorted themselves out and became an efficient and formidable force playing a very important part in the air offensive.

On 10th November we were escorting a small bomber force to the Le Havre area, which encountered heavy and accurate flak and two bombers were hit. It was a terrifying sight, they simply disintegrated into nothing. Four other missions that month were uneventful.

December was quite busy, I flew eight missions with or without bombers but nothing much happened. It seemed that the Germans had moved a lot of their squadrons to the Eastern Front where they were making an all-out effort to defeat the Red Army.

The Spring Offensive began in May and by the end of July the Germans had crossed the river Don. On 1st July Sevastopol fell to General von Manstein after a siege lasting 250 days. They made enormous territorial gains and moved as far as the Volga, but their lines of communication and supplies were extended and strained to the limits. A battle had begun thirty miles from Stalingrad on 26th August, and the Germans reached the city by 12th September. This was the beginning of a disaster.

Meanwhile on the Western Front, RAF one thousand bomber raids began in May on Cologne, Essen, and Bremen, with Polish squadrons participating.

In France, Laval assumed dictatorial powers in April and ruled like Hitler's agent. The Jews were deported from occupied and unoccupied France, and young Frenchmen were joining the *Maquis* to escape forced labour camps in Germany.

In Africa Rommel won at Tobruk on 20th June but paid for it at Alamein in October. On 8th November, US and British forces landed in North Africa under overall command of General Eisenhower in the biggest amphibious operation to date. Admiral Darlan became head of the French State in North Africa. The Germans occupied the whole of France after the African landing. The tide was turning, slowly but surely.

At Northolt Gp Capt. F. Rosier was the Station commander. He was a friend of Poles and Poland, liked and respected by all who knew him. There was always a fine spirit at Northolt, but more so at his time, and he livened up the Station with All Ranks weekly dances in the enormous Station Gymnasium which he faithfully attended. The Conga was *his* dance. It was a great treat to watch and great fun to participate. His WAAF driver would lead, with him behind her, firmly holding her slim waist, and the rest of the Station moving rhythmically all over the place like a great snake, up on the stage, down the stage, singing and laughing.

Some evenings he would be found alone in the guest room playing a violin, with a bottle of whisky and glasses on the table. Slowly the room would fill with people fond of music and whisky. Another bottle would appear, Polish songs would be sung, and one would feel amongst friends, relaxed and at peace with the world for a while.

There was to be a Mess dance at Christmas time and neither I nor Tadek Sawicz had any partners organised, until Sqn Ldr Nowierski, a well known Casanova and an awfully nice man, introduced us to a couple of nurses from RAF Uxbridge Hospital. Monica Agazarian, whose Armenian parents lived in South Kensington, was an Eastern beauty, dark, vivacious and full of fun, and Mary Guthrie - my partner - was a good three inches taller than me, one hundred per cent English, and a great girl for an evening out. The dance was a tremendous success and our partners loved every minute of it. When the tired band dared to take a break we played Polish records and the girls whirled around dancing the *Oberek* as if they did it all their lives. We took them to Uxbridge in the early hours of the morning singing Polish songs all the way.

Włodek Miksa acquired a small monkey which lived in his room and terrorised everyone who entered. She escaped occasionally, creating havoc in the Mess, and eventually she had to go, the Mess staff could not stand it any more.

In January 1943 I flew six times across the water. At one time fifteen to twenty FW-190s engaged 306 and 316 Squadrons, which shot down one-one-four. On the 21st W/O Jasiński collided with Wg Cdr Janus, our Wing leader, who had to bale out over the Channel near the French coast. I followed him with my wingman to the sea, making the usual 'May Day' calls on the emergency frequency, and saw him in the dinghy eventually. It was a bit misty there and we could not see much movement nor signs from him. Jasiński returned safely to England, but Janus was picked up by the Germans and joined the band of friends in the POW camps.

I made several visits to the theatre that winter, and remember seeing J. B. Priestley's 'Doctor's Dilemma', 'Blithe Spirit', a variety show at the Palladium with Tommy Trinder, and 'Hamlet' with an ex-ballet dancer in the main role. Unlike 'Macbeth', I found 'Hamlet' difficult, but to be in England and not to see 'Hamlet' was like being in Rome and not seeing the Pope.

We cheered the February news of von Paulus' capitulation at Stalingrad.

The Germans were evacuating the Caucasus and Rostov on Don; they were falling back along the whole front at last.

I flew for the last time with 315 Squadron on 4th February, and on the 13th I took over command of 308 Squadron, again to my great surprise. I was sorry to leave 315 and all my friends there, but the new appointment was a challenge. At 26 I was the youngest Squadron Commander in the Polish Air Force at that time, and the first one from the 12th Dęblin Cadets entry to be so appointed. Furthermore, I was the only Squadron commander with the Polish rank of Lieutenant, all others held the Polish rank of Captain or above. I had some misgivings about the appointment but I had no doubt that my duty was to accept and to do my best.

Two days later Northolt Wing flew a fighter sweep around Dunkirk.

I led 308 and compared them with 315. The weather was bad over France until the 26th but we had three reasonable flying days over the base and that gave me a chance to get to know them better in the air. Everything was going nicely until the 26th, when we flew twice somewhere around Dunkirk on both occasions. I felt a little pain in my stomach during the morning flight but thought nothing of it. After lunch we went up again and paraded over France at twenty-five thousand feet. My pain was getting worse. I felt better after tea and when somebody suggested the cinema in Ruislip I gladly accepted. By the time I returned to the Mess I thought there must be some reason for the pain as it was increasing again. I discreetly asked Dr Jarosz to my quarters and told him about it.

"Lie down on your back" he said, and when I did, he stuck a finger in the right side of my belly - I yelled!

"Right! Don't move, I am going to call an ambulance to take you to hospital. Nothing serious you know, just an appendix."

I was on the operating table at Hillingdon Hospital on the outskirts of Uxbridge the same evening, and when I woke up in a nice private room, a pretty nurse was sitting by my side. Thirteen was not my lucky number; I took over 308 on the thirteenth and thirteen days later I left them. *What* a way to go!

Next day the surgeon came to see me, explained what had happened, and why I had to have a plastic pipe sticking out of my belly. He thought they would keep me there for about three weeks and that I should be fit for flying when everything was firmly healed in about six to eight weeks, to be on the safe side.

I was certain 308 Squadron would have a new commanding officer within a day or two and wondered what they would do with me. I had no strings to pull, nor any contacts in high places and could not ask anybody what the options were. I thought it best for fate to decide.

Late afternoon on the second day Tadek Sawicz, Włodek Miksa, Andersz, Zygmunt Drybański, and a couple of other chaps came to see me. It developed into a tea party with several amused nurses popping in and out. I had to remind them that they were supposed to lavish their attention on their sick friend and not to flirt with the nurses, but I was promptly told to shut up, mind my own business, and that my turn would come later. They made me laugh several times which was very painful and so I asked everybody to talk about funerals, and how I would like them to behave at mine. There were some outrageous suggestions which brought more laughter and pain. In the end I asked the Ward Sister to throw them out but they would not go until they saw my plastic pipe and when somebody wanted to pour tea into it the sister had had enough.

Monica and Mary came to see me, dressed in their smart RAF nurse's uniforms, a few days later. They had a frosty reception from their civilian opposite numbers and were told to come in one at a time and for five minutes only as I was very ill. I hollered for Sister and when she heard that I was engaged to both of them she promptly lifted all restrictions. Monica and Mary had been coming to the Northolt weekly dances whenever they could make it, and gave me strict orders to get fit for a rumba as soon as possible. Both had had enough of nursing and had applied for training as ferry pilots. Apparently they stood a good chance and in fact succeeded later that year.

The 315 Squadron Mama sent me a huge parcel full of various biscuits, cigarettes, chocolates, and fresh fruit. I shared it all with the nurses and they were my daily guests for their tea breaks.

I was making good progress and eventually the pipe came out, and the stitches, and I returned to Northolt to convalesce. Dr Joseph Jarosz was going to Edinburgh for a week's leave and suggested that I should join him, which I gladly did. I had never been there before and was greatly impressed by that beautiful city. There were Poles everywhere, mostly Army, but by chance we met Gp Capt. S. Pawlikowski, ex Commanding Officer of the Fighter Pursuit Brigade in Warsaw, and then the Senior Polish Staff Officer at the Headquarters Fighter Command - a brilliant officer and leader, and one of the best senior officers in the Polish Air force. He was shot down over France on 15th May 1943 flying with young pilots half his age. He deserved to be spared for the fruits of the Allies' victory.

* * *

On 7th May I took over 317 Squadron at Martlesham Heath, Suffolk. My predecessor had already left and Flt Lt Z. Wróblewski, 'A' Flight commander, was acting Commanding Officer. The 'B' Flight Commander was Z. Janicki - both being my contemporaries from Dęblin. Flt Lt Weber was the Squadron Adjutant and F/O E. Młynarski Engineering Officer. The Squadron had thirty three pilots, including me - twenty two officers and eleven SNCOs, and of course the ground staff comprising all specialists required to keep the aircraft flying.

Our task for the month of May was to provide daylight cover for shipping of all kinds within our range. F/O W. Kirchner destroyed one enemy aircraft and Sgt Tamowicz damaged one during the month and other intruders were chased off. The squadron flew seven hundred and thirty-three sorties in eight hundred and ninety-nine hours.

On 2nd June we moved to RAF Heston, a neighbouring station to Northolt, where we stayed until the 22nd. Within days of our move an unfortunate accident occurred over the airfield on a training flight. Flt Lt T. Owczarski collided with Sgt Zych, the former landed safely with bent propeller tips, and the latter baled out unhurt.

On the 17th we escorted twelve Bostons in the morning to and from the target in France and although enemy aircraft were reported in the area they did not engage. In the afternoon we flew Rodeo 23 - low level approach to Ostend, a fast climb to fourteen thousand feet, and a look-see around. We did not find anything.

On 22nd June we were on the move again, this time to RAF Perranporth in Cornwall. We left our well-cared for aircraft in Heston and inherited Spitfire Vs in a rather poor state of health. 302 Squadron, commanded by Sqn Ldr W. Barański, moved with us at the same time and the two squadrons worked as a Polish Wing under Wg Cdr W. Żak. Our Station Commander was an RAF Squadron Leader of Administration Branch who looked after us extremely well with his small British staff; his was a satellite airfield controlled by the main base at Portreath. Our airmen and NCOs were accommodated in standard wooden huts with the usual facilities near the airfield, while the Officers Mess was right on top of a cliff in the requisitioned Droskyn Castle Hotel - the view over the bay was superb.

The first operation on the 24th took us to an enemy airfield north-east of Brest which was bombed by twelve Mitchells, our wing acting as escort. We all flew at low-level over water and then climbed rapidly to fourteen thousand feet. Over the target area Flt Lt Janicki's section of four (including F/Os Walawski and Ciach) attacked four FW-190s and were gone in a flash without a word. Everybody else wanted to join them, come what may, and my squadron disappeared in a few seconds. I stayed with my No. 2 behind the bombers with 302 closing in to escort them home. Most of our chaps returned singly or in pairs. Sgt Kostański was missing and nobody knew what had happened to him. Wg Cdr Żak was not very pleased with us and not without good reason. Walawski and Ciach claimed two-one-none FW-190s but Fighter Command did not confirm the claim[*].

Early on the 26th we escorted Typhoons to Landeda for a low-level attack. After refuelling we flew to Ibsley, home of the Czech Wing, and together with them we went to Argentan to meet Flying Fortresses returning from a raid. We waited for as long as fuel allowed but they never turned up. Apparently they changed the planned route and flew west into the Atlantic and around Brittany to England, but nobody knew about it. We spent the night at Ibsley, flew to RAF Ford, near Arundel, next morning to take part in another operation, but the weather deteriorated and we returned home.

Another escort of Typhoons on the 28th took us to Morlaix, 317 climbing to fourteen thousand feet near the target and providing rear cover.

On the 29th we did a lot of flying. From base to Ibsley, an operation to Argentan, landing at Middle Wallop for a second operation which was cancelled, and back home.

During July I led the squadron on six operations. We were frequently required to reinforce 11 Group in southeast England, which entailed flying from Perranporth below five hundred feet to airfields in the south east and night stops. For example: 25th July - Base to Martlesham Heath, Ramrod 154 (12 Mitchells sent to bomb Fokker factory near Amsterdam), refuelling, and again Ramrod 158 (12 Mitchells, target: airfield near Shiptel). No enemy aircraft encountered but Servicing Commandos (mobile aircraft servicing crews) stole my private watch left with its broken strap in my Spitfire map compartment at Martlesham Heath. The RAF came to my rescue and provided a service watch next day before we returned to base. 28th July: Base to Northolt, landing at night and stopping overnight. 29th - took off at dawn to Coltishall, Ramrod 22 (cover for 18 Marauders bombing an airfield), refuelling at Coltishall and back to base. Base to Middle Wallop - overnight stop. 30th - early morning to Manston, near Dover, operation to Merville, called off as we were crossing the French coast, refuelling at Manston and back to base.

During July our squadron shot down three-one-one enemy aircraft. The squadron flew two hundred and thirty-two sorties in three hundred and forty-seven hours. F/O Owczarski damaged his aircraft on take off, and W/O Leszczyński had a taxiing accident when a strong gust of wind overturned his aircraft. We lost F/O Ciach, F/O Felc, and Sgt Bartys.

F/O Felc had married an English girl a month or so earlier. They lived in a small flat in Perranporth village. I called on her. Her self control was admirable, but her pain must have been unbearable - she just froze. I wished she had cried before her landlady took her to another room. Probably I would have cried with her and shared some of her grief. As it was, I only had a few words to say and no way of showing her how deeply I felt for her. But what would that be to her? She had just lost her husband and her world was shattered.

The first operation in August was an escort of eight Whirlwinds - light twin-engined aircraft, carrying 2 x 250 pound bombs. They blew up four German 'E' boats and set one on fire in a small Brittany harbour. 302 Squadron went in first at low level firing at anything they could see, followed very closely by Whirlwinds, while 317 climbed and made a wide circle around the target protecting their withdrawal. No enemy aircraft appeared. The following three operations were uneventful, and then we were advised that the Wing was to move to RAF Fairlop on 21st August, a small airfield on the north east outskirts of London. Our stay in the Cornish holiday resort was drawing to a close.

---

[*]   They were credited with three damaged. *Ed.*

Perranporth was a very pleasant village in those days. In the centre, surrounded by lawns and shrubs, stood the Stork Club, the social centre of the resort. When we first went there nobody would talk to us. They served us with drinks, and took our money, but the staff and locals were definitely giving us the cold shoulder. We were surprised at the unfriendly reception and ceased trying to make contacts with them. This went on for about two weeks until a friendly matron and her daughter could not stand it any more and broke the ice. It appeared that our predecessors - Canadians - swore that every Pole carried a knife and that we would rape their daughters and knife their men. They believed them, but as nothing untoward had happened so far, they wondered whether there was much truth in it.

"Oh yes!" we assured her, "Your daughter is in mortal danger, and so are you madam. You are both too beautiful to walk the streets of Perranporth without police escort."–

The bubble had burst, and we had no problems from then on, particularly with holiday visitors and voluntary evacuees from London and the south east. Werner Kirchner and Deidre, a charming Londoner, were often seen together and later in the year they married. Friends from other squadrons filled all the spare bedrooms in the Mess, coming to this peaceful land for a break. Polish ladies from London and elsewhere, wives, daughters, and secretaries who had any interests in our two squadrons began appearing in the village. The weather was fine, the swimming excellent, and the fame of Perranporth as *the* place for a break spread far and wide.

There were problems too. One of the very young officers owned an old car with worn tyres and exchanged them for a better set belonging to an old car parked in the Mess garage, and never used by anybody. But the owner, a local man, kept an eye on his car and noticed what had happened. The Station Commander wanted to sort it out quietly, and so did I, but the aggrieved Cornishman wanted the police, the court, and his pound of flesh. My argument was that this was a prank rather than a serious crime, and any court would probably treat the young fool's first offence leniently. He certainly was not a thief. The danger was that the Polish authorities might finish him as an officer and a pilot. It takes a lot of time and money to train a pilot. He was an excellent flier and fighter and it was in everybody's interest to keep him flying. As a punishment I suggested that he should pay a sum of money to a charity to be agreed by the Station commander and the Cornishman. All was settled on those lines and I thought this was the end of the matter. However, a few days later Gp Capt. Bajan, our senior officer at Headquarters Fighter Command - he succeeded Gp Capt. Pawlikowski - arrived on an official visit and rebuked me for not reporting the occurrence to him. I said that we would have done so if we had failed to solve the problem locally. Admittedly, I did not act according to the book of rules but I was taught that rules were to guide you and not to think for you. I found out later that the indignant ladies from London, holidaying in Perranporth, passed the news to him via the grapevine. It seems they wanted the officer crucified.

I had a different problem soon after. Flt Lt 'X', detailed for readiness duty one morning, argued with his Flight Commander that it was not his turn and that he was very tired. This was unheard of and I had to do something about it, particularly as it was in my hearing and a lot of junior pilots were there as well. I took his turn in readiness, relieved him of all duties for one week and instructed him to take maximum rest either in the Mess or on the beach, but nowhere else. He was not to drink any alcohol in the Mess and retire to his quarters at 9 p.m. I also asked the squadron Medical Officer to examine him just in case there was something wrong with the chap. For weeks afterwards everybody was most solicitous about his health, to his great chagrin.

When we had arrived at Perranporth our men were appalled at the state of their quarters. Now that we were about to leave I suggested to the Adjutant that we should do the opposite, the name of our squadron was involved, and all that. They responded and left their huts fit for inspection by an Air Marshal. The Station commander could not believe his eyes, and telephone calls and letters of appreciation followed.

Our advance party received all aircraft at Fairlop on the 21st. The next morning the main party of ground staff arrived by train at a station nearby. I took all pilots to meet them there and thought this went down well. The Adjutant confirmed later that the men were surprised and pleased, apparently this had never happened before.

302 Squadron had its own Officer's Mess in a large mansion, whereas 317 had a primitive brick and corrugated iron, half-barrel shaped affair, sub-divided into a lounge, dining room, bar, and kitchen. Flt Lt Knapik and company promptly painted a slightly rude mural depicting a well known ballad about a King and a Princess who fell in love with a handsome fiddler (*Raz królewna...* etc.). A little WAAF Corporal was the Mess Management and looked after us admirably with her girls. Peggy was the Dining Room queen. In spite of the primitive set-up it was a happy Mess and the chaps from the posh mansion were calling often for a sing-song and a drink.

We went to work straight away and escorted bombers to their targets on the 23rd, 25th, 27th, 30th, and twice on the 31st. The respective missions were:
- 24 Mitchells - St Omer airfield
- 18 Bostons - Beaumont airfield
- 18 Marauders - Rouen airfield (recalled)
- 36 Marauders - St Omer ammunition stores
- 36 Marauders - Mazingarbe airfield, near Bethune
- 24 Mitchells - Le Foret de Hepdin

There were hardly any enemy aircraft to be seen anywhere. The squadron flew in August two hundred and thirty-eight sorties in three hundred and forty-five hours. From the second to nineteenth September I went up with my squadron on sixteen missions - thirteen with bombers and three fighter sweeps. On some days I flew more than once a day; for example, twice on the third, three times on the fourth, and twice on the eighth. The operations were of a similar type as the last six. Thus:
- 36 Marauders - Lille marshalling yard
- 18 Venturas - Target in a forest
- 18 Mitchells - Rouen area
- 18 Mitchells - Boulogne area
- 36 Marauders - Hazebrouck
- 72 Marauders - Ghent marshalling yard
- 36 Marauders - Amiens area
- 36 Marauders - Lille area
- 72 Marauders - Lille airfield
- 18 Mitchells - Neufchatel
- 72 Marauders - Beauvais area
- 12 Mitchells - Lens

German fighters engaged our wing on four occasions. 317 had a good day on the eighth when escorting seventy-two Marauders tasked to bomb Lille airfield. We were in the middle of a very large fighter escort and just before we reached the target a group of about fifteen enemy aircraft were approaching our formation from behind and above, and it looked as if they intended to dive to the bombers through us. I warned the squadron that as soon as they get a bit closer we would turn one hundred and eighty degrees anti-clockwise and meet them head on. This we did as on a training flight, and immediately the usual pandemonium started: guns blazing, aircraft turning, twisting, climbing, diving, and on the RT warnings and shouts. After a while I wanted to get everybody together again and invited them to join me at a certain altitude where I would circle to the left, and to my surprise we re-assembled very quickly and once again we were a force and a team not to be trifled with. By that time the bombers and escorts had disappeared from sight on their way home and it was time for us to do the same. I took the squadron down to low level and as we approached the coast we fired at coastal gun positions, vehicles, and a column of men marching along a road. The squadron shot down three-nought-one, and all returned safely.

On the eleventh I did not fly. I think Wg Cdr Żak led the squadron and again they had a good day shooting down three, nought, three.

Earlier in the month we had a Spitfire delivered by a lady ferry pilot - slim, very attractive, and speaking Polish. It was Second Officer Jadwiga Piłsudska, daughter of Marshal Józef Piłsudski. We were all bowled over by the event. It felt as if she had brought a nod of approval with her from the great man for what we were trying to do. I drove her slowly by the longest route to 302 Squadron Mess for lunch where Wg Cdr Żak and Sqn Ldr Wańka Barański and his warriors looked after her with gentle and tender attention. I wondered what she thought of us. There were, I think, eleven Polish ladies flying as Air Transport Auxiliary (ATA) pilots at that time, ferrying anything from Tiger Moths to Lancasters, and she was one of them.

A frequent visitor to our Mess was Gp Capt. Stannard from Headquarters Fighter Command - a staunch friend of Poles and 317 Squadron in particular. He was a cultured and courteous man of great personal charm and modesty. He liked our ballad about the Princess and the fiddler and sang with us, or hummed when he ran out of words.

Werner Kirchner brought Deidre to the Mess a few times and it was obvious theirs was not a light-hearted romance. A few months later they married. Something had happened to the Best Man and I was asked to step in at the last moment. My impromptu speech was not exactly brilliant but at least it was short enough not to be boring.

On 21st September we moved back to Northolt and on to Spitfire IXs at last. It was sad to say good-bye to our mural, Peggy, and the management, but Northolt was our home and we were glad to return. Our effort for September comprised three hundred and ten sorties, four hundred and ninety-four hours, and seven-nought-four enemy aircraft shot down. The victors were Walawski, Radomski, Zbrożek, Rudowski, Janicki, Martini, and two others.

Bad weather considerably reduced operational flying in late autumn. I flew with the squadron only five times in October and six times in November. All in all there were three fighter sweeps and eight bomber escorts, which included cover on two occasions for one hundred and twenty Flying Fortresses returning from day raids over Germany, four escorts of seventy-two strong Marauder raids and one of thirty six. They were bombing targets in northern France similar to those already mentioned. In October the squadron flew one hundred and sixty-three sorties in three hundred and four hours and in November one hundred and eighty-seven sorties in three hundred and twenty-eight hours.

In early December we spent a lot of time in Southend on range practice. Then the weather deteriorated and remained bad for weeks. I took some leave and on return I heard the dreaded news that, as from 1st January 1944, I would have a ground job. I handed over the squadron to Włodek Miksa. At the farewell drinks in the Orchard Hotel attended by both of us somebody gave the toast 'Le roi est mort, vive le roi!', and that was that, my war-time flying came to an end.

In 1943 the war was getting bloodier and nastier everywhere. In the East, after Stalingrad where Hitler lost three hundred thousand men, came the battle of Kursk in mid July. Hitler threw in seventeen Panzer divisions, half his total armoured strength, and lost. Having no mobile reserves left he had to transfer six of his best divisions from Russia to Italy. On 7th August the Red Army launched their summer offensive and pushed the Germans beyond the Dnieper river and, by December, west of Kiev. Of the three hundred and twenty German divisions outside the Reich they had, in November, two hundred and six in Soviet Russia, twenty four in the Balkans, twenty two in Italy, fifty in France and the Low Countries, and eighteen in Norway and Denmark. Another fifteen divisions were inside Germany in various stages of organisation.

RAF night raids on Germany caused vast destruction and heavy civilian losses. But Speer was able to maintain and increase production of arms even in bombed cities. Six million foreign workers and POWs were labouring for the German economy.

American day raids by the 8th USAAF Flying Fortresses began badly at first, but they soon improved and the day and night offensive continued and carried the horrors of war deep into Germany.

Britain was winning the vital battle of the Atlantic at last. The Africa Corps surrendered on 13th May and on 10th July the US and British forces invaded Sicily. King Victor Emanuel ordered Mussolini's arrest, and Marshal Badoglio formed a government.

But for us things went badly. News came that in April the Germans discovered mass graves of 4,143 Polish officers murdered at Katyn. Nothing was known of those who were in Russian camps at Starobielsk (3,920) and Ostashkov (6,500), they disappeared completely. When the Polish government requested an investigation by the International Red Cross of that unprecedented crime the Soviet Government broke off diplomatic relations with us. The crisis deepened with the untimely death of General Sikorski in Gibraltar, where his aeroplane crashed into the sea after take-off. S. Mikołajczyk, leader of the Peasant Party, became Prime Minister, and General Sosnkowski the Commander-in-Chief.

In April and May the Germans carried out the liquidation of the Jewish Ghetto in Warsaw. Out of 400,000 Jews herded there by 15th November 1940 when the Ghetto was sealed off, only 60,000 were still there. But some six hundred young Jews organised in twenty-two combat groups fought bravely for a month until they all died. Their leader was twenty-four year old Mordechai Anielewicz. This was but a part of the most hideous crime known. The Nazi anti-Jewish genocide was carried out on a massive scale in concentration camps at Auschwitz, Treblinka, Sobibór, Bełżec, Majdanek and others.

Roosevelt, Stalin and Churchill met in Teheran on 28th November. The Americans and Russians formed a united front and it is the American President and his advisors therefore, who bear the greater part of responsibility for the betrayal of Europe. The main subjects for discussion were Overlord, Poland, Balkans, Finland, Germany, and Japan. As for Poland, both Roosevelt and Churchill agreed Stalin's claim to the Eastern half of Poland. They hoped that once Stalin had satisfied his territorial appetite he would respect the real independence of the remaining part of Poland at least. This abrogated the Anglo-Polish guarantee of 1939 and the noble Atlantic Charter.

Chester Wilmot summed it up neatly: "Thus the Teheran Conference not only determined the military strategy for 1944, but adjusted the political balance of post-war Europe in favour of the Soviet Union" - (*Struggle for Europe*, page 142). The Polish government in London knew nothing of this.

* * *

During the next three months I held the post of Liaison Officer, first at Headquarters 11 Group in Uxbridge for about a month and then 9 Group, near Preston, Lancs. I had no clear terms of reference, and virtually nothing to do. Whether I was there or not did not matter to anybody. I had a desk and a telephone, but nobody ever called or telephoned. At Preston I shared the office with an RAF Flt Lt whose specialisation was photography. I never saw him doing anything in particular either, but he made two or three telephone calls every day chatting to various people and, I suppose, letting them know that he was still alive. As I was not on chatting terms with anybody at Preston I telephoned my friends at Northolt once or twice a week, keeping abreast of their news.

There was only one Polish unit in 9 Group at that time, 303 Squadron based in Northern Ireland. I should have been brought into matters concerning them to help if necessary, but all Headquarters branches were perfectly capable of dealing directly without any difficulties and there was neither any need nor desire on their part to raise any matters with me, even out of courtesy. As it was not in my nature to crawl around soliciting for business, I sat at my desk waiting for something to happen. And one day it did.

A very young and inexperienced Sgt Pilot of 303 Squadron returning from a training flight in rapidly deteriorating weather landed with retracted undercarriage and bent his Spitfire. This had happened to a lot of people and in each case the Station Commander blew his top, rebuked the pilot for negligence, or whatever, and endorse his Log Book accordingly in red. In this case however, the newly promoted and appointed Station Commander wanted to make a name for himself as a tough master and ordered a Court Martial, to the great embarrassment of his superiors and to the amazement of the Poles. The charge was 'wilful destruction of his Majesty's property in that…' etc. etc. Had our chief at Fighter command sent a defending officer with some knowledge of the law, and we had several of them, the case, in all, probability, would have been dismissed. As it was, Flt Lt S. Brzeski, an excellent fighter pilot but hopeless as a defending officer, soon manoeuvred himself into such a position that the court had to do something, and after the charge was changed by deletion of the word 'wilfully' the pilot was reprimanded. This was the lightest sentence the Court Martial could award. I was one of the four members of the Court and after Brzeski's 'defence' could do nothing else but agree regretfully with the others. I had one consolation however, the Station commander had made a fool of himself, the Court knew it, everybody on the Station knew it, and 303 Squadron did not hide their feelings either.

The Commanding Officer of 303 Squadron was Tadek Koc at that time, whom I knew from Lwów. He was a dedicated flier and excellent at his job. It was during my Northolt time earlier in the war when Tadek was shot down over Belgium or France. He was unhurt and luckily his first contacts were with friendly natives. They noticed that he was hardly five feet tall, very slim and youthful looking, and so they dressed him in schoolboy's clothing, and the escape organisation passed him from hand to hand across France and to Spain. He was back at Northolt within four weeks, and fortunately for him the squadron adjutant had not yet despatched his belongings to the special depot. Tadek was a thrifty fellow and had amassed more than the usual amount of worldly goods. On opening his box however, he found that his radio, alarm clock, and several other items were missing. He was furious and began a systematic search. People tried to help by amusing notes telling him who was wearing his cuff-links, that his radio was under a bed in the west wing of the Mess, and so on, until he recovered the lot and peace was restored again.

On my return to Preston I found a very important letter. It contained the conditions of entry into the Polish Air Force Staff College, together with an application form, which I filled in immediately and sent away. The possibility of serious studies appealed to me and it would also mean departure from 9 Group.

The next course - the fifth – was due to begin in April, and would be the first one divorced from the Polish Army Staff College in Scotland, and run by the Polish Air Force alone, in Weston-super-Mare.

In due course I was called for entrance examination, which consisted of one written paper and an interview by the College Commandant, Gp Capt. Tuskiewicz and three other senior officers. The most interesting part of the interview was questions regarding the operational use of the Polish Air Force in 1939. I spoke against dispersing squadrons to particular armies... I was all for concentration and mobility... all fighters under one command on airfields between Warsaw and Łódź... with refuelling and rearming facilities on landing fields near Krakow and north of Warsaw. All bombers under one command..., operating in large numbers on most important targets... always with fighter escorts. I raised several other points and answered probing questions. I concluded that although we could not have won on our own we might have given the army better support and inflicted higher losses on the enemy. About a fortnight later I received the letter of acceptance and joining instructions.

I spent one week at RAF Station Faldingworth, Lincolnshire, with 300 Polish Bomber Squadron on Lancasters, where I tried to learn something about their work, and then a month with the Polish Army Staff College at Kirkcaldy, Scotland. The army people gave us a crash course on land warfare with particular emphasis on armoured divisions. We studied in detail the infantry battalion in the field with maps, sketches, etc. in a howling wind, rain, and hail. The army staff were true professionals and I was greatly impressed by them.

Our proper Air Staff course began on 15th May and lasted six months. The college was accommodated in two requisitioned hotels, the Beach Hotel for the business side, and the Cabot Hotel for the Officers Mess and domestics.

It was a comfortable and civilised set-up, we even had our own Polish dentist, the beautiful Halina. I was very pleased to meet several of my old friends: George Radomski who was a Flight commander in 317 Squadron at Perranporth and now on the college staff as an assistant, Wańka Barański, ex Commanding Officer of 302 Squadron, Główczyński, ex Personal Assistant to General Sikorski, Langhamer, my contemporary from Dęblin, and the college adjutant, Adam Olszewski, ex adjutant of 315 Squadron where he was like a father to young pilots, he being a pre-war navigator of vintage years.

The course was thirty strong - seven Majors, seventeen Captains, and six Lieutenants. These were Polish ranks and did not correspond to our RAF acting paid ranks which were usually one higher.

The programme was similar to that at the RAF Staff College, Bracknell. The general part comprised studies of air strategy and tactics with particular emphasis on bomber and fighter operations, as well as reconnaissance, signals and supplies. Then came detail studies of Tactical Air Force Group, together with all supporting services. The last stage of that was syndicate work; we planned and fought our paper battles in Poland within the 1939 boundaries. Our enemies were Germans again but this time we fought them with Spitfires, Typhoons and Marauders and we had radar and good communication between aircraft and operation rooms. Our supply lines worked, and we were not running out of fuel. The umpires did not think we were doing too badly.

In addition to normal planned work everybody had to choose one book out of a set and write a précis and comments. We also took turns in studying the national daily press for one week and delivering a review of the week's events on Saturdays, followed by questions and discussion. We had several lectures by visiting RAF Staff Officers from Bracknell and Polish Staff Officers from London.

I found the course stimulating and enjoyed the hard work and the challenge it provided. I was certainly increasing my knowledge, learning to analyse problems, exercising judgement, making decisions, and generally widening my horizons. It was all good stuff, no matter what the critics said.

The seaside resort of Weston-super-Mare was very popular with the people of Bristol and other towns further north. Apart from a good range of shops, hotels, boarding houses, B and Bs, and cafés, there was also a large and very nice swimming pool, and a place of mass entertainment where there was music and dancing - a favourite with Americans.

George Radomski and I often called at the friendly Atlantic Hotel Bar for a drink, and several other Cabot Hotel residents would also trickle in and out during the course of the evening. Sometimes we ended the evening in somebody's house for the last drink and a chat and returned the hospitality in our Mess later.

Wańka Barański had a splendid Alsatian which kept him fit. He was allowed to bring the dog on a lead to the swimming pool and immediately all the toddlers wanted to stroke him. Little Hilary Pakeman succeeded several times and had to be rescued by Cecilie, her charming mother. She had a friend, Frances, and the two of them came for drinks to our Mess occasionally and to the Mess dance later.

An exclusive girls' boarding school invited ten officers to their dance. The youngest of us had to volunteer and I was one of them. The girls were like little flowers, warm, soft, delicate, and slightly shy and very sweet.

After we drank some strong orangeade - beer came later - they lost their initial shyness and were dancing like angels, chirruping and laughing merrily. We treated them as if they were most precious porcelain figures, but there was no need to treat their attractive mistresses alike who were also keen dancers.

Within days of my arrival at the college news came that after eight days of ferocious fighting the second Polish corps, led by General Anders, had taken Monte Casino on 18th May. The German Gustav line was smashed and road number six - via Casalina - to beleaguered American troops at Anzio, and to Rome, was wide open one week later when the Poles finished the job by taking Piedimonte.

Previously the Allies had mounted two offensives in this sector, both by forces within the 5th US Army; the first from 20th January to 14th February by American and French forces, coinciding with the Anzio landing, and the second from 15th February to 24th March by the 2nd New Zealand and 4th Indian divisions. When the British 8th Army took over the sector from the US Fifth Army the third offensive was mounted, and the Second Polish Corps was given the main task to take Monte Cassino and Piedimonte. The 13th British Corps, on the left, was to force the river Gari and move along the river Liri, to be followed by the 1st Canadian Corps, and the 10th British Corps to cover the right flank defensively.

Already brave men of five nations had fought valiantly for Monte Cassino, Americans, British, French, New Zealand, and Indian. The eyes of the world were focused on it. A myth was growing that this was an invincible fortress, but it fell, and the Poles took it.

Then the dreaded news of the cost paid for the victory came. The figures were staggering, about 900 killed and 2,900 wounded. The strength of the 2nd Corps before battle was 45,900, total losses were 4,199 - 9.1 per cent, out of which 924 were killed, 2,930 wounded, and 345 missing[*]. Contrary to Soviet propaganda that Poles did not want to fight the Germans, the Second Corps fought them to the end of the war - at Ancona, on the Goth lines, in the Apennines, on the river Sonio, and lastly at Bologna from the 9th to the 23rd April 1945. Total losses amounted to over 11,000. The ratio of officers to men lost was 1:3 - they were not leading from behind.

It was difficult to concentrate on studies and fight paper battles when real ones were being fought all over the world. Soviet troops entered Poland again on 4th January 1944; in 1939 they did it as Hitler's allies, now as his enemies. How would they treat Poland and Poles this time? The shadow of Teheran was hanging over us. Mr Churchill's speech on 22nd February in the House of Commons confirmed our fears, but still we hoped.

On 6th June the Allied Forces landed in Normandy. On 13th June the first V1 bombs fell on London...

I was working hard in July on a précis of a serious book when George Radomski came and dragged me out. He had something on his mind. He told me about two Polish WAAFs employed in the college - a mother and daughter. What a sweet girl the daughter was!

"Well, you are not going to marry her, so leave her alone!"

"One can't stay a bachelor forever."

"No, not forever, but it makes sense to wait until the end of the war, however it will end."

We left the subject then, but next year George married Halina, his sweet WAAF girl, and they lived happily for many years. Their fate, however, was a tragic one. First Halina's mother died of cancer, then their son, Andrzej, died of the same disease when he was about to complete his medical studies, and about two years later the same fate befell George.

A dramatic radio message was sent out of Warsaw, the first of many - "We are fighting" - it was 1st August 1944. General Tadeusz Bór-Komorowski, the C-in-C Polish Underground Army (*Armia Krajowa*, AK), ordered the Warsaw uprising to begin at 1700 hours on 1st August. General Monter was the Commanding Officer of the Uprising. Professor J. K. Zawodny gave the full story in his scholarly book 'Warsaw capitulated on 4th October. The cost was appalling':

	Poles	Germans
In combat on 1st August - AK soldiers	40,000	13,000
after 20th August		21,500
on some days up to		40,000
Numbers, approximate for the Polish side:		
Killed	10,000	10,000
Missing (killed?)	7,000	7,000
Wounded	5,000	9,000
Total losses	22,000	26,000

Sent to POW camps: 15,900 Poles (including 2,000 women AK)
About 3,500 soldiers merged with the civilian population
Civilians in Warsaw: Killed: 200,000 - 250,000
Evacuated during and after the Uprising: 700,000
Material losses: about eighty per cent of all buildings were destroyed.

[*] *Bellona* No. 1, 1958

Attempts made to supply Warsaw by air from Italy (1,500 kms) by 1586 Polish Flight and 148 RAF Squadron failed owing to enormous losses. On 4th August seven Polish and seven British aircraft took off for Warsaw, but only three succeeded in their mission and six were destroyed. In August and September there were only twenty three flying nights owing to bad weather or full moon. 213 sorties were flown in that time and losses were heavy. The Poles lost 37 Officers and 107 SNCOs. 110 Flying Fortresses of the USA Air Force dropped 1,284 containers over Warsaw in a day flight on 18th September, but only 388 were recovered by the Poles. The aircraft landed in Poltava and returned via Italy. This was not repeated because the Russians refused any more landing facilities on their airfields to Western Allies. They would not drop supplies to Warsaw themselves either.

It was with a heavy heart that we heard the news of the Uprising, and for the next sixty-three days we followed the desperate struggle and suffering of our people in Warsaw. And so did Polish soldiers, airmen, and sailors fighting on all Western Fronts helping to liberate Italy, France, Belgium, and Holland. Polish Communist puppets were taking over the country as the Germans were retreating. The AK units which contributed to the Red Army success, fighting Germans in Wołyn, the Wilno area, in Lwów, and Lublin were being arrested and disarmed. The Polish Government Manifesto of the 3rd October declared that "We have been treated worse than Hitler's allies, Italy, Rumania, Finland".

Eight days after the fall of Warsaw, on 11th October, Churchill, Stalin, Eden, and Harriman conversed about the Uprising during the Moscow talks, and Stalin assured them that failure to relieve Warsaw had not been due to any lack of effort by the Red Army. The Prime Minister 'accepted this view absolutely' and so did Harriman (Eden's telegram from Moscow to Sir Orme Sargent).

Our course was drawing to a close. The Commandant offered me a job on the College Staff, which I declined and asked instead that I might be posted to one of our squadrons in Belgium as a supernumerary pilot. He did not think that was a good idea and said he would recommend a staff job.

On 28th November 1944 I reported to Headquarters 84 Group (Rear) of the Second Tactical Air Force in Hertogenbosch, Holland. I was to relieve Sqn Ldr Z. W. Bieńkowski as a Polish Liaison Officer at the Organisation Branch. The Rear Headquarters was responsible for all logistic support of the group and to that end controlled appropriate units, a number of which were Polish, i.e. 411 Repair and Salvage Unit (RSU), 408 Air Stores Park (ASP), and 72 Motor Transport Light Repair Unit (MTLRU). The main headquarters controlled the sharp end i.e. flying Wings each comprising on average three squadrons. There were seven of them: 35, 123, 131 (Polish), 132, 135, 145 (French), and 146.

The 131 wing had 302, 308, and 317 Squadrons; its Commanding Officer was Gp Capt. Gabszewicz and T. Sawicz was Wing commander Flying, both outstanding and highly decorated officers.

The Commanding Officer of the Rear Headquarters was Gp Capt. Beaumont, a business executive of high rank in civilian life and eminently suited to his RAF job. I admired his dedication, efficiency, and leadership. Like him, most of his officers had war-time commissions - they came from all walks of life and on the whole did not have much time for regular officers.

I remember a meeting at which our Chief announced that a new Air Officer in charge of Administration, his boss, was due to arrive shortly straight from a high-powered staff course.

"How about staff papers and all that? He will expect it of us so everybody watch out" he said with a grin, to a roar of laughter. After all the war was approaching its end, if he did not like their spelling, he would have to put up with it. Not an unreasonable attitude, but the man in question served his country with distinction during the war and for many years after, he was a regular RAF officer.

"What did you do in the Staff College, Kornicki?" asked Gp Capt. Beaumont one evening in the bar.

"Oh, this and that, sir, like school, similar stuff as in the RAF place."

"Yes, but what in particular? What did you spend most of your time on?"

"Tactical Group, sir."

"Then you should know what we have and how to use it. Tell me…" and question after question followed for the best part of half an hour. "Well, Kornicki, if I broke a leg to-morrow you could take over, couldn't you? Ha! ha! ha!"

I did not mind his little joke but I began to realise that my staff course was a liability in a way, rather than an asset in that place.

I shared an office-cum-home motorised caravan with Flt Lt Rowiński, who worked for Personnel Branch and was quite busy - Polish names were difficult to spell. My chief told me on arrival that I was free to visit Polish units. "Take a jeep any time you want." He would call me when he wanted me. He never did, and if I wanted to see him he never had much time for me either. This was not surprising. Poles were becoming embarrassing allies and people in Polish units had very strong views on such things as the Allies' stand vis-a-vis the Warsaw Uprising. I never raised controversial subjects in the Mess but if asked for my views I spoke politely but freely, as I thought. This might have been undiplomatic but at least it was honest. There was a purpose behind some of the questions - the four or five Poles at the Headquarters represented a sample opinion of all Poles in the group. It was important for the chiefs to know how the events were affecting our attitudes and morale. Needless to say, my views were not endearing me to my RAF colleagues.

I was less than a month in Holland when the last German offensive began on 16th December - the von Rundstedt Ardennes Offensive. The 69-year old Field Marshal opposed the idea and so did Model, but they were eventually obliged to accept the plan completed to the last detail and endorsed in the Fuhrer's hand-writing "NOT TO BE ALTERED". Three armies were to strike on a seventy-five mile front: the 6th Panzer (Dietrich) north-west for Antwerp –(the main task), the 5th Panzer (Manteuffel) via Namur to Brussels, and the 7th to cover the southern flank. A special sabotage-trained force under Skorzeny of American-speaking, jeep-riding 'Commandos' was formed to carry out Trojan Horse operations.

By a supreme effort over three thousand new and repaired tanks and assault guns were sent to the front in less than two months and twenty-eight divisions were concentrated in the Ardennes without detection in the prevailing bad weather.

The 39 divisions of the US Army Group under General O. Bradley were deployed for attack on a two hundred mile front in three lots, the smallest - five divisions - was stretched over a hundred miles in the Ardennes sector, where the Germans struck. It was a complete surprise. Heavy losses, confusion, broken communication and general pandemonium followed. But the Americans fought stubbornly wherever they could, like at St Vith, for instance. The situation was grave.

Our Headquarters was alerted and ordered to pack up and move to the Brussels area. I drove our heavy caravan for hours in a slow convoy until we arrived at our destination at night.

Mist and low clouds were shielding the Germans during the first week of fighting until suddenly over Christmas the weather improved. In four days the Americans and British flew one thousand five hundred sorties striking at traffic, roads, railways, airfields, and cutting off supply lines in the Rhineland. Eisenhower placed all forces north of the break-through - the 1st and 9th US

Armies - under the command of Montgomery, who had reserves. "The Field Marshal strode into Hodges Headquarters like Christ coming to cleanse the temple" according to one of his officers, and promptly antagonised all American commanders. However he stopped the confusion, brought order into the battle and after Christmas the tide started turning against the Germans, by which time we had made a return journey to Holland.

Against von Rundstedt's advice Hitler ordered Model to re-group, attack Bastogne Salient, and try to reach the river Meuse. In support of ground forces all available German fighters - about nine hundred - took part in operation *Bodenplatte*, an attack on Allied airfields.

The day was 1st January 1945; the sky was covered with heavy low clouds, I thought it was going to rain when I walked to the Mess for breakfast. Suddenly I heard a roar of engines and saw about a dozen FW-190s to my surprise, flying very low over the town and practically overhead. This was duly reported to the appropriate people and I heard nothing more about it until later when I went to the Mess again in mid morning. I was passing a small group of officers when I heard one of them saying:

"It's the bloody Poles again."

"I am sorry, I couldn't help over-hearing, what happened?"

"Haven't you heard?"

"Heard what?"

"German fighters attacked most of our airfields, lots of aircraft were destroyed on the ground. Hardly anybody was flying, some men were killed."

"This is terrible, what have you heard of the Polish Wing?"-

"Oh, they came out of it best. They were flying and two squadrons caught the Germans over the airfield and shot down a lot of them, but they lost some aircraft and men too."

I drove to St Denis airfield, near Ghent, and saw several aircraft burned, including one four engine job. This is what happened. Early in the morning 302, 308, and 317 Squadrons took off to bomb their targets behind enemy lines. About one hour after they left approximately fifty German fighters - FW-190s and Me-109s - attacked numerous aircraft parked around the airfield and the airfield installations. 308 and 317 Squadrons, returning from their missions, caught the Germans unaware and shot down eighteen. The Poles lost two pilots, three corporal technicians, and over a dozen others were wounded. 302 Squadron returned last, after the battle was over. The Germans destroyed eighteen Polish Spitfires on the ground and several 'visiting' British and American aircraft whose departure was delayed.

The Second Tactical Air Force lost one hundred and forty-four aircraft destroyed and eighty-four damaged, and the Americans one hundred and thirty-four destroyed and sixty-two damaged. German losses were claimed to be three hundred and four aircraft and two hundred and fourteen pilots. This was the swan song for the Luftwaffe fighters.

Werner Girbig described in his book '*Start im Morgengrauen*' the operation '*Bodenplatte*' and gave a detailed account of the action by the First Fighter Regiment 'Oesau' on St Denis. He called the operation the demise of German fighters in the West.

The Germans could not take Bastogne, and by the 8th January their Panzer divisions were in danger of being trapped west of Houffalize. Hitler admitted at last that the Ardennes offensive had failed.

It was the Russians who benefited from the German defeat. They began their offensive on 12th January, took Warsaw on the 17th, and by 4th February reached the Oder and Neisse rivers. The

Allies paid dearly for the Ardennes offensive, they lost seventy-seven thousand men and a great deal of prestige vis-a-vis Stalin who exploited the advantage to the full at Yalta.

It seemed mad of Hitler to fight the British and Americans in the west and let the Russians advance into Germany and the Balkans. On the other hand, the September terms of unconditional surrender meant dismantling or destroying of industrial plant and turning the country into agricultural land, as the Romans had treated Carthage. No wonder that all Germans, even those opposing Hitler, would rather fight than accept those terms.

The effect of this strategy on Poland was disastrous. Stalin set up a 'National Committee of Liberation' in Lublin, all communists, and they ruled the country. Mikołajczyk, the Polish Premier of the Government in London, was prepared to cede Eastern Poland to the Russians, provided Lwów and the Carpathian oil fields remained Polish but, unable to gain support of his cabinet, had to resign. It would not have made much difference in the long run, except that the Russians would have had a formal Polish agreement to their robbery.

Roosevelt, Churchill, and Stalin met at Yalta between the 4th and 11th February in great secrecy. The terms of their agreement were announced on the 12th. General Fuller had this to say about it ('*Conduct of War*', page 294/5) "The Yalta Conference led to a super-Munich. It was agreed that Germany should be partitioned into zones, and each zone occupied by an Allied Army, (Berlin to be governed jointly); that unconditional surrender would be enforced, that forced labour would be imposed, and that twenty billion dollars in reparations, of which Russia was to receive half, should be considered. When Stalin agreed to take part in the United Nations San Francisco conference in April, Poland, for whose integrity Great Britain had entered the war, was thrown to the Russian wolves. Her Eastern Frontier was approximately fixed on the Curzon line; her Western provisionally pushed out to the rivers Oder and Western Neisse; and the Lublin Committee of Soviet stooges, which at the instigation of the Kremlin had, on 31st December 1944, proclaimed itself the 'Provisional Government of Liberated Democratic Poland', was, when diluted with a few members of the ... émigré government to be accepted on condition that free elections were held; but these were not to be supervised by neutral observers, as this might insult the Poles...'

Prime Minister Churchill invited General Anders to see him on the 21st.

Churchill: "You are not pleased with the Yalta Conference?"

Anders: "... a great misfortune. Poland fought abroad and at home... for the freedom of the nation... What am I to say to my soldiers? The Soviet Union, which was Hitler's ally until 1941, is taking half of our country and wants to set up their type of administration. We know from experience where that will lead."

Churchill: (very violently) "It is your own fault. For a long time I tried to persuade you to make a deal with the Russians and cede the land east of the Curzon Line to them. We never guaranteed the eastern border of Poland. We now have enough troops and do not need your help. You can take away your divisions. We will do without them..."

(Anders: *Without the last chapter*, page 315)

What Churchill said to Anders became the prevailing attitude of the British people to Poles for years to come, including our Headquarters. Gp Capt. Mümler, Polish senior officer at the main Headquarters, became a frequent visitor to my caravan after the terms of Yalta were announced. He tried very hard to find some hope where there was none. We talked for hours, in circles, feeling trapped and betrayed.

The Prime Minister spoke in the House of Commons on 27th February:

"The impression I brought from the Crimea… is that Marshal Stalin and the Soviet Leaders wish to live in honourable friendship and equality with the Western democracies. I feel also that their word is their bond. I decline absolutely to embark here on a discussion about Russian good faith."

At the same time the NKVD Colonel Pimienov sent a written invitation to the Polish Underground Leaders to attend a conference with General Ivanov, their safety being guaranteed. Sixteen attended, including the Polish Government Delegate for Homeland, S. Jankowski, chairman of National Unity Council, K. Pużak, the last C-in-C of the disbanded Home Army (AK), General Okulicki, nine representatives of political parties and others. They reached General Ivanov on 27th March stet. Was there no end to Russian good faith?

131 Wing moved from St Denis to Grimbergen (B.60) near Brussels. I spent as much time as I could with them, which gave me an opportunity to explore Antwerp and Brussels. The black market was flourishing. The two cities were always full of men in uniform, some of whom were dealing in all sorts of commodities for gold coins, cameras, gold watches, etc. It was impossible to cross the centre of Brussels without being offered several deals. Driving to Antwerp I saw, sometimes, V1 bombs passing on a parallel course and running about a twenty kilometre gauntlet of gun fire before reaching the city. A lot of them were brought down but V2s were unassailable and many exploded in Brussels.

Just as people in 131 Wing felt deeply about Yalta so did the three Polish supporting units. The robust Sqn Ldr Dąbrowski, Commanding Officer of 411 RSU, whose hands were full of extra work after the Luftwaffe attack, was in an ugly mood when I visited him, and swore in rage, but he drove his men hard just the same.

When our Headquarters moved to Breda I was billeted with a charming and cultured Dutch family in their beautiful old house. Breda was taken by the 1st Polish Armoured Division, of Falaise fame.

The division was commanded by General S. Maczek and on 1st August 1944 had joined 21 Army Group in Normandy under Montgomery as a unit of the Second Corps of the First Canadian Army, commanded respectively by Lt General G. G. Simonds and Lt General H. D. G. Crerar, all in all 13,000 souls and 4,431 vehicles including 381 tanks. They were delighted to be under overall command of the famous Field Marshal and forgave him his terrible faux pas which he made during his inspection in the UK by asking them what language Poles spoke amongst themselves in Poland, German or Russian?

At that time the 21 Army Group was locked in heavy fighting in the Caen area with six German Armoured Divisions (Panzer Gruppe West), which enabled the Americans to break through from the St Lo region and advance south, fanning out to the east and west. The Germans counter-attacked with most of the armour from the Caen area which had also a very strong static defence position. Montgomery ordered the Canadians to attack ('Operation Totalise') and after three days of heavy fighting the second stage began, culminating in the Polish division joining hands with the elements of the American 90 Infantry division in Chambois and then holding fast the elongated hill 262 (Maczuga – The Mace). Thus, as Montgomery said, the Poles became a cork in a bottle where the bulk of German Army Group B was trapped. The ferocity of the battle was incredible. At one time Chambois and hill 262 were cut off and supplies of ammunition had to be dropped by air but the division was not over-run and inflicted enormous losses on the Germans fighting desperately to get out of the 'bottle', which included taking over 5,000 prisoners, but it paid a terrible price itself:

325 killed, 1,002 wounded, and 114 missing. And so it went on through France, Belgium, Holland to Wilhelmshaven in Germany.

At Breda the Germans had very strong and deep defences facing four Allied Divisions advancing from the south west. Had it come to a siege of the city the artillery fire and air bombardment would have ruined it, but as it happened the out-flanking move of the First Polish Armoured Division, designed initially as right wing cover, proved more successful than expected and after four days of heavy fighting they advanced from the south west and took Breda, saving it from destruction. The inhabitants never forgot that.

It was fitting that fate decreed for the division liberation of the POW camp at Oberlangen on 14th April 1945, where there were 1,728 Polish women soldiers of the Home Army who fought in the Warsaw Uprising.

In Breda I met Capt. Bartel who had gone to the same school in Poland as I. He was a very nice chap and we met frequently while I was based there. He knew a lot of Dutch people and next day took me to a small private party. Our hostesses were a mother and three daughters, all musicians. They spoke very good English, as most of the Dutch people do, and I really enjoyed the evening. It was surprising what they could do with the few tins of corned beef which we brought. Then there was a solo violin concert in some office building where more than fifty people squeezed in. We were pleased to see the three sisters arriving just before the concert started, and chatted with them in the interval, but nobody else did. They left in a hurry while we talked to other people who were surprised we knew them. "They worked for the German controlled radio station, as musicians, which wouldn't be so bad but they also fraternised with German officers, you know, and we don't like that".

The Town Mayor threw a party in his large residence. There were lots of people of all ages, most of the ladies wearing long dresses, quite a 'posh' Do in fact. There was schnapps and wine to drink, and dainty eats including well camouflaged corned beef, and there was a gramophone too, so we, the younger set, danced with the daughters and mamas until midnight. Bearing in mind the shortage of practically every commodity, the hospitality of the Dutch people was embarrassingly generous. Their warmth and friendliness was evident everywhere and they understood us better than some of the RAF officers at Headquarters.

My host had two daughters; one was away most of the time and the other at home. She was engaged to a handsome Canadian Army officer. They looked well together and she was full of enthusiasm about their future. She was going to be a farmer's wife - not on a sixpenny farm, acres and acres you know, and horses to ride and this and that. He tried to tell her that it would not be all milk and honey, but she knew better. I hope she was right.

"And what will you do when the war ends?" he asked.

"I will be looking for a job. You don't happen to need a groom in your stables? I understand horses."

They thought I was joking and we all laughed; but I was serious, pretty soon I would need a job, any job, anywhere.

Eisenhower's broad-front strategy had been criticised in the past, and again when he unfolded his plan for the Battle of the Rhine: Montgomery north of the Ruhr, Bradley south of the Ruhr, and Devers in southern Germany. The chief critic was the Chief of the Imperial General Staff, Alan Brook, who changed his mind later when events proved the plan was right this time. By the end of March the Allies crossed the Rhine.

In the British sector Arnhem was still in German hands, but when the right time came a three day battle was fought and the town fell. The previous attempt, operation 'Market Garden' failed in September 1944 with terrible losses to the First Airborne Division and the Polish Airborne Brigade, the air drop of the latter being delayed for several days by bad weather. On the second day of the assault I was taken by a friend to the battle area, but well behind our infantry. We drove as far as the road was clear of mines, then on foot we followed signs of a mine-free path to the ruins of a large farm close to a brook. This was a strong forward position and the Germans fought there stubbornly before withdrawing. They left their dead behind - we saw bodies in a muddy trench near the farm. The war in the air was much cleaner.

131 Wing was moved to Gilze Rijen (B.77) in March. This was a vast Dutch pre-war airfield, used by the Luftwaffe throughout the war, with a number of buildings still left intact. The local people said that the Germans used horses and carts as aircrew transport in the end, they were so short of petrol. I spent Easter there with my friends. To jolly things up a bit they sent a lorry to France with a shopping list for the bar and kitchens. The expedition was very successful and drinks were cheap in their Mess for weeks to come. I bought a bottle of Champagne, packed it with straw in a strong box, and sent it to Ailsa's mother in appreciation of her sentiments towards Poland. My instructions were to open it on the nearest Sunday after church, but they disobeyed and kept it until I saw them again.

My predecessor who left Headquarters to command 302 Squadron became a prisoner of war by the end of February. About six weeks after his misfortune the same fate befell one of our best fighter pilots, Wg Cdr (Johnny) Zumbach, but the circumstances were vastly different. Johnny was a Polish Liaison officer in Operations Branch of the Main Headquarters, having even less to do than I. They had several little aeroplanes there to get around in and he could always take an Auster whenever he wanted. One day he flew to 131 Wing and returning in misty weather, with dusk approaching fast, he lost his way and landed behind enemy lines. To his surprise ugly Huns appeared out of nowhere and took him to the nearest prisoner of war camp. There, he demanded to see the camp Commandant and soon persuaded him that they should run the camp, more or less, together and that he would look after him when the Allies came. All this, and more, war and post-war adventures of the incredible Johnny Zumbach could be found in his book Mr Brown written in French, and its English translation: On Wings of War.

Johnny had a lot of contacts in Brussels. I was surprised when on one or two occasions a well dressed Belgian gentleman, having noticed that I was a Pole, promptly expressed their commiserations at his misfortune, assured me that he was greatly missed and expressed their hope that he would soon be back; they were right, he was.

All officers in Headquarters were forbidden to fly operational sorties. I managed to get a few training flights in my old squadron, but that was all. Spitfires in those days carried nasty little bombs, which was something new to me. The Wing was allocated a sector behind the enemy lines which was visited daily, sometimes several times, and anything which was moving or hiding was a target. In order to learn the bombing technique I needed to go for a course in England. It took me a long time to persuade my Polish chief to agree but, in the end, I succeeded. I was to leave in three weeks time and report to an airfield near Swansea on 8th May.

In the meantime the war was about to end. Field Marshal Model surrendered with 325,000 men in the Ruhr on 13th April. The disillusioned President Roosevelt died a day before. Stalin, the man to be so trusted, would not allow American Transport aircraft to evacuate their ex prisoners of war from the Soviet controlled territory, in contravention of the Yalta agreement, just as he ignored everything else he agreed to do. Churchill said:

"If we did not get things right, the world would soon see that Mr Roosevelt and I had underwritten a fraudulent prospectus when we put our signatures to the Crimean settlement." (The Second World War, Volume 1, page 370)

To make things worse Eisenhower, with President Truman's approval but against British wishes, halted on the river Elbe and abandoned Berlin and Prague to the Russians, being perfectly able to take both. By this act Poland was sealed off from the free world, being surrounded by Red regimes on all sides, and the communist barbarian state took control of half of Europe, advancing its borders by seven hundred and fifty miles.

Hitler married Eva Braun and both committed suicide on 30th April. The British advanced to the Baltic and saved Denmark from Soviet domination. The Russians captured Berlin on 2nd May and on the 4th an armistice was signed by Montgomery and the German High Command, providing for the surrender of German forces in the North West theatre, followed by unconditional surrender of Hitler's successor, Admiral Doenitz, on the 7th.

I had just arrived in England when the end of the war was announced. British people were dancing in the streets, singing and cheering. There would be no more dead or wounded, nor bombs; their sons and husbands would soon be home. Peace, glorious peace at last! I envied them.

I completed my course, learned to drop little bombs on small targets from low level flight, and returned to my Headquarters in Germany. We soon moved to Celle, and 131 Wing to Varrelbusch.

With the end of the war and Poland in Russian domination, Poles in the West had to search their souls and decide whether to return to Poland or to refuse to go back, come what may. We did not have to make any declaration one way or another at that stage, this came later when our units returned to England and were disbanded, but there was nothing more important in our lives at that time.

A couple of days after my return Gp. Capt. Beaumont invited me to go with him to 131 Wing - a friendly visit and a lunch there, he said. After a business chat with Gp Capt. Gabszewicz and a quick look around the airfield, all officers assembled in the bar wondering whether their visitor had something important to say. He had nothing official to communicate at all; he came to find out for himself what was the mood of Poles and what they thought of the future. It was in the dining room where serious discussion took place at the top table as we were about to finish the meal, everybody listening in silence.

"Well Gabby, what are you and your chaps going to do now? Anybody thinking of going back to Poland?"

"What are we going to do? How on earth could I tell you that? You tell us. As for going back that is something for everybody to decide for himself. Some people have wives and children there, others have widowed mothers. Not easy to decide, is it? Many came from the eastern half of Poland and that is behind the Curzon Line in the Soviet Union now. They have no homes to go back to."

"Surely this is too pessimistic a view? It was agreed in Yalta that Poland will have free elections and democratic government. People from Eastern Poland would, no doubt, move to the former German territories under Polish administration. You will re-build your country, the West will help, doesn't that make sense?"

"It would if it wasn't the communist Soviet Union who occupied the country. They have broken the Yalta agreement already. You cannot trust them, you will see."

"What about you, Kornicki? Would you go back to Poland? What do you think?"

"No, I will not go back to Poland. You know what brought us to France and here. You have won the war, but we have lost it."

"What will you do?"

"Does it matter? I don't really care where I live and what I do but one thing is certain, I will not embrace the communist creed on my knees and become a slave of my own free will."

The discussion went on a great deal longer with several people taking part in it. It was surprisingly orderly and our guest was afforded proper courtesies. I have tried to recapture the spirit of the conversation rather than the actual words spoken, particularly as in those days our command of English was only basic, but sufficient to express our thoughts clearly.

Gp Capt. Gabszewicz was appointed our senior officer, replacing Mümler who left for England. I heard from him that RAF Command was invited to stage a one week exhibition of British aircraft in Warsaw. Immediately I asked that I might be permitted to go there as a member of the ground staff, dressed as an airman. It was agreed at first by all concerned but at the last minute somebody from Intelligence vetoed my participation. The exhibition was opened by the C-in-C 2nd TAF, Air Marshal Sir William Sholto Douglas.

I was invited by Gabszewicz to lunch in No. 1 Mess (Gp Capts. and above) and as we were standing in the bar having a drink, Sir Sholto Douglas walked in with another officer.

"Ah, Gabby! Glad to see you. Just got back from Warsaw, have a lot to tell you."

"What does Warsaw look like, Sir?"

"Terrible, quite terrible, but about that later. I saw General Żymierski. We had a long talk and he wants you all back. He has plans for the future, he needs your experience and has a job for everyone of you. Right now he desperately needs two squadrons of transport aircraft; something your bomber chaps could do straight away. You really ought to go back and start rebuilding your country."

"When all the Russians leave Poland, when we have free elections, democratic government, rule of law, no secret police, no interference from Moscow, then we would return and nothing would keep us from Poland."

"But all this was sorted out in Yalta. We won the war, there is peace now, you are needed over there."

"What are you going to do if you don't go?" he said, turning to me.

I gave him the same answer as I did to Beaumont. He did not like it. The conversation became heated until his companion reminded him of a non-existent appointment, and with the words "You are wrong, very wrong" they left.

There were about ten senior officers in the bar, all listening to our exchanges. Some joined us; one said quietly that he understood our point of view; we had another drink and went to lunch.

Gp Capt. Beaumont had a brief conversation with me about the Russians again and mentioned some difficulties in dealing with them. A little later I heard that a whole train with supplies for British troops in Berlin had gone missing, including the military guard. The Russians denied all knowledge of it. He referred to it briefly in passing, saying there might be something in what we were telling him about the Russians.

Our Senior Personnel Officer was caught smuggling 'liberated' loot to England. This became a joke as apparently he was very hard on airmen for comparatively small black market offences. He was posted to England within a few days. At a farewell dinner for departing officers which he attended, hardly anybody wanted to speak to him. He had been downright rude to me in the past, but now he needed somebody to talk to, so he came to me.

"You have heard about my bad luck, haven't you?"

"Yes, I heard, but what had luck to do with it? It was against your own instructions; you asked for it didn't you, Sir?"

"Do you know that there were two Group Captains with me on the same plane, both loaded with loot, but the Customs men let them pass and only stopped me?"-

"Ah! that was bad luck."

"I bet you have done well for yourself, moving about as you do."–

This was an insult and I reacted with anger:-

"I know it would have pleased you to catch me on some illegal black market deal, however trivial, but you never did. Now that you are going I will let you into a secret - I was never a crook, sir."

The only 'liberated' item which I acquired during the war was a German-made camera called 'Lizet' with a good Zeiss lens. I paid two pounds and two hundred cigarettes for it to our Sgt Gałaj, no questions asked. I had no head for business.

The previously agreed democratisation of the Lublin committee by the inclusion of representatives of all political parties was to be negotiated in Moscow. On 13th June the Soviet, American, and British ambassadors - Molotov, Harriman, and Clark-Kerr - met the previously invited four members of the temporary government in Warsaw who were all communists, together with the four democratic leaders living in Poland, and three London Poles (one from London and one from Poland did not attend). On 28th June the composition of the new 'Polish Government of National Unity' was announced: sixteen ministers from the previous communist temporary government and five new nominees. Stalin's insistence that for security reasons his Western Border must have a friendly government in Warsaw - meaning a communist minority government - was fully satisfied. This, of course, was not a matter of security because no Polish Government could possibly represent a threat to the Soviet Union but was a matter of expansion, of gaining a gateway to the West, and domination of Central Europe.

Parallel to the above negotiations the Soviet Union arranged in Moscow for the trial of the sixteen democratic Polish leaders who had been invited to meet General Ivanov and had disappeared last March. The perfidy and brutality of the trial coupled with the timing was astonishing. Their barbarian and treacherous captors accused them of collaboration with the Germans and sentenced twelve of them to terms of imprisonment from four months to ten years, including General Okulicki, the last Commander of the three hundred thousand strong Underground Army (AK) which had fought the Germans for years. And yet the two Western Ambassadors were there, their Governments and the rest of the free world knew about it, did nothing, and watched the best leaders of Poland being thrown into jail, their only crime being a love of freedom and of their country.

On 5th July the 'Polish Government of National Unity' was recognised by Britain and America, and at the same time they withdrew their recognition of the constitutional Government of Poland in London, their sterling war-time ally.

In mid July Stalin, Truman, and Churchill met at Potsdam to talk about post-war Europe. Stalin had already settled the Polish question on his own, contrary to Yalta. The Polish administration was extended to the Oder-Neisse border. Seven million Germans were being kicked out of there and East Prussia, with the aid of the Red Army, and the Poles were moving in from behind the Curzon Line. This was endorsed with the proviso that the final status of ex-German territories, currently under Polish administration, would be decided by the future Peace Treaty. The Eastern part of East Prussia was to be ceded to the Soviet Union forthwith! They also agreed to help the Warsaw Government to arrange the return of Polish servicemen and civilians from abroad to Poland if they so wished... free elections as soon as possible... and whatever. It did not really matter what they agreed, the Soviet Union would do as it pleased. The fruits of victory were theirs. This was the end.

Years later I heard that there had been a move afoot in 131 Wing to fly away to Switzerland in protest of what was done to us. Had it come to that, and had I known about it, I would have gone with them. I felt a need for a defiant action of some kind, which stayed with me for a long time and against all reason.

Celle was a beautiful, ancient town, with a schloss, on the lovely river Aller which reminded me of Chester. An Infantry Regimental Barracks was on one side of the town and the German Army Gas School on the other. Our Headquarters took over the Gas School where we lived in luxury. The Officers Mess was a well-planned building with every facility one could wish for. The Germans must have vacated the place in a hurry, as they left the Mess cellar full of wine. The vast dining room had a gallery where a first class string orchestra played during dinner. The orchestra leader was an ex Lt Colonel of the Celle Regiment; he would bow elegantly when we applauded. The price of a bottle of wine for weeks to come was one shilling. We never had it so good.

I explored the unique collection of gas equipment, appliances, illustrations, etc. in several rooms, each one bearing the name of a different country. I went to the Polish room and found there samples of probably everything we had at that time, displayed and described in a commendable manner.

Some thirty miles south east lay Hanover. The city was in ruins, side streets full of rubble, quite impassable, with weeds growing here and there. The best place to visit was the Zoo with its restaurant and bar. It was like an oasis and well screened by trees and shrubs. People looked grim. I went to Bremen and Hamburg which were just as bad, but Lübeck's gateway stood firm and the town was in reasonable shape.

I saw refugees of many nationalities, some in dreadful camps. I met many Poles too. The futility of this war was unbelievable. It had to be fought though, but to beat one evil system with the aid of another, and to reward the latter by handing over half of Europe into its tyrannical claws was madness. The half of Europe which won, together with the Americans, would have to pay dearly one day for the betrayal of the other half.

On 6th August the Americans dropped the first atomic bomb on Hiroshima, killing about eighty thousand people and destroying four square miles of the town. Two days later the Soviet Union declared war on Japan and entered Manchuria. The second atomic bomb fell on Nagasaki on the 9th, and on the 14th Japan surrendered unconditionally, and from that day the blessings of peace descended upon our planet, God help us all.

The only way we had to avoid being asked "Why don't you go back to Poland?" was to stick with Poles, but that was not always possible. There was never any shortage of people who asked that question, as with the advance of peace war-time officers were leaving and regulars were coming in, but in reduced numbers.

I began to think what to do next. I thought I would start by revising mathematics - it could be useful if I managed to get into a Technical College. This became a joke among Poles in Headquarters and they were frequently checking my knowledge of tables, which of course I mastered in Wereszyn when I was a boy. Polish units had organised a number of vocational courses, using their varied skills and brain power, and swapping their men around quietly. Unfortunately they were too far away for me and so I stuck to my maths. It was more difficult in English, I had to learn a whole new vocabulary, but I persevered.

A friend rang from 131 Wing and invited me to a party. The honoured guests were to be Polish Prisoners of War from the Warsaw Uprising, in skirts, now liberated but still living in their camp. They brought them early for the day, lorry loads of them. How they must have laboured on their dresses and hair dos, but they would have been just as welcome in rags and bare feet. Our war was soft by comparison with theirs and I felt humbled in front of these girls, who so wanted to be just girls again.

The familiar face of Lt Kwiatkowski of the Second Mounted Rifle Regiment in Hrubieszów appeared suddenly. He was married to Hala, sister of my school-friend Władek. He shook hands, unable to speak for a while. He was a prisoner of war for over five years, his wife was in another camp and he was on his way to her. I asked for her address.

"Was there anything I could send her through the Red Cross?"

"Yes, Californian Poppy was her favourite perfume. She would love that. Thank you."

The British Army on the Rhine - (BAOR), new title for British Land Forces - had an Officer's Holiday Centre for war-weary warriors in Bad Harzburg, a splendid spa, with several hotels. Food was reasonable and there was wine and music. Fraternisation with Germans was forbidden, but nobody worried about hostesses, who knew more hostesses. Our meteorological officer who was a forester in civvy street, went there with me for four days. He was very much at home in the forests of the Harz mountains and looked at trees quite differently from me. While I admired the colour, shape, and size he would talk about the health of the trees, their diseases and how to cure them, their propagation, life and death. He was a most interesting companion on our daily excursions until late afternoon. For our protection we carried big sticks and service revolvers. According to our map the Russians were about five kilometres to the east.

"Avoid the bastards; they could lock you up if you strayed into their preserves" we were warned by the management.

One day, walking in the woods, we found ourselves dead opposite a hut which was a Russian Border Guard Post. A couple of unarmed moujiks were standing outside while the third one, armed with an automatic weapon was walking along a brook. We were within less than a hundred yards and decided to withdraw quietly. A few minutes later we met over a dozen civilians, men, women, and children, carrying well-loaded haversacks and walking up a hill on a converging course. As soon as they saw us they ran away in silence and disappeared - escapees from the Red paradise.

At last my posting to England arrived and on 25th November 1945 I reported to No. 3 Polish Personnel Holding Unit at RAF Station Newton, former Polish Initial Flying School, near Nottingham. I had lost my acting rank of Sqn Ldr, which I had held for almost three years, and reverted to that of Flt Lt. The Education Officer told me that all courses at Nottingham Technical College were full and there was, in fact, a queue of British ex-servicemen for everything going. Not surprisingly they had a priority in their own country, but there was a full-time course run for Poles only by a Textile Chemistry Department. Perhaps I could join them. I tried, and with a little persuasion, I did. It was a one-man show. An ancient lecturer taught various subjects in the morning and organised laboratory work in the afternoon with a storeman-cum-assistant. The subjects taught were inorganic and organic chemistry, textile chemistry, natural and artificial fibres, spinning, weaving, knitting, dyeing and finishing. Our laboratory store had everything we needed including pure alcohol which the old boy used to pour into a test-tube, top it up with water and knock it down just before the lunch break. It was a two year course designed to produce dyeing and finishing technicians for the textile industry. There was a good bus service to Nottingham and transport was no problem. At first I was frequently offered lifts by motorists passing the bus stop but I soon started to wave them on preferring to travel by bus rather than answering the same old question for the umpteenth time. Some people were quite aggressive, others did not understand why we disliked Russians, some thought it downright unpatriotic to leave one's country which was obviously so in need of every pair of hands to rebuild it. There was no end to original thoughts and gratuitous advice:

"Best go home, what could you do here? You don't know anything useful, only flying; you really ought to go home" or

"You can't even speak English properly. Go home."

"Who do you think will give you a job while English lads are looking for them too? Go home."

"We are sick and tired of foreigners. Go home!"

"We are really sorry for you chaps; you had a rough deal, but that's life, don't know what to say..." -

This was a bit below the belt and I lashed back, but only when I felt cornered. At least they were honest, I thought, so what the hell, I will play their game and see what happens; they are fair-minded people and are bound to come round sooner or later.

I invited 'Dear Auntie' and Ailsa to our Mess dance after Christmas. It was very nice to see them again. They met several of my friends, Stan Marcisz and Karol Rajchert amongst them, and we all had a most enjoyable time together. They had come one afternoon to Northolt in 1943 while staying in London and were greatly impressed by three squadrons of Spitfires taking off for an operation across the water; they counted them out and they counted them in, all thirty-six of them. But that was now ancient history.

Towards the end of February 1946 I received my first letter from Poland at last. My Mother, three brothers and their families were well but living in difficult conditions. My Father had died on 23rd July 1942. He went to the village, felt unwell, sat down under a lilac bush and died; a most fitting death for him. It was a hard blow, I loved my father dearly.

I continued my course and although I was not a science man I acquired some taste for chemistry. A fascinating subject, I knew very little about it and was learning from books and in the laboratory as much as I could. Everything physical in the world is to do with chemistry; everything you see, touch, taste, are elements; and what was it that created and arranged them so? The believers in God have an easy answer, but the unbelievers have none, and their evolutionary theories do not answer the question how the Universe began and when. The world is full of wonders, but of all its marvellous things and creatures it is only the Homo sapiens I have some reservations about.

In the summer of 1946 I decided to try for a University course. There were no places in the UK but Dublin was possible, and if they would have me I could get a grant from the Education Authority in London dealing with such matters. My interview at Trinity College was successful; they accepted me for a three year degree course in Commerce and London agreed my grant. I was elated. About a week before departure to Dublin I telephoned London to tell them I was leaving England in a few days, when to my dismay I was told that my grant was cancelled and that I should get a telegram to that effect on the same day. I did.

3

PART III - 1945
EXILE

In the meantime the new Labour Government was faced with the problem of what to do with the Polish forces in Italy, Germany, and Britain. The Foreign Secretary, Bevin, tried hard to encourage us to go back and pressed for early demobilisation. He had to manoeuvre between the commitments made at Yalta and Potsdam and the stand of the Polish puppet government and their masters, the Soviet Union, vis-a-vis those commitments, as well as the stubborn view of the Polish Commanders. General Anders, General Kopański, Vice Admiral Świrski, and Air Vice Marshal Iżycki maintained that the Polish forces should not be demobilised, but should wait until free elections and the Peace Conference were held re-establishing independence and a democratically elected government, when they could return to their country. As the Polish government in London was no longer recognised, the Foreign Secretary had to deal with them through his Service chiefs. General Anders was very outspoken in his orders and declarations to his troops. The pledge "... to continue fighting for the freedom of Poland regardless of conditions in which we might have to live and work", read in all units on the 'Second Corps Day' celebrations in Ancona on 15th June, was published in the British Press. London demanded an explanation. Anders said that the pledge he had signed was the pledge to his soldiers, reflecting their feelings and beliefs.

Towards the end of May the British Government announced its decision regarding Polish forces:

1. Gradual transformation of Polish Armed Forces into Polish Resettlement Corps (PRC), whose aim was to find employment for those who did not wish to return to Poland.

2. The PRC will have a military character within the British armed forces; it will be commanded by Poles and retain Polish character.

3. Once all PRC members were found employment, the corps will cease to exist but not before two years had elapsed.

During a House of Commons debate Mr Churchill asked the Foreign Secretary how many Poles wished to return to Poland? The answer was "23,000 up to 20th March, and 6,800 after 20th March."

"How many remain?"

"I think about 100,000 overseas and about 60,000 here, if I remember correctly" said Bevin.

These decisions put an end to the Polish Armed Forces. They were accepted by our Commanders who declared their willingness to co-operate, and their appreciation of the good will of the British Government regarding the welfare of their men.

On 8th June the Victory Parade was held in London. The column, twelve abreast, was nine miles long. Thirty Allied nations marched: Czechs and Norwegians, French and Iranians, Mexicans, Ethiopians, even the Seychelles Pioneer Corps. But there were no Poles. They had been barred from taking part by the British Government, for fear of offending Stalin. A small group of twenty-five Polish Battle of Britain pilots who were invited declined the honour once they knew that neither the Polish Army nor the Navy would be represented.

During 1945 and 1946 many voices were raised in the House of Commons favourable to Poland and Polish Forces. There were letters and messages from people in the highest places, including HM King George VI (message to President of Polish Republic W. Raczkiewicz, 8th May 1945) and comments in the press. Mr Bevin said:

"...when men have fought with you, or stood by you, it is against our religion to let them down..." (House of Commons 21st February 1946).

The Times' comments on the statement of Mr Bevin in the House of Commons on Polish Armed Forces contained this passage:

"... History records few instances of armies of the strength of the Polish Forces under British command having fought so long and so gallantly as exiles, or of men who took such risks, not to seek safety, but to face the further risk of battle when they reached their goal.

No fewer than 83,000 Polish troops served in France in 1940 of whom 27,000 reached the United Kingdom. Nearly 70,000 left Russia for the Middle East in 1942 (about 120,000 according to General Anders), out of over one and a half million Poles deported to the Soviet Union. By means of secret evacuation service from the Continent another 12,000 escaped to join the forces in the course of four years.

The Battle of Britain - during which Polish fighters shot down some fifteen per cent of German Aircraft - Tobruk, Cassino, the Falaise Pocket, Arnhem, these are only a few of the names associated with Polish arms. At sea, on land, and in the air the Poles proved themselves good fighters and good comrades.

Those who love courage and endurance in the depth of adversity must wish these men well, wherever they may go."

Of course, we did not want to go anywhere except to our own country; nothing else mattered.

The number of British decorations conferred upon officers and men of the Polish armed forces from 1940 - 1945, were KCB - four, CB - eight, DSO - fifty-one, DSC - twenty-eight, MC - forty-nine, DFC - one hundred and seventy-eight, MM - fifty-three, DFM - seventy, BEM - nineteen. It was ironic that while Polish soldiers were honoured on battlefields, their country was betrayed by politicians and sacrificed to Russia as a price for her co-operation with the West. There was neither justice, nor wisdom, nor honour.

My last day in the Polish Air Force was 18th December, 1946, my thirtieth birthday and the day I joined the PRC camp at Framlingham, Suffolk. That put a stop to the Nottingham Course, just two terms before finals. I was allocated a bed, a wardrobe and a chair, in company with several other officers in a 'Nissen Hut'. We had a solid iron stove in the middle and took turns to keep it going all day and night. The winter of 1947 was very hard and some people still remember it.

Tadek Sawicz, ex Commanding Officer of 315 Squadron, ex Wing Commander Flying 131 Wing, and now reduced to the rank of Squadron Leader, was the Camp Administrative Officer, responsible to the RAF Station Commander, Wing Cdr Boffe. The Commanding Officer had a twelve bore shot-gun and my good friend Ksawery Wyrożemski had one too. A small party of three or four guns was formed which enjoyed rough shooting on the airfield and several acres of adjacent woods, where bombs were stored during the war. I went with them occasionally, acting as a beater sometimes. The woods provided very good shelter and food for pheasants which flocked in from the farmers' fields around. The Commanding Officer was a bachelor with a busy social life and one day suggested that I should keep his gun and use it whenever I wished, as long as I could provide him with a brace of pheasants for week-ends. This was a great idea and Ksawery and I wandered with our guns almost every day.

I remember shooting my first woodcock - had to use both barrels though - and a sad episode with a large hare. I was walking across the woods when I spotted him sitting motionless on the ground. I stopped, picked up a twig, threw it towards him with one hand, and quickly raised my gun, aimed, and as the hare jumped I shot him. To my horror I found a poachers gin-trap around his hind legs. He did not get a sporting chance after all. I declared a truce for the rest of the day.

Boffe had his weekly brace and occasionally Stan Przelaskowski, and other people too. What remained was hung for a while and cooked in large pot on top of the stove, or in Ksawery's private apartment next door. A hat would be passed around for a bottle which would brighten things up a bit. We were not starving in the Mess, quite the contrary, in spite of all commodities being rationed, the food was good, and our quarters although Spartan, were adequate considering that there was absolutely nothing to do.

I took a correspondence course in Plastics Chemistry. This was a new field and I thought it might lead to something, even though I could not to do any laboratory work. Several chaps had useful contacts in London and were digging themselves into civilian occupations of all kinds with little or no pay. Rewards were not important as the RAF paid us normal salaries according to our rank. We were permitted to do that, subject to immediate recall if necessary.

Early in the spring I met little Pat Williams by arrangement, at one of London's Main Line stations. She had come to see her cousin, Cecilie, off to Scotland, and so did I, but she did not know I would be there. It was a bit of inspired match-making by Cecilie, for which I shall remain in her debt for ever. We waved her off at 9 p.m. and found ourselves standing on the platform, two strangers eyeing each other.

"Have you time for a drink?"

"Yes, thank you, but I will have to go home soon."

The next half hour passed remarkably quickly. She was easy to talk to, smiled readily and sweetly, and looked fresh and lovely. An English rose - I thought - probably with a thorn or two. Must meet her again. This was soon settled and before she left we had a very brief conversation on a mundane subject.

"Can you knit?"

"Yes, I can."

"Good, if I buy the wool, will you knit me a pullover?"

"Yes" - with a little hesitation.

We both smiled and she was gone. It was a good beginning.

In due course I bought grey wool, she knitted me a very nice pullover and we started meeting about every three weeks at first, and more often later. It became clear to me very soon that this was not a casual friendship but something rather special and very precious. I wanted to be with her all the time, and how marvellous it would be if I could marry her. At the same time I started agonising about practical things such as jobs, a place to live, the future I could offer her, and where? Would she go to Poland if a miracle happened, and I was sure it would one day? I might have to emigrate somewhere if I could not live in England. Would her parents approve? Most of the time I thought it was madness, and not fair on Pat, but we kept meeting just the same, and eventually we spelt out our feelings for each other - it was marvellous!

I had hardly any civilian clothes at that time, apart from a tweed jacket and grey flannels. I needed one good suit, not so much for social reasons as for job interviews, and asked some friends to recommend a good tailor. I followed their advice, selected a navy blue pin stripe material and thought no more of it. I was not particularly impressed with the street full of tailors nor with my tailor's establishment. I thought they were a bit surprised when I walked in, but they were polite if somewhat stiff. Some time later I was asked to come for a fitting and having met Pat shortly before my appointment, I asked her to accompany me and tell me what she thought of it all.

"The material is good. I wonder what sort of a job they will make of it" I said, as we turned into the tailor's street.

"Is this the street where your tailor is?" asked Pat, eyeing the sign which read Saville Row.

"Why? Have you heard of it?"

"Yes!"

"Here we are, come in."

"This one? Oh!"

They smiled at us nicely as we said "Good-bye" and as soon as we were outside Pat asked me -

"Have you asked the price of your suit?"

"No, do you think I should have?"

"Perhaps you should prepare yourself for a bit of a shock, but you will certainly have the best suit ever - it will be made by one of the best tailors in the world, in the most famous tailors street in the world. I must tell my father about this" she said, with a twinkle in her eye.

Perhaps the cost of my suit should remain a secret, but the quality and workmanship should not. The suit became like a magic wand sometimes. A hotel manager who saw the name 'HUNSTMANS' on the box, when I collected it, started treating me with unusual reverence. An Air Commodore who saw it for the first time at RAF Brampton Officers Mess stopped dead and exclaimed "Good Lord, I thought you were our new C-in-C". The C-in-C had a similar suit in grey as his wife had noticed. I wore it for all important social occasions and job interviews, and felt comfortable and confident in it. It has been my best suit since 1947 and still is. Hunstmans should buy it back for their museum!

Framlingham had no means of teaching us anything useful, nor was there anything in the district either. Other PRC camps were in a similar position. The Air Ministry tried to help by offering attachments to various branches like Accountancy, Equipment, etc. at selected RAF stations. I chose accountancy and was detached in July to RAF St Athan, about twenty miles west of Cardiff. It was the largest station in the country and the Accounts set-up was headed by a Wg Cdr, with three officers, several NCOs and men and women clerks. I soon found out that as an ex-pilot I was really rather a nuisance to them. The Chief had a friendly chat with me, ascertained that double-entry book-keeping was a mystery to me and I had no knowledge of their procedures - I would not have been there if I did - and passed me over to a very bright young sergeant who was slightly embarrassed and did not know what to do with me. He gave me a copy of his accountancy course notes which I copied in long-hand

and tried to learn. Later I was allowed to make a few entries in one of the personal ledgers, everything being checked and double-checked. I made a few suggestions to my chief how I could make myself useful, gain some experience and learn more, but it was explained to me that I was not properly trained, could make a hash of things and waste a lot of their time and, therefore, it was not possible to give me any responsibility at all.

"Just watch and learn what you can, or study something else if you want to."

It was not written that I was to become a financial wizard. Therefore I arranged with the Educational Officer for some help with my English. I was in luck there. A National Service Corporal who was a teacher by profession took me in hand with great enthusiasm and made sure that a bit of his knowledge passed on to me. I also took an evening course in Organic Chemistry at Cardiff Technical College where I went twice a week. They had a good laboratory there and I remember making chloroform.

I enjoyed the Cardiff theatre where I saw, among others, "Lady Windermere's Fan" and an opera performed by Welsh amateurs. Sometimes I invited my English teacher along. He was about ten years younger, intelligent, courteous and full of zest for life - a thoroughly nice fellow. He invited me to his home for a week-end - his parents would be pleased if I would come, they had a large house and a fine garden. I declined with apologies. I was sure they would have been very hospitable and nice to me, but I also thought they were probably sorry for me and I could not accept their hospitality in the circumstances I was in then.

I wrote to Ailsa and her mother, told them about Pat, and that I intended to ask her to marry me. They were surprised and hurt that I had not mentioned her before. The three of us had had a very special relationship for years, we were like a family, and perhaps the two ladies thought we might become one. I had never mentioned marriage nor love to Ailsa and, not counting an occasional hug or two, treated her more like my favourite sister. I asked their forgiveness for disappointment and hurt I had caused them and thanked them for their wonderful and never-to-be-forgotten friendship. What the three of us were, four could never be, and with sadness I said good-bye to them.

The events in Poland followed their predictable path. The elections held on 19th January 1947 were not 'free and unfettered'. All reports by Western observers confirmed that, and in particular Arthur Bliss Lane, the American Ambassador. A wave of terror before and during the election, coupled with fraud resulted in a 'landslide victory' for the communists. Out of four hundred and forty-four seats only twenty-eight were won by the opposition led by Mikołajczyk's Peasants Party, which had no representation in the government at all. Mikołajczyk's life was threatened and he escaped to America in October. In spite of that the free world continued to recognise the fraudulent gang as legitimate government of Poland.

In July Russia forced Poland to reject Marshall Aid, which was so badly needed for the reconstruction of the country, and gave nothing in compensation. The country was in the grip of the Red terror and nothing could change that in a hurry.

I thought that the best way I could serve Poland was to be a Pole here in a foreign country, a voluntary exile, for ever protesting by his presence the wrong done to Poland. To do that with dignity, I must live a normal life and stand on my own two feet, four if Pat married me.

I proposed, Pat said "Yes", her parents approved, and the two of us celebrated the engagement at a New Year's Eve Ball at the Park Lane Hotel in London. Someone stole Pat's evening bag from our table, but we did not make any fuss about it.

A few weeks later Pat's parents and the two of us visited Mr and Mrs Gardiner in East Grinstead - Auntie Lil and Uncle Bill to Pat. They lived quite close to a unique hospital where the patients were mostly Hurricane pilots with terrible facial burns - 'standard Hurricane burns' they called it. This was Dr McIndoe's place, the only man who could make them look human again. He did wonders with his saline bath and skin grafts, using his scalpel like a sculptor, working bit by bit on faces, noses, eyelids. It was a long and very painful process alternating between hope and despair. Death was an accepted risk in war, but losing one's face and looking like a monster was not an acceptable alternative. McIndoe had to rebuild their will to live as well as their faces.

Uncle Bill was the Manager of the Whitehall in East Grinstead, which was a fairly large enterprise comprising a restaurant, bars, dance/banqueting hall, and a cinema. He and Dr McIndoe became friends and the Whitehall was known as a sort of extension to the hospital where the first steps towards rehabilitation were taken by patients. A word of friendly welcome from Uncle Bill followed by a drink, then another, and another, would be the normal routine on the first call; getting drunk helped. A meal in the restaurant and a dance were further steps in the right direction. Local civilians played their part admirably by treating them as if nothing untoward had ever happened to them. Pat's cousin, Cecilie, attended one of these dances having been told by Uncle Bill that the chaps did not look exactly like God's gifts to girls now but, given time they will, so she had better behave herself.

It was sometime in 1941 when Geoffrey Page and a few inmates conceived the idea of forming a club. They called it the 'Guinea Pig Club' and Uncle Bill was one of the founder members. He attended all their East Grinstead reunions during his remaining years having won their hearts and their friendship for his contribution to their recovery. At the end of the war there were 644 members, British mostly, then Canadians, some Australians, Poles, Czechs, and Americans.

Pat's parents intended moving to Guernsey in the spring where her father was offered the position of manager of the Old Government House hotel, the best hotel on the island. He was glad to leave the City restaurant - the 'Palmerston' - which he had run since leaving the Army in 1945. He had served in the Army Catering Corps in the rank of Major, and was Catering Advisor for North West Army district. Comparing notes, we discovered that he had been responsible for the Transit Camp near Chester and was there when hundreds of Poles, myself included, arrived from France in 1940.

Pat was in the ATS (Auxiliary Territorial Service). She enlisted as a trainee Draughts-woman but apparently there was no training in that trade organised at all, and nobody organised any. She was posted from one dead-end temporary job to another, as a one finger typist, a member of the mobile 'Salute the Soldier' Campaign team, or as a clerk, always supernumerary, being passed on as a problem for somebody else to solve. In desperation she wrote to her MP, the case was investigated and she won an apology from the ATS 'Queen Bee' herself. They offered her a provisional place for training at pre-OCTU (Officer Cadet Training Unit) but the war was ending, so she packed her bags and left eventually. Of course this could not have happened in the WAAF.

We were married in the morning on 6th March 1948 in the Catholic church of Pad-dington Parish, and again before the Registrar afterwards. As Pat was an Anglican, and the old Priest disapproved of mixed marriages, he did not waste much time on us, but the Registrar made a jolly good PR job of it. The family and friends 'gathering' with a wedding cake, speeches, and alcohol took place at the Café Royal. Of my friends I invited Wańka, Halina and George, Przelaskowski, Polek, Ksawery, Kulesza, and others - they soon livened up the proceedings.

We had a three day honeymoon at the 'Ye Old Felbridge Hotel' in Sussex, travelling by Green Line bus. Pat wore her lovely 'new-look' dress; it was warm and sunny, we were young and happy and full of dreams.

We started our married life by saying "Good-bye". Pat had a job and stayed in London in a bed-sitter, and I was in a Camp on the edge of the beautiful village of Castle Combe in Wiltshire.

There were still eight months left of the PRC's two year contract with pay and, so far, I had made no progress towards resettlement except getting married. I wrote to several firms describing my very limited knowledge of chemistry and asking for the opportunity of gaining some experience in any field they could use me, without pay, for at least six months. Those who answered said the same thing "We regret… it is against our agreement with Trade Unions to employ anybody without pay, and we also agreed that jobs with pay must go first to British ex-servicemen". Hard, but reasonable in the circumstances.

There were always Italians and Frenchmen in hotels and restaurants. Perhaps Poles could join them? I made a few direct approaches in answer to advertisements for trainees in the weekly 'Hotel and Caterer' but to no avail either. Then I heard of a six months 'Hotel Management Course' run by the PRC at Borde Hill Camp in Sussex. I applied and was accepted for the next course starting in July.

I was coming home most weekends and Pat came to Castle Combe several times. I invited her mother to come as well before she left for Guernsey, and she loved the village and the woods full of bluebells. There was an antique shop there and we often stopped and gazed through the window at the beautiful things inside. We could not resist an oak folding table with some woodworm and bought it for five pounds. Stasio Przelaskowski bought us a pair of lovely six-inch vases, one of which survives to this day.

Before I started my course we moved from the tiny flatlet in Warwick Avenue to a bigger place at Cranwich Road, N.16, which was an attic flat with a kitchen, living room, bedroom, and use of a bathroom. The landlord provided a few sticks of furniture to which we added Pat's bureau, the oak table big enough for six, and our wedding presents, which included a most attractive set of china with a pattern of quails and a nature background, in blue. Pat made the place feel like a home, but her essential items were not all crossed off yet. Apparently the thing we needed most, in early June, was a bedspread and Selfridges was the place to look for one. Before we entered the store I drew Pat's attention to a fine display of beautiful ladies' summer dresses.

"Aren't they elegant? Why don't we buy one or two of those instead of a bedspread?"

"Oh no! We do need a bedspread."

"Why? The top blanket looks perfectly respectable. We can always buy one later. Let's go inside and try one on, just for fun, see how you like it."

"Oh well… yes, no harm in trying, but we must be sensible, we really *do* need a bedspread."

In the end we were very sensible and bought the dress. Pat looked lovely in it.

The Hotel Management course was reasonable. There were over twenty of us, all officers, mostly Air Force, but there was a sprinkling of male and female khaki uniforms as well. We were taught the principles of double-entry book-keeping, hotel tabular ledger, etc.; buying, storing, and control of foodstuffs, culinary terms, restaurant French, menu planning, restaurant organisation and table service; beer, wines and spirits, bar and cellar work, dietetics and practical cookery by demonstration, as there was only one kitchen range available. The 'Chef' was an ex British Army Officer who had done some cooking as a POW and learned more afterwards. They also taught us how to teach ourselves touch-typing. We had several machines and practised a lot, achieving a staggering thirty-five words a minute in the end, more or less accurately!

It was interesting to hear what other chaps were doing. Gp Capt. Mümler, for example, was learning how to make Austrian and Swiss cakes in a Polish set-up in London, something I wanted to do before my course began but they were full up. Karol was a waiter at Regent's Palace hotel and looked splendid in tails. Ksawery was in the building trade as a free-lance plasterer, and this and that. George was a transport manager in a firm owned by his English friend but did not like fiddling Government returns, which was part of his job. Wańka was a production controller in a small engineering enterprise set up by a few Poles in someone's back garden; later they emigrated to Brazil. Włodek Miksa married Angela, rented small premises and embarked upon trials of a plastics process with a clever scientist or two, which led to the development of 'leather cloth' and a multi-million pound enterprise. He started by buying up war-time black-out curtains, and discarded electric irons for the recovery of their heating elements. He soon discovered that wearing his uniform with ribbons, DFC, and other gongs, was very useful; people treated him sympathetically and some would not take any money either.

Stasio Przelaskowski was on a surveyor's course at the London Polytechnic; as an ex artillery officer he already knew a great deal about surveying. Stan Marcisz was looking after the grounds of a hospital in Bristol. Jasio Wiśniewski was tinkering with second-hand cars; just to clean, polish, and sell again at a profit; he was not much of a mechanic and knew it. Werner had had a two year degree course in chemistry in Poland and was accepted by London University to finish it. One chap had chickens and lived on eggs, another had pigs, a small group rented cellars under a bombed factory and were farming mushrooms. Mietek started a scrap iron business and with luck, hard work, and perseverance built up a prosperous enterprise supplying some most strange things all over the world. Jasio, Lulu, and relations, bought or rented a Welsh hill farm and astonished the natives with their methods and hard work. Johan Zumbach left England and became a successful international smuggler and soldier of fortune; he organised a little air force for Tshombe and fought in his war (see his *On Wings of War*). A group of senior officers was employed by one of London's prestigious hotels cleaning silver and were known as the 'Polish Brigade'.

Before my course ended Pat and I had an interview at the Hotel and Catering Department of Simonds Brewery in Reading. They had an on-the-job training scheme for young married couples with a view to employment as joint managers in their small hotels, of which they had hundreds. Pat's father made preliminary soundings and it all went well for us. We were to report on New Year's Eve to the Red Lion Hotel in Basingstoke, in about a month's time. Meanwhile, I was given a solo examination in all subjects, passed well, and was given a splendid certificate before the course ended. On 18th December 1948 my two year's PRC contract expired and I was demobilised, collected my civilian outfit comprising a sports jacket, grey trousers, a pair of shoes, and a hat. At the same time my bank account was credited with a 'war gratuity' of some three hundred pounds and I became a civilian with a ration card and identity card. I had to report to the local police station wherever I lived, once a week, I think. Pat became a foreigner as soon as she married me and she was already reporting dutifully in London to the Police for the previous nine months, to their great amusement; until the rules were changed, and later she became a loyal Briton once more.

We put our worldly possessions into store and reported as instructed, only to find out they had no need for us for another two days. We stayed in a small hotel outside Basingstoke feeling a bit deflated, but at least we did not have to pay the bill.

The management of the Red Lion was a Mr Chmurow (wrongly pronounced as Chumro) and his English wife. They had a son at Cambridge reading French. Mr Chmurow was of White Russian origins and a victim of the Communist Revolution. He made his career in Simonds via London Hotels, where his previous job had been that of Head Waiter. He was about five feet tall, of solid build and suffered from fibrositis in his right shoulder, sometimes very severely. He had some sort of a grudge against Poles going back several hundred years probably. His wife was concentrating on the kitchen, she was an excellent cook, hard-working but morose and unfriendly. She loved her son, but nobody else much. I do not suppose she smiled at us once while we were there, always looking for faults, always disapproving - a thoroughly miserable woman.

The hotel had about fifteen bedrooms, a dining room to seat about thirty-five, a bar, and a resident's lounge. The Public Bar, a scruffy hole with a fireplace as its only redeeming feature, was in a small building across the yard.

It seemed that they had lost the services of a barman and as it was the quiet season they did not engage another, thus I became the barman in no time at all, under the watchful eye of the Red Lion Napoleon. I also did the cellar work, prepared draft orders for supplies, received deliveries and kept a stock book. In my spare time I cleaned and white-washed the cellar which was in a dreadful state, and did other useful jobs.

Pat soon became the 'porridge queen', leaping up from bed at four a.m. and cooking the stuff in the old-fashioned way, helping with breakfast, learning the 'Simonds' book-keeping system, helping with lunch in the kitchen or dining room and, after a short break, helping with teas and dinner until, quite exhausted, she fell into bed and was fast asleep when I crept in, sometimes after midnight. Once she was sent, whilst at an outside function, to fetch a gallon tin of ice-cream from the hotel; she ran, fell, and the ice-cream spilled over the floor. Nobody was around, the floor was clean, and what the eye does not see...!

Our joint pay was five pounds a week. On Mondays, our day off, we would distance ourselves from the Red Lion as far as possible immediately after breakfast, and travelled by bus to Pat's birthplace - Winchester - which we both liked very much. On one such expedition a lovely ladies' hat with a feather caught my eye in a window of a fashionable shop. We stopped and discovered that the hat was part of a smart Spring outfit which included a skirt and a coat, all in an elegant shade of grey. It did not take me long to persuade Pat to have it. "Oh no! Too expensive" was her first reaction, but everything was her size, she looked very chic in it and it did her sagging morale a power of good. Mrs Chmurow made a catty remark when she first saw it, but we did not expect anything else.

Early in March, on a very quiet day, both the Chmurows went to Reading leaving the two of us in sole charge. Quite unexpectedly a coach-load of people arrived and asked us to provide lunch for them. Pat, cook and waitress, did wonders whilst I was selling a lot of gin, whisky, and beer. The customers departed well satisfied and left behind a lot of money in the till. We were all very pleased with ourselves, until the Chmurows returned. They assumed it had been a disaster, we could not have coped satisfactorily by ourselves, and they began an inquisition, giving no credit to anyone for anything. We were both appalled at their behaviour. In the evening Pat was kept up late to do some accounts. When the Manager checked her work he found an error and was rude about it. Pat stood up to him and said that he was unfair as she had been on her feet all day with hardly a break owing to the coach party, and she was very tired. What did he expect? If she never made mistakes, she would not require training.

Next morning he called us both, assessed my progress as barely satisfactory and proceeded to criticise Pat; I disagreed, a sharp exchange took place and I informed him that we would seek an immediate interview at Head Office, as we could work for him no longer. Our appointment was in the afternoon of the same day. The upshot of the interview was that trainees ought to watch their step as a rule, but as Mr Chmurow hardly ever approved of anybody, they were not surprised at what had happened. They listened to our version and moved us to the Ship Hotel in Reading forthwith.

The Ship was a very busy Commercial Hotel with about thirty bedrooms and a good restaurant, bars, etc. We both had a wider experience there, being moved around quite frequently. I was a successful Wine Waiter and Pat was soon working on her own in the Reception Office, or running a small Cocktail Bar, where she once served a non-resident after licensing hours and was reprimanded by the Ship's Captain. The residents who were present almost tore him apart - how was she to know? They had been responsible for smuggling him in, it was not her fault. On the whole we had a pleasant relationship with the management, which is more than I could say for some of our guests, a very well known comedian, for example. He stayed with us for a week taking part in a Reading Variety show. He was unreasonable with his demands for constant attention, often rude and vulgar to waiters, bar staff, receptionists, and even Pat. A thoroughly unpleasant man, we were all glad to see the back of him.

Simonds had a nine bedroom old-fashioned place on the river at Wargrave on Thames called the St George and Dragon Hotel, about three miles from Henley-on-Thames. An ex Welsh Guards Officer and his wife ran the place until their marriage broke up and she left him. It was May 1949, and we were offered the job. Our joint salary jumped from five pounds a week to forty pounds a month.

It was a dear little place with restaurant, two bars, sun lounge, gardens sloping down to the river, and a mooring place for boats cruising on the Thames. Bill Wyatt's boat-hire business and workshops were next door to us, below our car park. He was a good friend and a helpful neighbour.

Joe was our six foot tall barman. 'Brooky', a middle-aged waitress-cum-chambermaid was our guide, mentor, and staunch friend. The rest of the staff were Poles: Jan - the chef, Frankie - the waiter, Leo - the kitchen porter, Leo's wife - the washing-up woman. We also had a part-time local cleaner. As I was passing the kitchen on the day of our arrival I heard someone saying, in Polish -

"I wonder what this bloody man will be like?"

"You will soon find out" I replied, also in Polish; there were signs of consternation and a lot of coughing followed!

Whenever any of them had a day off, Pat or I stepped in, depending on who had the more time. Pat's main job was office work: accounts, bills, money, banking, bookings, etc., while I was concentrating on the bars and kitchen, including supplies and stock control.

Our contract stipulated that one of us had to be on the premises at all times. There was no provision for a weekly day off, neither together nor separately. Unlike our staff we were not protected by the 'Hotels and Catering Wages Act' and were working seven days a week, for less money. It was quite all right for one of us to be absent in the afternoon of course, but by 1800 hours we were usually both needed, even in the quiet period of winter.

I knew nothing about cooking and decided to spend as much time as I could in the kitchen working under Jan's instructions. When he had a day off we would devise an easy menu for me to handle. Usually some dishes would be pre-cooked in our refrigerator requiring only re-heating and finishing, to which I would add a 'cooked to order' selection such as omelettes, fish, liver, mixed grill, etc.

We had a crisis soon after our arrival when Jan fell ill suddenly and Pat had to cook Sunday lunch. She weighed an enormous piece of beef and calculated she needed about ten hours to roast it! But her Yorkshire pudding was superb and her rice pudding, with sultanas, gained high praise too.

The previous management had concentrated on attracting well-to-do people from the district, bending the licensing laws a bit, and working on the assumption that *one* of them was worth *ten* village customers in the public bar. I became very unpopular with some of the big spenders by sticking strictly to the licensing laws, and soon lost them, but new customers took their place to our relief. The Public Bar was filling up with villagers very nicely and whenever Joe asked for help I left the posh customers to him and served the natives. Pat did the same and the two of us became well acquainted with them. They were pleased to get some attention from the Management, having had hardly any in the past.

One evening a fellow, who was by then well fortified with Simonds Best Bitter, dropped a remark that the village was wondering about us -

"What do you mean *wondering*?"

"Well, of the past three managers, one ran off with the barmaid, another ran off with the till, and the wife of the third ran away with his best friend! So you see, we are wondering what *you* are going to do?"

Pat and I promised to think of something nice for a change, and we did: just over a year later Peter was born.

We had two permanent residents. Mr 'B' was a large jolly and affable retired man who was greatly preoccupied with the activities of the Wargrave Sailing Club - he was their Admiral. The second, Mr 'L', was almost as ancient as Mr B, but still working and commuting to London every day, and was like a grizzly bear, large, unsmiling, silent, and a rather private person. He was very friendly with one family in the village and entertained a lady and her daughter to dinner almost every week, but usually without the lady's husband. It was, as the gossips had it, a *ménage a trois* of sorts. We got on very well with the two gentlemen but the two of them disliked each other intensely.

In the western corner of our garden, right on the edge of the water, grew an alder tree which obstructed the view of the river. Mr L wanted the tree cut down while Mr B wanted it to stay. Whenever we met in the garden, the two gentlemen, ignoring each other completely, would address their remarks directly to me -

"When are you going to cut that tree down?"

"I wouldn't like to see that tree cut down, it's fine where it is."

I managed to stall by telling them that the tree belonged to Simonds and who was I to cut down their trees? But the pressure went on:

"Cut it down"

"Leave it alone"

"Cut it down"

"Don't do it"

Week after week it went on like this until I could stand it no longer, grabbed an axe and with a few strokes felled the tree, to the shouts of protest from one and cheers and applause from the other. The view was much better with the tree no more, Mr L was right, but Mr B was grumpy with me for the next few days.

Throughout the summer river craft were mooring outside the hotel, some staying overnight, some only for a drink or a meal, up to four boats at a time. There were regular customers amongst them, particularly those who lived in Reading - the owner of the Reading Laundry empire, and 'Leo the Lion' being the most frequent week-end visitors. The latter was a retired actor or magician, tall, handsome, fancied himself as a ladies' man, hence the 'lion'. He brought the comedian Max Miller several times. The 'Cheeky Chappie' was everybody's friend. Jokes, laughter and noise would fill our saloon bar whenever he appeared.

When Ascot week came - a very important week for the St George and Dragon calendar - the river people and dozens of others, dressed for the occasion, would stop for a drink on the way to the races, and again on the way home. We had a preview of fashion, and ladies' hats in particular were worth seeing, but I would have rather watched the horses. Eager to do business I welcomed coach parties to our Public Bar. It was as if a typhoon hit the place. In half an hour they would consume vast quantities of beer, gin and orange, port and lemon, cherry brandy, and advocaat. It would be all hands on deck, Joe serving ladies and gentlemen and Pat and I the rest. They called her 'Darling' or 'Dearie' and I was 'Hey! Fellow'.

I encouraged Jan to try cooking new dishes with the aid of Saulnier's *Le Repertoire de la Cuisine* and Escoffier's *Guide to Modern Cookery*. We improved the image of our menus by adding to old English favourites like leek and potato soup, steak and kidney pie, etc., such simple but exotic sounding things as Consommé Mimosa, Sole Bonne Femme, Canard Orange, and others. Slowly we started building a reputation for reasonable food and our Dining Room trade began growing. The normal price for a three course lunch or dinner was five shillings with sixpence, or one shilling extra for expensive food like salmon or duck. Meat was still on ration and we used a lot of poultry and fish. I had a standing order for weekly supplies of fish, and oysters in season, direct from Grimsby, buying the rest from Tony Shaw, the village fishmonger who also sold poultry, as did the butcher. I asked them both for a drink one day and suggested that I should buy 50% of my poultry from each of them.

"Fair?" I asked.

"Oh yes! Very fair" they assured me as we had another drink, and another.

Two weeks later the butcher made me a proposition, having established that I bought about two hundred pounds worth of poultry per summer month.

"If you buy all your poultry from me, I will give you 10%. Times are hard, I need more trade, your idea about 50% each was very nice but business is business. Think about it."

"What do you mean 10%? Would that be a discount on your bill?"

"No, it's for you, in cash, into your pocket, normal practice in trade you know."

I felt like telling him to go to hell but decided to play it cool.

"Well, I am not sure but I will think about it and let you know."

A few days later our Head Office man came to lunch, checking on us in a way, but he was a fair and courteous man and we both liked him. I told him about the butcher's proposition and said that I could not take the money for myself as I was paid the agreed salary, but if he wanted me to take it, how should it be entered into the hotel accounts? He was silent for a while, then said:

"Unbelievable. I never heard anything like it before. How much would that come to?"

"At least twenty pounds a month in summer."

"That is half of your monthly salary. I think most people in your place would take it, and they probably do."

"I don't know about that, but I would appreciate your advice on how to handle the butcher."

The upshot of his advice was to decline, as the butcher would try to exploit his advantage by over-charging for inferior goods - I still had no head for business.

Soon after Ascot came Henley Regatta week. We were packed out all week, restaurant, bars, teas in the garden, and of course all rooms let. Bill Wyatt moved a lot of his punts to Henley where he was hiring them out for a day or a whole week and making a good profit. He worked very hard and slept with his boats, guarding them against intruders.

We had some idea what the Henley crowd was all about when they over-spilled into our place. They were big spenders and drank a lot of Charles Heidsieck, vintage of course, and fresh salmon and strawberries with cream were very popular too. I wished we did not serve afternoon teas though; at two shillings and sixpence a head we had to sell eighty teas to collect ten pounds - too much work for too little money, but we gave them good teas and hoped some would come for lunch or dinner another time. A sprat to catch a mackerel, as 'Brooky' would say.

The third big date was the second Saturday in August - Wargrave Regatta. The event was well known by the river people way up and downstream. Some of our customers booked rooms for a week, or week-end, a year ahead. We had two sittings for lunch and dinner booked solid and served additional meals in the Residents' Lounge. Head Office was very helpful and sent us additional staff but did not interfere otherwise, which was wise of them. The Regatta Races took place all day and were watched by hundreds of people; some on our side and some on the beautiful meadows on the Shiplake side, lining the route along the bank and cheering their favourites. In the evening a wonderful display of fireworks was set up dead opposite the St George and Dragon on the other side of the river, with catherine wheels as a Grand Finale. It was a great day but terribly tiring. Pat and I were on our feet from early morning until well after midnight. After the last customer went the place looked like a battlefield: there were glasses everywhere, inside and outside, in the garden and in the flower beds, and cigarette ends littered the place. By breakfast time next morning the hotel looked reasonably respectable again and we were bracing ourselves to face a very busy Sunday.

Our takings for that week were over a thousand pounds - a new house record. "Well done" messages came from Head Office which reminded me of war-time signals, except that it was beer, not blood that we were spilling in Wargrave.

A dinner was booked for Gp Capt. 'X' and three officers from Bracknell for about 9 p.m. They arrived an hour earlier and were enjoying their drinks in the Saloon Bar. At the appointed time Frankie informed them that their dinner was ready but they continued drinking and would not move in spite of repeated requests. Jan put their main course in the hot-plate and left at his usual time while Frankie and I waited. They came into the empty dining room at about 10 p.m. and were served with soup which was well received. The main course was in a sorry state but I gave it to Frankie to serve it to them just the same. The senior man complained that the meat had dried up and that it was horse meat and not beef as on the menu, and wanted to change it for something else. I explained that our cook had gone, that they were one hour late and that I was not going to start cooking anything else for them at that hour. They nibbled at the meal, left most of it, asked Frankie for cheese and fruit, and ordered four glasses of port. The time was gone ten-thirty p.m. and I could not serve alcohol to non-residents in the dining room at that hour. The senior man did not accept my explanation and became rude and abusive to the embarrassment of his companions who tried in vain to mollify him. It was an unpleasant situation and I asked them to leave. As they were staggering out, one of the party said -

"What about the bill?"

"I don't want your money, just go" was all I could say.

I was vexed and disappointed that a very senior officer should have behaved in this manner, but it was obvious that he had a drink problem which was getting out of control. It was up to the rest of his party to ensure that nothing untoward occurred, regrettably they let their own side down.

This was not the end of my problems with RAF customers. Another fine Sunday brought a lot of people to the St George and Dragon again. Pat was busy somewhere and I had just answered a telephone call in our office when a tall and distinguished looking man came in and complained that he and his wife had been waiting in the bar for ages and the barman had served other people out of turn and ignored them. I apologised, suggesting that Joe had not meant to offend them and that I will bring their drink to them myself, which I did, having found a small table for them in the Sun Lounge with a fine view of the river. I offered to do that again if he so wished; he thanked me politely and I thought all was well. Fifteen minutes later he caught me in the office again -

"Look here!" he said angrily, "Your barman ignored me again and answered me back in a rude manner. This is intolerable! I will complain to Simonds, I am a shareholder, here is my card." He stormed out. As I was looking at his card, which read Air Vice Marshal somebody, another man came in and said -

"The man who just left your office, was he complaining?"

"Yes, about the barman, he said he was going to write to Simonds."

"Well I was in the bar and saw it all, he was quite unreasonable and your barman was right. If you have any problems because of him I would be glad to say so to your bosses; here is my card."

The second card read: Sqn Ldr somebody.

"I think you ought to know who that man was" I said, handing him the other card. "In the circumstances perhaps you shouldn't stick your neck out for me, particularly as I don't think he could do much harm."

"Well, no matter who he is, I stand by what I said and you may use my name if you have to."

We shook hands and he left.

Among our regular Bar customers there was a boat builder. He owned an old family business going back several generations and ran it with his sons. He kept an eye on us in a sort of fatherly way. Several younger villagers liked our bar and Simonds Best bitter, as well as a not-so-young Paddy, the Irishman. He was a free-lancer of sorts, and his fortune vacillated from good to bad. When the going was rough he looked very neglected, unshaven, broke, thirsty, and sometimes hungry. We tried to help, I with beer and Pat with food.

Our local homosexual, a professional man, was usually an agreeable Saloon Bar customer. Sometimes he would join a crowd of young men in the Public Bar, and spent a lot of money buying them drinks. They laughed behind his back and made crude jokes about him - it was a sad spectacle.

Lady 'X' was the local celebrity. They ate with us but drank in a nice old pub, the White Hart, further along the road. She complained in the bar once that her gin was watered. I gave her a sample and took one myself for analysis, both being sealed and signed. I thought it necessary to challenge that dreadful accusation and sent my sample to Head Office. To my surprise - they hit the roof.

"How do you know that your gin was not watered down?"

"Of course it was not."

"Nobody is suggesting that *you* did it, you wouldn't have given her a sample if you did, but had it never occurred to you that somebody else might have done so before it reached you, or your Barman? If she had been right we would have ended up with a court case and a lot of bad publicity, which wouldn't do you any good either."

"Oh, sorry!"

"Yes, well, things like that *do* happen you know. If in doubt about anything DO ring us up."

The Malcombs had an engineering firm near London and sometimes stayed for a weekend, or came for a day to have lunch and an hour on the river and back home again. She wrote sloppy books about nurses and their romances and could not write fast enough to satisfy her publisher. The couple and their son frankly admitted that the only good thing about the books was the money. They played amusing games by tossing impossible romantic situations at each other. She also answered letters from love-stricken females in one of the women's magazines, but when she was too busy, her son gave equally good advice.

In mid-summer we employed Barbara as a General Assistant. She had just returned from Tripoli, where her employment as a nanny came to an end and she was looking for a job. Pat had known her in London and we were glad to have a friend working with us. She fitted well into our set-up and was a great help with afternoon teas, in the bar, and in the office - a popular girl, everybody liked her.

I wrote to Head Office and asked for a small entertainment allowance. I reckoned I spent at least thirty shillings a week buying drinks for customers. It was difficult to avoid it, particularly as some insisted on buying me a drink. I received a short and sharp answer - "No allowance, we do not expect you to buy drinks for anybody". Easier said than done, I thought.

Once a week Pat balanced her books and sent a financial summary to Reading. Occasionally the books refused to balance and she was deficient by a shilling or two. There were penny slots in the Ladies' Lavatories - this source of weekly income became useful for such contingencies.

Late in autumn we spent two weeks on the beautiful island of Guernsey with Pat's parents - our annual holiday. When we returned we found a letter from Head Office with a hundred pounds bonus, and a hundred pounds per year rise in our joint salary, very gratifying.

We had a full house at Christmas. All our guests were nice people and we knew most of them but backgrounds were mixed and I wondered how they would all get on. Fortunately there were no snobs and a good time was had by all. They treated our staff admirably, invaded the kitchen and showered them with gifts and drinks and good wishes.

Pat had been pregnant for several months. It was not a secret any longer and when the news spread around, customers knitted bootees. It seemed they wholeheartedly approved of the forthcoming event and fussed over Pat endlessly. An ancient doctor of ninety years of age attended her and made a reservation at a Maidenhead Nursing Home. Pat developed an aversion to sweets and chocolate and ate oranges and pears by the ton, causing a decline in restaurant profits.

Barbara wanted to take a shorthand and typing course in Reading during the quiet winter months, and worked part-time only until the end of March. She promised to stay with us throughout the following summer and we gladly agreed.

I rushed Pat to the nursing home in the middle of the night by taxi, returned to the hotel, and telephoned impatiently throughout the next day. In the end I decided to see for myself how things were progressing. When I arrived at about seven p.m. Peter had been born and all was well. I was thrilled to meet my son. The date was 1st May 1950 - Labour Day! Although weighing seven and a half pounds, he looked incredibly small, like a doll, with a mop of black hair, a dear little chap. I was overjoyed and Pat looked very happy. Good messages, flowers and things were sent to her. I could not balance the books and took the lot to her, claiming ignorance of Simonds' accounting system.

Joe had an argument with Head Office. He wanted to train for management but they would not hear of it. It appeared that he took his revenge during the last month of his employment - but less said about that the better. He was eventually replaced by an excellent young man, Henry Fleck, who was a Jewish refugee from the Continent, the only survivor of his family.

When Pat brought Peter home in mid May we were beginning to get busier. She had Peter with her in the office, or in the pram outside the window, where people crept up to have a look at him. We had no private sitting room, work and sleep were alternating so rapidly that there was no time for sitting except in winter. Peter was very popular with our staff and 'Brooky' doted on him.

One day Pat was feeding him in our bedroom when a harassed Frankie told her that a customer demanded to see the management and would she come.

"Sir was busy in the kitchen."

"Right" she said, "Hold Peter like this and here is the bottle. You feed him while I see to your customer."

Frankie was terrified and thrilled by the experience.

Barbara's attitude towards us changed unexpectedly at the end of May. She became difficult, complained about too much work now that we had Peter, did not like her food, had headaches and was tired - nothing seemed right. Early in June there was a stupid scene over her lunch and things could not be tolerated any longer; I dismissed her with one week's wages in lieu of notice and she looked rather dumbfounded. It was obvious she wanted to leave, but not like that. Head Office did not question my action but some customers did, particularly those who liked flirting with her.

Three honeymoon couples stayed with us for a week, all at the same time. One was very secretive about it and had a room with twin beds, poor things. Another couple was related to the top echelons of the company. Their choice of a simple river-side hotel surprised us. They were a charming couple and looked after Peter on many occasions.

Count Wiszniewski, his wife and small son stayed for three months. They had bought a house requiring a lot of work done on it and it was taking longer than anticipated. He had a papal title, was a financier of some kind and spent a lot of time on daily telephone calls to the city.

Stasio Przelaskowski - now Stan Carlton - joined the RAF and before his departure to RAF Station Habbaniya in Iraq, stayed for a week with his wife. She was very attractive and a vivacious lady with lovely blonde hair. The marriage was not a success and this was an attempt at reconciliation. Stan's background was that of landed gentry and he and the Count got on like a house on fire. Sadly Stan's marriage failed and he later married Jane, also an attractive blonde, some years later.

Week after week we were taking more money than the previous year. I engaged some part-time staff, including university students for short periods. We converted part of the sun lounge into a small dining room with seating for over twenty, including a small bar, which enabled us to accept an occasional coach party for lunch. Ascot week and Henley Regatta were very busy again. The top man from Head Office looked in one Sunday, taking in what was going on, kept out of our way, and magnanimously granted us two pounds a week entertainment allowance before leaving.

A few days later I had a dizzy spell after leaving the kitchen during the lunch period. I sat in a corner of the hall with closed eyes for a moment when one of our regular gin and tonic customers appeared, had a quick look at me, and dashed to the bar where he shouted to Henry:

"Quick! A double brandy! Your boss has fainted."

I thanked him and escaped with the brandy to my office, thinking how kind of him to buy it for me - until Henry asked for the money later!

"Can you do one lunch at about two p.m. to-day for a VIP lady?" asked a male voice on the telephone.

"Yes, of course, what name please?"

"Brown. I am her chauffeur."-

We were intrigued. At the appointed time she arrived - a beautiful young woman. Brooky met her and showed her into the dining room, which was almost empty at that time. Mr Brown went to the Public Bar to recharge his batteries with Simonds Best Bitter. The lady had Jan's special chicken pie for the main course and enjoyed it. She chatted to Brooky about the village, river, boats, and said she would love to come again and spend a few hours on the river. It was Greer Garson, the film star, on location in England. The news spread around and everybody wanted to know when she was coming again. I hoped we would keep it a secret lest we frighten her away, but it was not to be. She came for a late lunch when several other people had booked lunch for the same time but they were discreet and all was well. After lunch she went on the river in a rowing boat with Mr Brown rowing. They came back about two hours later, Mr Brown dripping with water. He had fallen in just as he was getting out of the boat and was still laughing about it. Brooky gave her tea in the garden whilst I sorted out Mr Brown. I lent him my new pair of grey flannels which he promised to send back next day. He never did, and we never saw Greer Garson again, she was a lovely lady.

Another film star, an American of Italian origin and name, spent a couple of hours with two of his friends in our Public Bar drinking beer and playing darts with the natives. He was instantly recognised and won everybody by his modesty, good humour and easy friendly ways. He was almost one of the crowd but for his accent.

We beat the house record again and were looking forward to our holiday. Once again it was Guernsey, but this time we flew from Southampton with Peter in a Carrycot, in a biplane, a twin-engine Rapide, which looked like a vintage model to me.

Autumn in Wargrave was wonderful. Downstream towards Henley the bank on the right side rose to a considerable height, with a variety of trees popping their heads one above the other, clad in leaves of all shades of gold, brown, and red, glittering in the afternoon sun - unforgettably beautiful. The left bank was a green meadow extending far and wide with Shiplake village on the horizon - peaceful and restful. Upstream, beyond the railway bridge, dozens of boathouses and various craft were moored on both sides, and there was also a lovely lazy backwater winding its way among old overhanging trees, cottages with colourful gardens and lawns running right down to the water, and a couple of exceptionally pretty houseboats with geranium pots on them. We loved the river.

As time went by we wondered whether Head Office would rent a small flat across the road for us, to give Pat and Peter some privacy. Henry, a most reliable chap, could sleep in the hotel in a single room, and our room could be let. We asked, but they refused. They were not really keen on management having babies; joint management meant both part-ners working full time. Another hundred pound bonus and a raise of salary did not dispel our gloom. If our basic needs were not understood, what was the future with them to be? What was to prevent them giving us a month's notice and engaging a childless couple? Once Peter started running around he would either drown in the river, or be run over in the road, unless we tied him to a tree with a long rope! A roof over our heads - that seemed the first priority; we became obsessed with the thought. Then Pat had an idea.

"How about one of those twenty-two foot caravans? They have everything, a small flat on wheels, cheap to run, we could move anywhere, even Wargrave had a camp site."

We bought it and parked it on Bill Wyatt's grounds, adjacent to the Hotel Car Park. It cost six hundred pounds; we paid for it in cash and instalments. It could be sub-let, it gave us security, we ceased to be homeless. It was a lot of money to pay for peace of mind but it turned out not to be a bad idea.

We said good-bye to Jan, our Chef, with sadness; he had found a better job for less work and left. Frankie married in late August and we all helped to get his quarters redecorated, cur-tains hung, and made his room in an adjacent building look nice. Unfortunately they parted company about three months later, his wife left him and they divorced in due course.

Our new Chef was a large Austrian woman sent to us by Head Office. She would have been an excellent cook for a large family, but I dreaded the thought of next summer with her in charge of the kitchen. Soon she embarrassed us when she cooked Vienna steaks and left a piece of paper which read 'Wall's sausage meat' buried in one of them. We lost a customer.

The future still looked bleak for us until a day in March when an advertisement in the Daily Mail declared "One thousand Pilots Wanted Immediately... RAF expanding... six year engagements with one thousand pounds gratuity... apply Adastral House, etc. etc."–I It did not take us long to decide. Six years would allow time for a brother or sister for Peter who would be of school age by then, and with a gratuity and savings, we could hope to buy a tenancy of a neglected pub, and with our capacity for work, make a success of it. I applied and was called for interview.

The board of four officers with a Gp Captain in the chair, put me under a microscope for a good thirty minutes, referring to my record of service which they had in front of them. I was asked to wait in another room - I would be called again soon. Ten minutes later the youngest member of the board called me to another room and said -

"What would you say to an offer to join the RAF in the rank of Flight Sergeant?"

I was dumbfounded.

"If you only intended considering me as an NCO you should have said so at my initial enquiry, and neither of us would have wasted any time. I have a job, as you well know, and am not desperate to become a sergeant. You have brought me here under false pretences, good-bye to you!"

As I was storming out of the room I was asked to return, he had something to say. I was curious and we re-entered the room and sat down.

"I am sorry, but I had to ask you that question."

"Well, you have my answer, what else do you want?"

"I now want to ask you a second question - will you join as a Flight Lieutenant?"

"Yes, I will, but why couldn't you say so in the first place?"

"Orders from above. The first question was obligatory for everybody."

"Getting your pilots on the cheap aren't you?"

"Right, and you would be surprised how many officers will be wearing sergeant's stripes".

It took about three weeks to complete all the formalities, whereupon I received an allowance to buy new kit which was promptly ordered from a military tailor in Reading. I was required to report to RAF Hendon, near London, on 26th June 1951, and I gave Simonds my notice to that effect. Mr Davies, our chief at Head Office, and his deputy Mr Wadlow, whom we liked to think of as our friend, were surprised. I explained the need to give Peter more attention as he grew older, leaving less time for hotel work according to our contract. Even stretching a point, we could not live in one room indefinitely, we had asked for the flat and been refused; that, together with our desire to have one more child made us decide to leave. They had not realised how serious we were about the flat and felt a solution *could* have been found to our problems, but it was too late, I was committed. We received a nice letter from Mr Eric Simonds, one of the Directors, who expressed regrets at our leaving, wished us well and suggested that we should write to him in six years when I would have left the RAF, as he wanted us to work for the company again.

Peter was presented with a wooden horse on wheels by the staff on his first birthday. They also organised a professional photographer so that everybody, including the parents, could have a photograph of him. They were really fond of the boy and were always willing to keep an eye on him. Sometimes Pat hid him from the customers and parked the pram outside the kitchen door where he could sleep undisturbed. Once awake and demanding attention, Jan would call Pat. Peter behaved well, did not cry much and did not let the side down. This was reported to Head Office, and they were pleased to tell us so.

The new Manager took over at the St George and Dragon Hotel in June and we moved into our caravan parked in a beautiful camp site on the edge of a Thames back-water. There were only two or three tents there and a large caravan, apart from us. We were about five hundred yards from the Wargrave shops and Pat started house-keeping again. Our caravan had a small room at one end with two single beds, and a bath under one of them. The central section had a double bed which folded into the wall, a table, shelves, chairs, and an excellent anthracite-burning stove which kept us warm in cooler weather and heated water for the bath and washing. The front section was a well-equipped kitchen with a full sized Calor gas cooker, sink, cupboards, etc. and a toilet compartment.

We were given two weeks holiday with pay as a parting gift from Simonds and it *felt* like a holiday; we had time to play with Peter at last, to walk, and to read again.

On 26th June 1951 I reported to RAF Hendon and was sent to RAF Finningley, near Doncaster, on the next day for a three month flying refresher course. Pat and Peter stayed in Wargrave. There were several refresher courses run at different stages, some on single engine trainers - Harvards - and some on twin engine war-time bombers - Wellingtons. I was selected for Wellingtons after an extensive period of nothing but solid ground school and an examination in several subjects. Our course was about twenty-five strong and we were split into small groups with a Qualified Flying Instructor (QFI) in charge. I was the only Pole on this particular course, but I was also a 'British Subject' of 1950 vintage, and formally no longer a 'bloody Pole' which, incidentally, was not always a derogatory term. We also had 'bloody' Irishmen, Scotsmen, and of course 'bloody' Englishmen. On reflection, perhaps 'bloody' Poles were still more 'bloody' than the other three groups, but that did not matter any more.

"They are all failures, couldn't make it in civvy street you know" I heard two senior officers talking about us in the Mess Bar.

"Have to have them though, but they will be gone in six years, be patient old boy."

That view was not wholly without substance, as I had already discovered talking to my fellow officers. But still, put like that, it looked as if those two thought of us as lesser mortals, good enough for plugging holes temporarily in the sadly depleted RAF after a post-war mad bout of demobilisation fever, and nothing else. I did not like to hear it said so bluntly but there was a lot of truth in it. As far as I was concerned it was of no consequence. I was in the RAF for the money, aiming to secure an economic base for my family, and nothing else mattered.

It was strange to start flying again, and on the old Wimpey at that, but not as difficult as we were led to believe. Half way through the flying programme my group was taken over by a new QFI - a Pilot Officer - who had been instructing on single engine aircraft in his last job. He was not all that brilliant on a Wimpey, as I soon discovered. He took me up to eight thousand feet to demonstrate single engine flying, to be followed by landing on one. He switched off and feathered the starboard engine, let me handle her for a while, took control again himself and proceeded to descend. When we were on the final approach I was convinced we were too high and said so.

"We will be all right, don't panic" he said. A very short time later he realised that he was too high, gave full power to the working engine, and started un-feathering the second. We did not have enough speed to maintain height and direction, our aircraft was veering to the right, losing height steadily and aiming at hangars on the edge of the airfield. I thought this was the end, the bloody fool was going to kill us both. Fortunately the starboard engine burst into life and we cleared the hangar roof with a few feet to spare. He climbed and flew away shaken and silent until he heard the message to land on two engines in his own time, which he did. Walking with our parachutes to the crew room we had a brief conversation.

"They will give me hell for this" he said, looking very worried.

"Why did you take this job? You cannot, and must not, instruct on Wimpeys; you need a refresher course yourself."

"You are right there."

"Blame me for this mess as much as you like; I am a pupil and allowed to make mistakes."

"Do you mean it?"

"Yes, but it won't help you all that much as it was your job to prevent me from getting into a dangerous situation, which you failed to do, and you have no excuse for that."

My young instructor disappeared next day; I hope he survived.

A group of about fifteen Iraqi pilots were training simultaneously with us on single engine aircraft - first Harvards, then Spitfires. They could not land the Spitfires and I watched them bending one splendid machine after another until they demolished the lot, and were sent elsewhere to do more mischief.

I completed the course without further incident and was posted to the Signals School at Swanton Morley. I had one week's leave and moved Pat and Peter and our home on wheels to a caravan site at my new station. There were about a dozen officers' caravans parked on the edge of the camp. The site was bleak with flat, uninteresting fields on three sides and a road to the camp on the fourth. The NAAFI Family Shop was about fifteen minutes walk away in the camp. Once a week there was a bus to East Dereham, a small market town. Without a car we were prisoners.

Our next door neighbour was a Czech Officer with an English wife and two little girls. He had taken his bride to Czechoslovakia in 1945 and all was well for a while, until the communists began taking over. A wave of terror and intimidation started before their rigged election. He was made aware that unless he voted communist his ration card would not be renewed. They decided to try to return to England. They had a plan. He pretended to play fast and loose with women for a while, and then he disappeared. She waited until her mother sent a pre-arranged telegram about the death of a fictitious aunt, which meant that her husband was safe in England, whereupon she told the authorities that her husband had deserted her and that she wanted to go back to her mother. It worked. The authorities did not want the burden of an unsupported English wife and children.

My job was very dull. Two hours flying in the morning and two in the afternoon in a single engine Proctor, carrying a Signals trainee and his radio equipment. These fellows were sending and receiving Morse code messages while we were flying them along laid down routes - the same every day. This went on for a month until I was sent for a two month pilot's navigation course to Shrewsbury in Shropshire in early November. Pat was left alone and probably had the most miserable time of her life. She was used by one couple, who had a car and went out frequently, asking her to keep an eye on their children at night. Other neighbours noticed this and when the Mess had a Ball before Christmas, they organised a baby-sitter for Peter and took her with them and looked after her admirably. There were no long weekends in those days and it was impossible for me to get home and back in one and a half days. I came home for Christmas and had a marvellous welcome from Pat and Peter, I wished that I did not have to leave them again for so long while both of them were vulnerable.

In January 1952 we moved our home to RAF Lindholme and No. 5 Navigation School, some twenty miles from Doncaster, where we expected to stay for at least two years. Lindholme was a war-time bomber base and had enormous concrete circles for parking heavy aircraft, which were connected by a network of roads and taxi tracks. Several caravans were parked in those circles when we arrived, and we were shown into one of them. We shared the site first with a well-off US Air Force Sergeant and then with another poor British family like ourselves. They had a toddler daughter, Mandy, who became Peter's great friend. Our water was supplied by a mobile RAF tanker parked strategically in the centre. We had a twenty gallon tank on two wheels which I used to refill daily and Pat did not have to carry buckets of water as other people did. Milk was delivered and some other tradesmen called, otherwise there was the NAAFI Family Shop for provisions and nothing else other than Doncaster. It was a grim set-up and we looked more like gypsies than peace-time RAF officers and their families.

I was flying twin-engined Ansons. My Flight commander was a Pole but, regrettably, we did not get on very well together. He had been commissioned from the ranks, which worked very well in most cases but on rare occasions the selection boards made mistakes and I thought his commission was a mistake. He had a chip on his shoulder and probably thought I might be a threat to his elevated position. An autocratic and snappy little Napoleon, keeping his distance as befitted a post-war Flight commander, he had no time for anybody below the rank of Squadron Leader - in a word, a crawler.

The job was pretty dull. I was carting navigation officers around the sky on refresher courses who had come back to the Air Force as I did. The only excitement in that sort of flying was provided by the weather - fog, icing, gales - and occasionally a navigator who lost his way and had to ask the pilot the way home.

Our social life was limited to exchange visits between caravans, or the Officers Mess. The Service Messes at that time were run on the 'Men Only' principle, officers in skirts being tolerated. A room was set aside in every Mess where wives and friends could be entertained to drinks, but not meals. Once or twice a year there would be a formal Ball and occasionally an informal dance.

At Whitsun we went by train for a one week holiday to Ambleside in the Lake District. We were blessed with fine weather and walked for miles with Peter in his push-chair, or on my back over rough ground. I took them to Grasmere, to Wordsworth's cottage, the village church, the hotel at which I stayed during the war and, of course, we walked around the beautiful lake. It was a break Pat needed far more than I, being cooped up in a caravan all day for months on end.

In August Pat announced that there would be four of us by next April - it was great news. Peter's brother or sister was going to be born in Doncaster. I was certain it would be another boy, after all I had five brothers and the three who survived had seven sons and only two daughters between them

Towards the end of August I was converted to Wellingtons, which meant over four hour trips with several navigators prowling around inside and working simultaneously. 'Automatic Pilot' was not to be used as hardly any were serviceable and flying by hand was a bit tiring, but I preferred it to Ansons. The war-weary engines of our Wellingtons suffered from chronic oil leaks and chaps were making emergency landings all over the country. A Czech pilot whose engines seemed to leak non-stop, particularly at night, rebelled and went to the Station commander and announced he had had enough of emergency landings, and was not going to fly Wellingtons any more and did not care what the RAF did with him. He was an excellent pilot and was posted to a Fighter School to fly the 'Vampire' jet aircraft, and we were all green with envy. A typical navigational exercise would take me from the base to north-east and north-west, Scotland, Cornwall, Felixstowe and base, with sandwiches and coffee, day or night.

News came that our Navigational School was to move out of Lindholme to Langford Lodge airfield on the edge of Lough Neagh in Northern Ireland. The effective date was to be 15th November. The new station had no Married Quarters, but the RAF would pay for the shipment of caravans. We were promised an organised site near the airfield with water laid on and tradesmen calling, as well as the NAAFI shop. The airfield had been closed since the war and over one and a half million pounds had already been spent on runways and buildings, bringing work to the province. We wondered where our second child would be born, and were advised of a nursing home in Antrim.

Pat and Peter went to stay in Newcastle with her cousins, Cecilie and Ron, and were to fly from Manchester to Nutts Corner in a week's time, while I despatched the caravan to Liverpool, flew to Northern Ireland and brought it from Belfast to Langford Lodge Caravan Site, which was a large, gently sloping field with some debris of demolished war-time buildings. There was a nice corner on top of the field for only four caravans with its own water point in the centre. It had a hedge on two sides, remnants of a drainage system on one, and a road below. I parked our caravan there, connected waste water pipes into a drainage system, and had it all in working order before Pat arrived. I met her a couple of days later in Belfast. They had not flown owing to fog and came by boat from Liverpool. It had been a dreadful journey in rough seas, but they perked up driving the twenty miles to the camp which was like Lindholme, in the middle of nowhere, only worse. To Pat's surprise, I told her I had to go on duty, would be back for lunch, and that a man would call selling some sausages! Unfortunately, my 'Napoleon' needed me and I was not given a day off to see my family settled. She has never forgotten her welcome to Northern Ireland.

In our corner there were two very nice couples, each with one child - Smith was a young Education Officer and Gordon Senior a Flying Instructor. The fourth caravan belonged to my Flight commander who, incidentally, had a very nice English wife and two children.

With the onset of winter the weather started deteriorating - low clouds, mist, rain, howling winds, and frost. The occupants of three caravans were drawn together, the fourth stayed aloof. Gordon was detached in December to Bishops Court airfield, some thirty miles away on the east coast with a small group of our pilots. They were brought back home for weekends. Our airfield was to become fully operational in mid January.

On 4th January I too was detached to Bishops Court. Sqn Ldr Paterson, Commanding Officer of the Anson Squadron, knew full well that Pat was six months pregnant and Peter not yet three years old, and yet he saw fit to send me away. The man must have been a sadist.

While I was away a terrible storm blew up with winds gusting to ninety miles per hour. The gale sank the Stranraer-Belfast ferry, the Princess Victoria, with a loss of over a hundred lives. The caravans on our exposed site were battered by the winds which lifted one side up a few inches and then dumped them down again. Pat was terrified and feared it would overturn and catch fire from the Pither stove, which had to be kept alight for warmth, and sat with Peter ready to abandon the van. The worst time came later at night. Smith, the Educator, rose to the occasion and collected Pat and Peter, and Pauline Senior and her son, to his caravan where they stayed all night drinking gallons of tea. The fourth caravan weathered the storm well on its own, all the family 'present and correct'.

While still at Bishops Court I heard that Langford Lodge would not re-open after all, that some pilots would be posted to Bishops Court, including myself, and others to England. I immediately enquired about the caravan site and was shown a field about a mile from the camp at the end of a muddy lane with three or four caravans on it. There was no supply of fresh water except from an aircraft fuel tank adapted for the purpose. I went to the Station Medical Officer, described our circumstances, and asked him to back me up in my contention that the caravan site without fresh water was not fit for anybody, let alone a mother-to-be. He agreed and offered to put it in writing if necessary. I had decided that nothing on earth would make me move Pat to that terrible field and that we must go back to England, even if it meant leaving the RAF.

All detached pilots were recalled to Langford Lodge where we heard the dreadful saga of gales, frozen water stand-pipes with barely a trickle of water for more than half an hour a day, and our poor wives and children going through hell like that on their own. What was it all about? The war was long over, there was no need for this self-imposed misery, it was downright stupid to treat people this way.

Feeling in a fighting mood, I went to Paterson, my Squadron commander, and requested to see the Station Commander formally.

"What do you want to see him about?"

"I want my posting changed. I cannot go to Bishops Court."

"Why not?"

"There is no organised caravan site there. The only water on site is a stinking aircraft fuel tank, unfit to drink. The doctor agrees with me. I cannot possibly take my wife, seven months pregnant, to that place. It is downright dangerous, and you know it."

"And you think the Commanding Officer will change your posting?"

"I am certain he will when he hears what I have to say."

I went to see the Old Man, who agreed with me immediately and arranged everything with one telephone call to Headquarters Flying Training Command in my presence. He told them I must proceed immediately, as there was very little time left, to any station near a hospital or a nursing home - my job was of secondary importance.

"Halfpenny Green, near the RAF Hospital at Cosford, she could have the baby there, will that do?" he asked. I thanked him warmly and went to tell Pat, she was very relieved.

Our departure from Belfast was marred by long delay. The three of us and the caravan were stuck in the harbour waiting for the boat which arrived some five hours late owing to bad weather. We embarked and spent the night in harbour waiting for the gales to simmer down, and eventually arrived at Liverpool about twenty-four hours late. Pat and Peter were met by her father, who took them to Sheffield while I travelled with the caravan to my new station, arriving at night.

Next day I looked around and found a private site, just vacated, in an orchard near the village pub. Ours was the only caravan there, with water and beer on tap, and a peaceful and pleasant setting. Pat and Peter joined me a few days later and I called on the RAF doctor to make arrangements at RAF Cosford Hospital. There was less than two months left before the confinement. A great commotion resulted as Pat's medical papers were somewhere between England and Northern Ireland, and she had to have more examinations and tests straight away.

My job was similar to before and even more boring. I was flying trainees at No. 2 Air Signals School this time, over a couple of laid-down routes, day after day. Ansons were not exactly very exciting flying machines.

The RAF doctor took Pat in an ambulance to hospital during the night. Remembering how long it had taken to deliver Peter, I did not telephone until about noon next day, and was surprised to learn that Richard had been born several hours ago, and that all was well, and *why* had I not bothered to enquire earlier? My wife was waiting for me to show some interest in the event. I rushed to hospital with pink roses which I had managed to find on the way, made my apologies to all concerned, and most of all to Pat, and all was forgiven again. It had been a very easy birth this time, Richard was a bouncing chap in good voice.

While Pat was in hospital Peter stayed with his grand-parents. He had some adjusting to do on his return, particularly to being woken by his younger brother at night as they were sharing the end room. Pat was coping well with the two boys like the good trooper she was, but it was not easy. Nappies had to be boiled in a big zinc container on top of the Calor Gas stove. The laundry did not call and we had no car to take it to Wolverhampton. Everything had to be washed by hand; then there was the shopping, cooking, and everything else. I began to wonder whether we had done the right thing in leaving Simonds. I had never thought we would be moving our home on wheels so many times, including Northern Ireland. Richard had been booked into three different places before he was born. This was quite intolerable, what were my Commanding Officers thinking about? Why did I not protest? If that was to be our life for the next four years then I must start looking for alternatives.

A solution of sorts came within weeks of Richard's birth. I read in the latest Air Ministry Orders that pilots and navigators on short engagements might apply for a full career with permanent commission, and with a pension at the age of fifty-five, in ground branches such as Equipment, Catering, Air Traffic, Administration, and Accounts. We had a conference and decided that I should apply for Catering Branch because of my past experience in that field. We had realised that it was impossible to save any money out of my pay, therefore at the end of six years we would only have the thousand pound gratuity - not enough to buy a tenancy. Ground jobs were more static than flying jobs and with two small children we stood a good chance of a Married Quarter. I would, of course, lose one pound a day of flying pay, which would reduce our income a lot, but we would have security and I might even be promoted if I worked hard enough. On this basis I applied, passed the Selection Board and was posted to RAF School of Cookery at Halton for a two month Catering Officer's Course. I moved Pat and the children and the caravan to a farmer's field near Sheffield in May, where her parents were going to keep an eye on them.

It was a lonely spot. Apart from the farm and another house some distance away, there were no buildings for miles. Pat's mother brought supplies from Sheffield two or three times a week by bus and a travelling grocer called at the farm once or twice a week. I could not come home every week-end as we worked on Saturday mornings, but there was a Whitsun break and a couple of other week-ends when I managed to get away.

Just before I came home for the first time, Pat was woken early one morning. There were strange groans and heavy breathing outside the window. She sat up, alarmed. The window was slightly ajar. And there, staring in, were the large eyes of... an inquisitive cow. The farmer gave me a few sticks and some wire and I made a fence around our preserve.

My course consisted of two parts, one was paper-work including a very involved accounting and supply system, and practical cookery. I had some problems with crème caramel on the final examination, but the rest was all right and I passed, together with seven others. I was quite surprised to hear that I was posted to RAF St Athan, the biggest station in the UK. I had been there before, wasting my time in the Accounts Section during my Polish Resettlement Corps years.

Again the four of us hit the road like gypsies and parked ourselves on a scruffy little field with a couple of dilapidated war-time buildings, in company with several other caravans. It was a grim site. I had just completed two years service in the post-war RAF, having moved our caravan and family to Swanton Morley, Lindholme, Northern Ireland, Halfpenny Green, Sheffield, and now St Athan; booked Richard into three establishments before he was born, and spent six months away from my family on three courses and one detachment. It was time I stayed in one place for a few years, and moved to a house before winter.

My career as a Station Catering Officer (S.Cat.O) in the RAF started on 27th July 1953 at St Athan. The Station controlled No. 4 School of Technical Training in East Camp, Maintenance Unit in West Camp, with the airfield in between, and three small satellite units in the area. S.Cat. O was responsible for ordering, store-keeping, issuing and accounting for food-stuffs, as well as direct control of food production in four Airmen's Messes in East and West Camp, altogether feeding about two thousand eight hundred men. His involvement in catering for satellite units, Sergeants' and Officers' Messes was limited to daily issue of supplies and accounting for them, as well as advice on catering matters if required.

This was the set-up I walked into straight from the course and without any previous experience. No wonder my reception was somewhat unusual.

I reported to the Group Captain in charge of Administration who took me straight to the Station commander, Air Commodore Baker-Carr.

"Sit down, Kornicki" he said. "I think there has been some mistake in sending you here straight from the course. This is the biggest station in the RAF and naturally we expected an officer experienced in this field. We have nothing against you personally but I feel you should start in a smaller place. Don't you agree?"

"Yes, Sir, I do."

"Well then don't unpack, we are trying to change your posting as soon as possible. In the meantime understudy Lamprell, you might learn something."

"Yes, Sir!" I saluted and left.

Somebody had made a tremendous blunder. The Commanding Officer was right; who was the idiot who thought of posting me here? I felt ill-used. I had to tell Pat of my reception and she too was appalled at the position I was in through no fault of mine. For about a week I watched the man I was supposed to replace, in action, until I was called to see the Commanding Officer again. This time the Gp Capt. Administration stayed with me in his office.

"Well, Kornicki" he said, "We have lost the battle, we have to have you. What do you say to that?"

"Nothing, Sir."

"Nothing at all?"

"No, Sir. What ever I say now would be wrong. If I said I wanted to stay here then the moment I put my foot wrong, as I inevitably would sometime, you would say that I should not have accepted the job. But if I said I did not want to stay here the Catering Branch would say that I was afraid even to try it. I am bound to lose either way and therefore I will say nothing. It is up to you to say whether I stay or go, but I resent finding myself in this situation."

"You seem to know all the answers. Right, you stay. Thank you."

I left his office feeling very angry at the treatment meted out to me.

Sixteen new houses were about to be completed in East Camp as Officers Married Quarters. The allocation of Quarters was on a points system - so many points for each year of marriage, each child, length of family separation for Service reasons, etc. On this basis a waiting list was prepared and amended as people moved in and out of the station. There were never enough Quarters on any camp. I filled up the form and was glad to know I was on the top half of the waiting list.

The Station had also a fully equipped RAF Hospital to cope with young trainees as well as hundreds of wives and children of Service people living in Quarters and private accommodation in the area. The RAF School of Physical Training, known as 'Muscle Mechanics', was a lodger unit - they lived in the gymnasium and swimming pool. The Station was renowned for its sports activities, rugby, football, athletics and swimming being the most popular.

I had over two hundred and fifty staff under my, more or less, direct control in eleven Messes, out of which 60% were locally employed as civilian cooks, kitchen hands, cleaners, etc. The office side was concerned with accounts and daily balancing of income and expenditure, as well as store-keeping, and was in the hands of two very experienced civilians. Two RAF Warrant Officers were assisting me in supervision of kitchens and dining rooms, and anything else which needed doing. I worked hard and could be seen hurrying on my RAF bicycle from one Mess to another, arriving early, leaving late, and looking in on Sundays.

The Commanding Officer and Gp Capt. Administration worked in East Camp but lived in West Camp. Driving home for lunch, or at the end of the day's work, one of them would make a surprise call almost daily at first, and about three times a week later, at one of the three Messes during meal times. They would walk through the kitchen, look at the food being served and ask a question or two of any man about food. Once a month we held a 'Station Messing Committee Meeting' chaired by Gp Capt. Administration. The committee comprised elected representatives of various units and sections, airmen and airwomen, who were invited one by one to comment on food during the previous month.

"Any complaints?" was the standard question, and then discussion of menus for the next month would take place. Minutes of these meetings with the Catering Officer's replies to points raised were passed to the Chairman and the commanding Officer for their comments, and at the next meeting they would be read, discussed and passed by the Committee. This was a standing procedure at all RAF Stations at home and abroad.

Food was the only thing any airman could complain of to his heart's content. It was a safety valve in a sense; if things went wrong at work, leave was cancelled, an officer or a sergeant bloody-minded or unfair, if a chap had a girl-friend problem, or was miserable for whatever reason, he would take it out on food. It was the job of the Orderly Officer visiting Messes during meal times to listen to those moans, check their veracity on the spot and report.

The visitations to the Airmen's Messes by the two top men at St Athan continued for six months and stopped when the Air Commodore made the following comment in the Minutes: "There were no serious complaints about food for the past six months. Well done caterers".

Life in our caravan was very hard for Pat. I was so absorbed in my work that I could hardly think of anything else. It was a challenge, a lot depended on it, any other catering job after St Athan would be easy, I wanted to succeed, I was tense and jumpy.

Our field became very muddy in the autumn rains, but at last we were allocated a Married Quarter: No. 20 Burley Place, a new three bedroom, semi-detached, fully furnished house, with a garden in front and at the rear. We moved in in November, sold the caravan for three hundred and twenty pounds, bought a washing machine, and rented a television set. We had never had it so good! Christmas at home with Pat and the boys, a nice fire crackling in the sitting room, it was bliss. Our neighbours were very friendly. Sylvia and Jan Monsell, an Anglo-Polish couple with two boys older than ours, sold us a cot for Richard. We were settling in very nicely. Of course it was more expensive to live in a house. Rent, coal, and electricity bills took quite a slice out of my pay and there was usually nothing left at the end of the month, but we managed.

In spring I passed a driving test in Cardiff and bought an old Standard Saloon car for one hundred and ninety-five pounds. This depleted our reserves considerably, but we were able to drive to the beaches and countryside that summer and, of course, shopping in Cardiff on Saturdays - a great family expedition.

The non-public account under my control - which accrued from the sale of swill to pig farmers - grew into several hundreds of pounds and I decided to start a small 'food factory' in a disused kitchen. To that end I needed to buy one dough-dividing and moulding machine, install two large electric mixers and have minor works services done. The plan was to produce eight hundred yeast buns a day and move on to additional things later, using our own labour. The Commanding Officer showed great interest in the scheme and gave me full support. Two months later we had the first lot of buns baked and the first bun fight to celebrate the occasion.

In the summer of 1954 I took promotion examination 'C', for the rank of Squadron Leader, and passed in all five subjects outright. I had worked six months in my spare time in order to jump that hurdle and was glad to leave it behind me. There was a nod of approval from the Commanding Officer, particularly as a number of officers had only partial passes that year. I now had the qualification which would enable me to be promoted at some point; I began to feel more confident and more secure in my job. I thought I would last the course and survive St Athan after all.

Peter started school in the spring of 1955 and to my astonishment they were teaching him the Welsh language of all things, but not for long, as I was notified of an overseas posting to Singapore in about three months time. Our neighbours had had a tour of duty there and told us what a great place it was and we looked forward to an adventure with a promise of better things. Pat put the sewing machine to good use and made tropical dresses for herself and shorts and shirts for the boys, while I bought second-hand khaki shorts and shirts from a retiring officer, and a white dinner jacket. But it was not written that we should ever see the Far East. The Catering Branch - in my view the worst branch in the RAF at that time - changed my posting, at very short notice, from Singapore to Malta, without a word of explanation.

We packed all our worldly possessions, including the sewing machine and knitting machine, into wooden crates for despatch by rail and sea to RAF Luqa, our destination. The splendid cot for Richard was bought back by Jan and Sylvia as they were expecting their third child. A week before our departure a railway strike began. We were to travel by rail to Stanstead but this was no longer possible. To avoid an overnight journey in service buses or lorries, Pat's father picked us up in his car and we camped in their small London flat for a few days. He had changed his job in recent months and moved south again. On the 13th June 1955 we took off for Malta in an ancient York aircraft. A brother caterer booked a hotel for us and assured us in his letter that a flat could be found in a day or so. It was an expensive hotel and we could not stay there long - five pounds a day for two small rooms was a lot of money. I found a two bedroom, ground floor flat with a courtyard in Sliema. It was rather poor but in a reasonable area and very near the sea. Peter started school at the Convent of the Sacred Heart. We were anxiously awaiting our crates from St Athan, having brought little with us on the aircraft, but the strike went on for weeks and a pile-up of freight and delay was inevitable.

My job at Luqa was a welcome change. I was in charge of the Officers Transit Hotel, catering for the needs of passengers of the three Services and their families, as well as RAF Transport crews, in transit to the Near and Far East, be it for short or overnight stops. I could accommodate about ninety people including families, partly in modern buildings with all facilities, and partly in spartan Nissen huts. The reception desk, kitchen, and dining room were manned twenty-four hours. All the staff were Maltese civilians, with the exception of two or three members of Malta Forces recruited to support the British Forces on special terms. A similar hotel was run for other ranks, catering for much larger numbers.

My right hand man was Mr Borge, officially a charge-hand. Mr Farrugia and Mr Hilli were Accounts Clerks, Fredu and George were Barmen and Helen Cuell ran the shop with her sister Monica. The rest of the staff were cooks, kitchen porters, waiters, batmen and cleaners - about sixty all told. The main building comprised a large hall with reception desk and shop, lounge, bar, billiard room, kitchen, dining room, and my office. The bar and shop daily takings were locked in my safe. I maintained the Cash Book, did my own banking, cashed cheques for visitors, etc., and of course I was responsible for all services to our visitors.

The Station commander, Gp Capt. F. W. Thompson, was a splendid man. He had a difficult station to run with two Maritime Squadrons flying Shackleton aircraft as the main force controlled operationally by NATO through the RAF Air Headquarters in Valletta. There were other units as well and the airfield was used jointly by civilian airlines with everything that that might entail.

The island was still like a fortress. Sliema creek was full of destroyers. There were five sub-marines on station with their mother-ship at the Ta'Xbeix end of the creek, and the Royal Navy Docks employed over ten thousand Maltese workers. The Army had a battalion of troops at St Andrew's Barracks and the Maltese had their very own Royal Malta Artillery Regiment. There were primary schools for British children in various places, a grammar school run by the Navy, and an Army hospital. Main recreation facilities included a golf course and club house near Luqa, an Officers' club, and Tigne Beach Club in Sliema, a sailing club and several other facilities. With so many Service people on the island everything was bursting at the seams.

I liked my job. There was scope for initiative and enterprise and the Commanding Officer gave me a free hand within the financial limitations on the public side, pointing out areas for close attention, the food being one of them. I found Maltese cooks a hard-working and willing lot and we soon improved menus, introduced a wider choice, cooked dishes to order, and managed to keep that side of the business running smoothly.

When our crates were off-loaded in the courtyard I noticed a strange smell and on opening the first one we were both horrified to see that everything was damp, covered in mildew, and rotting. The crates had obviously stood in water somewhere and there was a water tide-mark on them. All our possessions, apart from my Service clothing, were ruined - this was a disaster! I contacted the Lloyds Insurance Agent on the island who inspected everything and agreed that, with a few exceptions, the whole lot was destroyed, including the knitting machine and a sewing machine, both covered in rust and jammed solid. He wrote to his superior in Marseilles, who wrote to London, who wrote to St Athan, who wrote to British Rail, who wrote to the Shipping Company, who wrote back... and so on, meanwhile we were writing directly to Marseilles and London demanding compensation. In desperation Pat sent all copies of the correspondence to her father in London who went directly to the Insurance Office and demanded to see the Managing Director. When this was refused by the office wallahs, he refused to budge until they relented and arranged a meeting. The top man was appalled at the delay and ordered an advance to be wired immediately, promising to settle the remainder within a few days. We were into November by then, it was getting cold and the family needed warmer clothing. When it was all settled eventually we found ourselves heavily out of pocket due to some items being wrongly listed under 'household' and not 'personal', or vice versa, and the insurance company refused to compensate for the loss of them at all. I thought it was a crooked deal and have never trusted insurance companies from then on.

We spent the insurance money on essential clothing, reviewed our finances, and decided to acquire a small car, duty free, with the intention of returning with it to England eventually, We chose a Standard 8 Saloon, paying a small down-payment and fifteen pounds a month for two years. Pat started taking driving lessons with a Maltese instructor and learned all sorts of local tricks, such as stopping a car whilst going downhill without use of the brakes. She passed her test first time and drove safely, gaining confidence in avoiding Maltese drivers. One day she was driving up a steep hill through Sliema and stalled at a point where five streets met and the intersection was controlled by a policeman. She re-started, was waved on, and stalled again. The policeman stopped all traffic in all directions, came to Pat, bowed and said "Madam, the road is all yours!"

Our flat was hot in summer and plagued by mosquitoes. We moved, and our next flat was a portion of a fine house owned by a Maltese doctor in the excellent residential area of Ta'Xbeix. It extended upwards over three floors and included the use of a flat roof over-looking Sliema creek and town. We also had a small shady garden with flower beds and a well.

Pat's parents came in May for a holiday and were lavishly entertained by several business contacts. We tagged along, enjoying good food and drinks on somebody else's expense account. We took them around the island, including a trip by ferry to Gozo where we stepped into the past. People lived very close to nature there and should have been saved from the invasion of developers in the years that followed.

My hotel shop was making a meagre profit, merely enough to pay the wages of Helen and Monica who ran it on alternate days, keeping it open for 10 hours every day including Sundays. The three of us discussed the poor performance of the enterprise and agreed to introduce new and more profitable lines, with the object of making the business viable, their jobs more secure, and providing a better service for our customers. The first successful new lines were original Malta-weave skirt lengths, Czechoslovakian earthenware beer mugs in two sizes, and small coloured glass animals. Other things followed and turnover and profits were steadily going up. Our flower garden became a source of income too. The shop sold bunches of flowers cut to order as available in a given season - violets, stocks, gladioli, and asters, to our local and transient customers.

Bar profits went up substantially when I started buying sherry in bulk and selling it at a discount to customers who brought their own bottles. However this was illegal and I had to stop it. I tried everything I could to build up the non-public account, and when I had two thousand pounds in the bank I suggested to the Commanding Officer that we might buy a carpet for the main lounge, some water-colours painted by local artists to adorn bare walls, increase wages for the shop girls, and put some money aside every month for a Christmas bonus for all staff. We also dug a well which would fill in winter and keep the gardens going throughout the summer. Water was at a premium and we needed a lot of it for our ambitious plans. We grew, used ourselves, and sold surplus artichokes, tomatoes, lettuces, and other vegetables. This helped to improve the standard of food and was noticed by the Commanding Officer. He often brought his lunch guests to our place rather than the beautifully appointed Officers Mess across the road, a splendid place, with a circular dancing area in the garden below a long veranda. A summer ball in Luqa was an important social event bringing together the cream of Maltese society, top echelons of NATO, Army, and Navy people on the island, officers serving at Luqa, and their wives and guests.

A Married Quarter became available at Luqa in the summer, which was only about three hundred yards from the Transit Hotel. We had a ground floor, three bedroom flat in a block of six flats on three floors. Outside the kitchen window there was a small bare patch of ground where I tried to grow a few flowers but nothing survived the heat except zinnias. There were neighbours for Pat, a safe area for the boys to roam about and play with other youngsters.

A weekly initiative known as the 'milk run' by a Meteor aircraft carried a couple of dozen bottles of fresh milk to a British base in Tripoli and brought back an equivalent number of duty free bottles of gin. A friend took me on one of those trips and soon after take-off I heard the familiar "You have control". I had never flown a jet before and was surprised and thrilled by the excess of power, stability at different speeds and the ease of handling. It was a joy to fly her. Our 'pay load' was vastly superior when I flew as a supernumerary pilot on a Shackleton to Gibraltar, but that was all above board. We loaded the aircraft with crates of alcohol in the presence of Customs officials, flew it to Gibraltar and brought it back to Luqa duty free,

Rising tension in Poland, Hungry, and Egypt was followed by important events in 1956. Great Britain, France, and Israel were confronted with a new situation after King Farouk was deposed in 1952 and a series of revolutionary changes took place, culminating in the emergence of the Egyptian Republic under Colonel Nasser. The British forces had left the Suez Canal Zone in 1955 as a result of the denunciation of the Anglo-Egyptian Treaty in 1951. Col. Nasser started buying arms from Czechoslovakia, increased trade with the Soviet Union, and when he recognised Communist China, Britain and the USA withdrew their offer to build the High Dam on the Nile. Nasser retaliated and seized the assets of the Suez Canal Company (24th July). Britain and France protested, the USA proposed international control of the canal, the United Nations deliberated, and Egypt refused to budge. In September French troops started arriving in Cyprus and the Anglo-French force was getting ready for action. In the meantime Israel attacked Egyptian guerrilla bases which were harassing their frontier settlements (29th October). The British and French called on both sides to cease fire and pull back from the canal in order to safeguard it, but when Nasser refused, the bombing of Egyptian airfields began and on 5th November the British and French forces landed in Port Said. Next day a cease fire was negotiated and in December the last of the Anglo-French forces left Egypt.

Malta was an important staging post for all three services during the Suez crisis. The two airfields - Luqa and Takali - were stretched to their full capacity and my Transit Officers Mess was in the thick of it. I doubled the number of beds in all rooms and in the final stages converted our large lounge and billiard room into dormitories. Air Headquarters Malta arranged for more staff and we coped reasonably well. We had no problems with our transients except for a couple of complaints from the most junior officers, who thought that sleeping in a lounge/dormitory was 'not on' really. However, when told that the chap snoring on the next bed was a Brigadier they shut up and walked on tip-toe.

I found it easier to sleep on the job than be called out at all hours and have the family disturbed by door-bells. For a while I was a visitor at home whilst Pat and the boys came to the hotel shop to have a quick chat with me, or just wave if I was too busy. I was no exception, other people did the same, in fact we all worked like beavers, led very ably by Gp Capt. Thomson, who seemed to be everywhere at once.

When it was all over and the homeward trek began the mood was different, our men felt ill-used by politicians and resented being let down in such a humiliating way.

Poland was in the grip of a Stalinist type regime under President Bierut, until his death in March 1956, almost exactly three years after Stalin's death. Then Khrushchev denounced Stalin as a tyrant at the twentieth Party Congress, putting an end to the infamous era of that vile man. In June Polish workers in Poznań rebelled, demanding higher wages, and serious riots took place. Wages were raised but scores of people died. The Party was shaken however, and outspoken criticism of the regime was voiced at the September session of the Polish Parliament. Gomułka - expelled in 1949 - was re-admitted to the Central Committee of the Communist Party in October. At the same time the Primate of Poland, Cardinal Wyszyński, was released from detention, and so were his bishops soon after. These events were described in Konrad Syrop's book *A Spring in October*, 1976.

Hungary, too, was simmering with discontent and resentment at Communist rule. On 23rd October a great demonstration of sympathy for Poland took place although there was fear of Soviet armed intervention. Students demanded free elections, withdrawal of Soviet Forces, neutrality for their country like Austria. People took to the streets, and security police fired on them. Soldiers ordered to disperse crowds joined them instead, distributing arms. On the next day, Russian tanks opened fire, which brought about a full scale rising in Budapest and throughout the country. Overnight Communist rule was swept aside and replaced by Revolutionary Committees. Nagy - the hope of the nation - negotiated withdrawal of Soviet forces and on 1st November formed a Coalition Government. He released Cardinal Mindszenty and cabled the United Nations that Hungary withdrew from the Warsaw Pact and was asking to be recognised as a neutral country. This was more than the Russians could take and a shooting war started in main industrial towns. The bitter struggle against the Red Army lasted a week. Nagy and one hundred and fifty thousand Hungarians fled to the West. Kadar and his Communists took over. The Hungarian 'Spring in October' was very short indeed.

The following year ran very smoothly. It began with the New Year Honours List - a well deserved CBE for Gp Capt. Thomson and a sprinkling of OBEs and MBEs for the most deserving cases. It had never entered my head that I could possibly be amongst them, but I received a personal letter from the Old Man saying that he had hoped to see my name on the list, etc. He left us early in the year on promotion and a new man took over, alas, not a match for the old warrior.

Our last summer in Malta was very pleasant, the best of the three we spent there. The boys learned to swim, jump, and dive from the board at Tigne Beach Club and off the rocks. It was fun to take a picnic lunch to the beach at week-ends and enjoy the sweetness of the close relationship between the four of us. Richard started school at four and a half years of age at the Convent. They handled the little ones with loving care and patience. It was a fine way to begin and we were glad he had a full term before we returned to England in December. We travelled on the troopship 'Dunera' to Southampton in very agreeable company and felt as if we were on holiday. A fitting end to a hard, but very satisfactory, overseas tour of duty.

We stopped in Streatham over Christmas with Pat's parents and then moved north to RAF Wilmslow, quite close to Manchester. This was an unusual place, all my hungry 'customers' were female. I was catering for WAAF recruits, hundreds and hundreds of them, marching, saluting, left, right, and about-turning, parading, shouting 1! 2! 3! this or 1!, 2!, 3! that. The Officers' Mess was unlike any other place I had ever seen - 90% women - young and attractive, displaying large portions of pretty legs, reading love letters and exchanging confidences about their current and ex-fiancées. The less fortunate ones were propping up the bar like old campaigners. I felt as if I was trespassing at first, but lost that feeling very soon. They were all right, very smart, efficient and cheerful. I did not mind the flapping eyelashes any more and rather enjoyed the sight of a good pair of legs.

We lived at Padgate, near Warrington, at first and then moved to a Wilmslow Married Quarter. This meant a change of school again. Over the next year and a half the boys did not make much progress and, having thought and talked about it for several months, we decided to look for a good school around London, buy a flat or house somehow, and establish a permanent family home. This we did. Pat went to Guildford with Peter and in two days flat had the boys accepted at St Peter's School at Merrow, and arranged a bank loan and a mortgage for a two bedroom maisonette which she had found within a short walking distance of the school. We could only discuss it by telephone, but agreed to go ahead, with a view to moving in before the start of the 1959/60 school year. Summer was only just beginning and we had time to look for a few sticks of second-hand furniture and plan our finances.

We did our sums carefully and bearing, in mind mortgage payments of £14.6.8d a month, rates, communal maintenance charges, interest on the bank loan, school fees, school uniform, etc. we needed an additional source of income. The car had to go, but not before the expiry of the two year HM Customs requirement, or import duty would be levied. Was I likely to be promoted? I was forty-three years old, there were very few senior posts in the Catering Branch, and if they did not promote me after Malta then I was most unlikely to be noticed at Wilmslow. It made sense, therefore, to transfer to the Supplementary List and be compensated for loss of promotion prospects by a higher salary and pension in my current rank. I took a pen and wrote:

"Sir,
I have the honour to request that I may be transferred from General List Commission to Supplementary List as soon as possible. My reason for this request is that I see no hope for promotion and I am losing financially under the terms of my present agreement.
I am, Sir, Your obedient servant"

To my astonishment I was promoted to the rank of Squadron Leader, which I had first held sixteen years previously, and was posted to RAF College Cranwell as from October 1959. I was very pleased on three accounts: more money and prestige, shorter distance to travel home for week-ends, and going to a place which was the RAF counterpart to Dęblin in the pre-war Polish Air Force.

Cranwell was a fascinating place, a world of its own, buzzing with social and cultural activities, lectures by interesting people, sport, games, parties, drinks - never a dull moment. My job was to feed hungry airmen of various sections and units of the station supporting every aspect of the College life. The top man at Cranwell was the Commandant. In my time the post was held by Air Commodore Spotswood, the future Chief of the Air Staff, a great man who served Cranwell well. His deputy was responsible for all aspects of Cadet training, and the Station Commander for all supporting services.

The main college building was quite splendid and in a lovely setting. The long dining room set for formal dinner, tables adorned with silver, Tintoretto and other fine pictures on the walls, looked a treat. It was home for the senior entry in its third year of training. Passing-out parades were held in summer and winter, the reviewing officers being prominent Commanders from the three Services. In 1961 HM the Queen honoured the College, and she looked pleased watching a superb march-past by her young officers to the tune of the 'Lincolnshire Poacher'. Later she had lunch with them and their guests, making it an unforgettable occasion for them, their proud parents, and delighted friends. For a finale they had a traditional Ball and danced until the early hours of the morning. I watched every passing-out parade and thought of Dęblin.

I lived in the main building of the Officers Mess and had the nicest single quarters ever - a sitting room overlooking the garden, and a bedroom. The furniture was old fashioned, very pleasing and comfortable. A big chair upholstered in green buttoned leather was a beautiful piece and I made it the main subject of a small water-colour depicting a corner of the room.

My two good neighbours were men destined for high office. Wg Cdr Brice became Air Commodore and Director of Physical Fitness Branch. He thought that I ought to know something about unarmed combat and practised his skills on me, which meant that I ended up flat on my face on the corridor floor with him sitting triumphantly on top of me, unless I first managed to twist his finger to breaking point, pull his ear, or stick my finger in his eye. Nobody was hurt of course, and it was all good fun. Padre Ashton became Chaplain-in-Chief with the rank of Air Vice Marshal, and a Bishop after that.

The Mess was full of young officers, Flying Instructors, Education Officers, College Flight Commanders, and the usual lot of Engineers, Suppliers, and Administrators of all ages. There were two other Poles living in the Mess and commuting home at week-ends. Both were Flight Lieutenant pilots, flying Valetta and Varsity aircraft for cadets training to be navigators. Toni Brent lived in London and John Baxter (ex Zabłocki) on the south coast. Toni had a car and I often travelled with him and John to and from London. The maximum speed he could squeeze out of it was about fifty miles per hour. His main problem when driving back on Sunday was not to fall asleep at the wheel, and I was expected to talk, sing, or make any other noises I could to keep him awake, for it was usually about two a.m. by the time he parked his chariot.

Young Barry Pearce, a supplier, was a man who understood nature, knew a lot about wild life and game, and was my mentor in these things. He undertook to rear pheasant chicks for the 'Cranwell Shoot' and had a hundred of them in the Mess garden. I was his helper; we fed them, looked after them, and eventually released them into a large field of kale maintaining a feeding point for a while longer. He had a twelve bore gun and was shooting pigeons in winter by the sack-full, which I was converting into various pâtés, half for me, and half for him.

Father Beresford-Young was a fiery and lively Catholic Priest. He thundered at his flock in church and fraternised with the opposition in his spare time. He had a substantial win on a football pool with his sacristan, which enabled him to attend monthly dinners organised by the Food and Wine Society in London and make occasional visits to Rome.

"Do you play bridge?" he asked me as soon as we met.

"Yes, would love a game."

"Good! We have a proper bridge club and play duplicate once a week, international points scored and all that, next meeting on Tuesday, must dash to a social engagement, never a moment to myself here!"

For the next two years we often played as partners and managed to irritate each other on some occasions, but on the whole it was an enjoyable association. I found the Commandant a good and agreeable partner, and a formidable opponent. His wife was charming, but an erratic player. Just before I left Cranwell Father Young was about to retire from the RAF to become a parish priest in Surrey - he was terrified!

It was in the summer of 1960 that I started to examine and think about my attitude to the Church. I had been a practising Christian until the age of nineteen when I fell into the category of lapsed Catholic. I had rebelled, but I thought God knew what was happening to me and why, and that I could not find any answers myself. However, I never gave up prayers completely. In my Spitfire PK-C two small crucifixes were wired firmly on the left hand side, close to the instrument panel, by a couple of mechanics who looked after that machine as if their own lives depended on it. I was deeply moved when I saw them for the first time, as I strapped myself in before take-off at Northolt. The tensest time in those days was the period just before the engine burst into life. After that, one was on the job and too busy to think about anything else. The two crucifixes were always there, to be seen as I was getting into my seat. One day a simple prayer of my own came into my mind and stayed with me to be repeated before every flight:

O Holy Maid, who Częstochowa's shrine
Dost guard and on the Pointed Gateway shine*,
Have mercy on us.

I remember it to this day. When I was leaving 315 Squadron those two fine men gave the crucifixes to me as a parting gift, mumbling their good wishes shyly. Their precious gift I still possess. The upshot of my thoughts during long walks along the Lincolnshire empty lanes was that I decided to re-join the church, freely and willingly.

I was very interested in the Cadet's selection methods and talked to the members of the Selection Board in the Mess, or just listened to them discussing marginal cases. The candidates stayed at Daedalus House situated in fairly large grounds separated from the rest of the camp. They were put through various tests which lasted several days. I was impressed by the meticulous analysis of the results, followed by the agonising process of deciding who was in, who was out, and why. The board was assisted by ad hoc co-opted members, usually a headmaster and a psychiatrist to narrow the margin of error. But errors were inevitable and a few chaps slipped through the net, only to be found out later, just as at Dęblin. Our methods however, as I experienced them twenty-three years earlier, were not as advanced and effective as those in Cranwell.

Our life as a family was still plagued by lack of money. We sold the car to pay off the bank overdraft, reshuffled educational policies and a life policy, and acquired some essential bits and pieces for our home. Once or twice we ran out of cash completely so that there was not enough to afford the railway fare to come home. We promised ourselves that this must not happen again.

Our pleasures were simple; we took advantage of the lovely Merrow Downs and the fine countryside beyond, and walked whenever weather permitted, to Newlands Corner, St Martha's Church on top of a hill with woodlands below and around it, to Albury - where we often stopped in the garden of the Drummond Arms - and further to Blackheath and Dorking following the Pilgrim's Way. From spring to autumn 1961 the four of us, and Bobby our dog, walked seventy-eight miles according to my log, the distances varying from three to ten miles. The *Ladybird Book of Wild Flowers* was a constant companion and by the end of that year all of us could identify common specimens staring at us as we walked the narrow paths in single file, with Bobby reconnoitring ahead. It was always sad to say quick farewells on Sundays but by then we had already made plans for the following week-end and had something to look forward to. While I was only

---

* Drawn from the early lines of *Pan Tadeusz*, by Mickiewicz, and referring to the miraculous images of Our Lady at Częstochowa and at Wilno.

a week-end husband and father, Pat never complained nor wavered from the course we had set for ourselves. When she fell down stairs and broke a couple of ribs she still managed to smile in spite of the pain and assured me she was not ready to die yet. She became familiar with hammer and nails, screws and screwdrivers, rawlplugs, a saw, paint, quite an expert with fuses, mender of electric items, as well as designer and builder of an electric train layout.

To fill the spare time in Cranwell I took a Pitman's Correspondence Course in intermediate bookkeeping, and soldiered on into the early months of 1962 when I was posted to RAF Steamer Point in Aden.

We reacted to the Aden posting with mixed feelings and finally decided that Pat and the boys would join me at the end of the next school term and remain until September 1963 - one full school year and two summer holidays. This meant three months separation at the beginning and six months at the end of the tour. It was a high price to pay for the sake of the boys' schooling, but that was the choice we made and had no regrets about it, being fully determined to give them as good an education as was possible under the system, so that they could stand firmly on their own two feet in life.

I disembarked in Aden early on the morning of the 9th March after a long and tiring flight and gasped for air. I felt I was breathing a warm and humid mixture of gases. My predecessor must have guessed how I would feel for he took me straight to the airport bar and softened the first impact of the Aden climate with a cool bottle of Fanta orange juice. He then whisked me around quickly and in the course of the working day, ending at 1300 hours, I had reported to the commanding officer, Gp Capt. Hanlon, his Senior Administrator, Wg Cdr Harry Bumford, and met a number of section commandeers whom I needed to know.

RAF Steamer Point was spread between the Arab town of the same name and the sea. Its function was to provide logistic support for Headquarters Middle East Command, which was a joint Headquarters for the three services, each under its own commander, all three being of equal rank and serving under the C-in-C Middle East Command - in my time Air Chief Marshal Sir Charles Elsworthy. The Station was responsible also for the RAF Hospital, a signals unit at the Saltpans, and British civilians under the Financial Adviser's Department at Headquarters. The sharp end of the RAF was at Khormaksar, a fully equipped modern airfield open for business day and night. About twenty miles along the main road was the garrison town of Little Aden with an Army regiment on station. The Royal Navy was showing the flag on a couple of mine sweepers and marking time, with a few men only looking after their installations, but prepared to expand quickly if required.

I was feeding several hundred airmen, soldiers, and sailors in one vast Mess, keeping an eye on another four smaller Messes, and supplied fruit juice, lemonade powder - known as 'jungle juice' - and salt tablets to families of service personnel serving at Steamer Point. About 30% of my staff were British - they were the 'chiefs', and the remaining 70% were Arabs - the 'Indians'. The former spent most of their time in a small preparation area which was air-conditioned, while the latter worked in the hot-as-hell kitchen with steam boilers, ovens and chip-fryers going full blast. I was drawing my foodstuffs from a Services Supply Depot which had regular shipments of frozen meat, fish, and dry goods, contracting locally for fresh vegetables and fruit, and buying the rest from the NAAFI shop.

The enormous Mess dining room was largely bare. With the Commanding Officer's blessing I decorated it with Masai shields, spears, bows and arrows, warriors' masks, zebra skins, and colourful Indian rugs which I bought in Nairobi. I called in on Stan Carlton - ex Stasio Przelaskowski - who worked as a surveyor for the Kenya Colonial Government and lived outside Nairobi with his wife, Jane. They were very hospitable and he helped me with my purchases, haggling expertly and saving us a lot of money.

A cold buffet counter made by the Station Workshop enabled us to serve a variety of cold meats and salads, which were less popular than I anticipated. Our customers were very conservative in their tastes, had everything with chips, and were partial to steamed puddings.

I settled into my job fairly quickly, there were no serious moans about food and I had the full support of the Commanding Officer and Harry Bumford, my bridge partner. I was very pleased to renew acquaintance with AVM F. Rosier - ex Station Commander at Northolt, and Padre Ashton from Cranwell time.

The Officers' Mess was a fine colonial type single storey building with a large patio, perched on top of a cliff with the sea immediately below to one side and overlooking lovely Tarshyne Bay on the other side, where blocks of flats were dotted around within a stone's throw of the sea. The Officers' Club complex had a restaurant, bar, swimming pool, and a garden full of trees and shrubs providing shade, a rarity in Aden.

My quarters comprised a large room, veranda, and a shower, in an old fashioned Indian-type building. There was a large fan suspended from the ceiling and an unusual arrangement of windows on two opposite walls - they were on two levels, one low and one high near the ceiling, four in all, allowing movement of air but never letting any sun inside. My room was by far the most comfortable and healthy, unlike the air-conditioned small rooms in new accommodation blocks.

The three months passed very quickly. Pat let our maisonette to a nice Army couple from Aldershot and landed at Khormaksar very early one morning, hoping to fall into my arms straight from the aircraft, but I was not there! I had enquired about their time of arrival at about 2200 hours on the previous night and then went to bed. However the ETA had been advanced by over an hour and I did not know about it, consequently I found them hot, tired and dejected, sitting on their suitcases. All other husbands and fathers met their families except me, I felt terrible.

Our three bedroom flat in Maalla was on the third floor in a brand new six storey building. The rooms were small and hot, and only one bedroom was air-conditioned. Mohammed, my batman, and family cook for extra money, did not like the place at all. There were several blocks of flats in Maalla occupied by Service families, mostly on one side of the main street near the water's edge of Aden Bay, while shops, warehouses and Arab flats were on the other side. A family clinic with several doctors and nurses was in the middle of the area coping with dysentery, food poisoning, prickly heat, cuts which did not heal, sick headaches, etc., and sending more serious cases to the RAF Hospital. They were always busy making calls and dealing with long queues of patients.

I had one week's leave and took the family around Aden. It was a different world. Steamer Point had the best shops, full of goods of every kind, all duty free, trading all day and every day. Arabs were sleeping on light wooden beds in the street, beggars at their well-established pitches, their bodies deformed with legs or arms missing, and some were blind. There was a market with stalls under cover, loaded with fresh fruit and vegetables of the highest quality, beautifully displayed, a slaughter house in a far corner where goats were killed, butchered, and sold as required, bloody and swarming with flies; a fresh fish stall next to it and usually sold out in the morning; suspicious characters wandering around trying to sell watches strapped to their arms from wrists to elbows to European passers-by, or radios and cameras, probably stolen; street sellers of everything saleable; tall Somali women in their colourful saris walking gracefully among Arabs as if they were Queen of Sheba; movement, noise, bright colours, smells, heat and thirst, from early morning until late at night.

Further west was Maalla with Anglo-Arab-Indian populations, and further still the road divided, left fork leading to Khormaksar and beyond, and the right fork under the Main Pass bridge to Crater, the teaming, stinking, revolting Arab town, terribly over-populated and without sanitation. A steady stream of illegal immigrants from Yemen seeking work, penniless and destitute, was swelling the population of the Colony. They lived in wood and cardboard shacks on the rocky mountain slopes above Crater, Maalla, and Steamer Point. A heavy rain or sandstorm meant disaster for them as those who were weak and under-nourished caught pneumonia and died prematurely, yet they continued to come.

Starting from Maalla one could climb a well-established path to the top of Aden's highest mountain, Shamsan. The view over Aden Port, the bay and far beyond was breathtaking. When we embarked on our expedition some weeks later we almost turned back at the start as the path ran through an area which was a Yemeni open-air lavatory. There was a saying that if you climbed Shamsan you would never be posted to Aden again. Gp Capt. Hanlon was serving his third tour in Aden and could not have heard of the magic powers of Shamsan.

The most English-looking corner of the colony was a housing estate near the Shell refinery occupied by British employees. A row of bungalows stood above a road on a gentle rise facing a fine enclosed bay and sailing club with dozens of dinghies moored and milling around. Each bungalow had a beautifully kept lawn in front and small trees and shrubs to the sides and back. It was an oasis lovingly watered every night - a bit of England on the edge of the desert.

Not long after their arrival, the family was struck down with dysentery in the middle of the night. By morning the three of them were in poor shape but there was nothing wrong with me. We agreed that Pat should call on the clinic as soon as it opened and I would come back after the Commanding Officer's Conference. The nurse claimed that the doctor was fully booked with calls all morning but fortunately the doctor over-heard the conversation and description of symptoms and ran after Pat, catching her up just as she was entering the block of flats. He questioned her about food, was her husband affected and did he eat the same food and, anyhow - where was he?

"He is at the CO's conference" said Pat.

"Conference! At a time like this? He should be here looking after you all. I will see he gets here quickly!"

I was listening to a discussion on discipline problems when the Commanding Officer was called away to take an urgent telephone call. He came back and said that I was wanted at home immediately - "And don't come back until your family is capable of looking after itself" he added as I hurried away. It was different to Northern Ireland.

I still have a copy of 'The Dhow', a combined Forces Newspaper, Aden, Friday 14th September 1962, 'circulation exceeds two thousand seven hundred copies'. A quick glance at the contents reveals what life in Aden was all about –

... C-in-C Middle East command, Sir Charles Elsworthy promoted to the rank of Air Chief Marshal... Salute for Sultan. At 9 o'clock on Tuesday 18th September 1962, D Battery third RHA will

fire a nine gun salute from Fort Morbut to mark the arrival of Nasser Bin Aidrus Aulaqi, the Sultan of Lower Aulaqi, at Government House where he will be paying a courtesy visit on His Excellency the Governor. Nasser… became sultan when his father was murdered some fourteen years ago. …The advance party of 9th/12th Royal Lancers (Prince of Wales) arrived by air in Aden 5th September. The remainder of the Regiment will arrive by sea aboard the Oxfordshire on 29th September. … The French Minesweeper 'La Dieppoise' calls at Aden… luncheon and cocktail party on board… A party of British Members of Parliament visited the Forces in Aden… On their arrival at the Second Battalion in the Federal Regular Army, they were welcomed with feux de joie from the local tribesmen… FOR SALE Ford Anglia 100E Dec. 1959, low mileage, excellent condition £250.

Towards the end of August we moved to a Married Quarter at Tarshyne Bay. It was a lovely flat on the second floor in a block of six, with three air-conditioned bedrooms and a big sitting room. Two sets of French Windows led to spacious balconies, one on the sea side and the other opposite. With both doors open there was always a gentle movement of air through the room. Sleeping in air-conditioned rooms was a mixed blessing. Admittedly one slept well but a wall of warm, sticky air would hit you hard on leaving the bedroom in the morning and it would take a while to get used to it again. We devised a system whereby the air-conditioning was switched on two hours before bed-time and switched off at the same time as the lights. By morning the temperature throughout the flat equalised and there would be no shock. We were also saving money as air-conditioning was just as expensive as electric fires to run. The 'cold' shower was always very warm and brought no relief. Usually I had at least three showers a day, one in the morning, one before lunch, or before the afternoon siesta when all clothing was discarded for washing, and one on return from the beach in late afternoon. We walked in swim-wear from the flat to the beach carrying towels, mats and books, wearing flip-flops - the sand on the beach was too hot to walk on in bare feet.

The Aden sea was infested with sharks and swimming was allowed only in the area protected by a shark net. There were dreadful stories of sharks taking people who merely paddled in shallow water. A Commanding Officer's wife, some years back, had had her leg mutilated and died of loss of blood and shock. The net was anchored to the bottom of the sea and kept up by colourful floats over a large area, and that was where we swam from early spring to late autumn. For the rest of the year the net was taken out because of very heavy seas, and the swimming pools came into their own, teaming with humanity.

In the winter months when the temperature was lower by a few degrees we had open-air cinema shows on Tarshyne Beach, run by the Officers' Club. It was the only time when ladies brought cardigans for the evening chill. All cinemas were open-air affairs - four walls and no roof. In summer it was purgatory and we kept away from them unless there was an outstanding programme worth suffering for.

The social life was very lively. After Pat had signed the Visitor's Book at the Governor's place, and made her calls according to the 'Customs of the Service', invitations started arriving, mostly to cocktail parties which were a popular form of entertainment. It was too hot for anything else except small dinner parties. A good venue for cocktail parties was the beach. There were several very big bandas with concrete floors, lighting, slatted roof for shade in day time, and no walls. The Officers' Club arranged drinks and food at a price and people could throw a party without any bother. Whenever we were invited to one of them I walked with my gin and tonic to the water's edge and listened to the murmur of the sea in total darkness or glittering in the moonlight. When my glass was empty it was time to walk back, and there, under the brightly lit banda roof, were ladies in their colourful, flimsy dresses and men in light-weight suits, talking, laughing, sometimes singing, as if they were on a stage. Arab waiters dressed in white uniforms with red sashes and red fezzes passed drinks and platters of dainty canapés while a cook attended a portable charcoal grill where sausages and other things were sizzling. Other parties were held in private houses and in the Officer's Mess, where the patio setting on the edge of the cliff with the sea below was quite superb. We often danced there in winter. The 'Twist' was all the rage at the time.

When the boys started school in mid September Pat found herself a job as a typist in the Financial Adviser's Office at Port Morbut at the princely salary of £25 a month, less four pounds ten shillings local tax. Mohammed was delighted; at last he had the flat to himself and a free hand to do his job in any order he liked. His routine was simple; he was obliged to arrive daily for work before we left, except on Sundays, wash breakfast dishes, clean the flat, cook and serve lunch, wash dishes again and depart. He lived in a room adjacent to the flat. He also did some shopping for us in the market whilst Pat shopped at the NAAFI. The first curry he cooked for us was as hot as hell; we could hardly utter a word of praise, drowning it in gallons of jungle juice and gasping for air. He was a robust Yemeni Arab of about forty-five years and had worked in the colony as a batman for several years, but his wife and children stayed behind. Once a year he went home for a month, loaded with gifts and extra money from me. We liked and respected him and he was content working for us. He was fond of the boys, secretly procuring forbidden catapults for them which they used for shooting salt tablets from the balcony at anything that moved. As soon as we confiscated one lot the next appeared, the three of them were endlessly conspiring.

Aden Port was one of the busiest in the world, ships coming and going all the time and about twenty in the harbour on any day. We saw great liners like the Canberra, Argentina, Oriana, Caronia, merchant ships of all nations, including modern vessels of the Polish Ocean Line, British aircraft carriers, frigates, destroyers, and even the Royal Yacht Britannia. When a large liner came and stopped for a day or two, the passengers swarmed to Steamer Point shops, some taking taxis for local tours to Maala and Crater, all looking very pale, all wearing hats. The shops welcomed them warmly and raised their prices sky high, making the most of their opportunities. Shopping at such times was difficult for us as it was necessary to be recognised as a local resident before making a purchase at normal prices.

"Don't tell the ship people what you paid for this, will you?" was the usual request.

On Christmas Eve Pat went on a marvellous Carol singing expedition organised by the Methodist Minister. They hired a lighter and packed it with volunteers to sing carols to ships all round the Harbour. They sang *Silent Night* to one large ship. Back across the water, a few moments later her German crew replied with *Stille Nacht*. Others joined in or waved in appreciation.

At the land-locked end of Aden Bay there were several wooden dhows, some just skeletons, others in various states of dilapidation, and some used as homes with added upper structures and decorated with intricate designs in bright colours. But there were still a few sea-worthy dhows in deeper water.

Several Poles served in Aden at the same time as I did. Four Flight Lieutenants at Khormaksar, and one Squadron Leader joined me at Steamer Point towards the end of my tour. We met occasionally in our homes and even managed to sing Polish songs once or twice. But there was no group cohesion of any significance as we were all too pre-occupied with our own affairs, jobs, children, or bank overdrafts. Stasiek Andrzejewski was catapulted from Dęblin into the 1939 war simultaneously with me. He had a distinguished flying career, attained the rank of Wing Commander and was the last Commanding Officer of 307 Polish Night Fighter Squadron. His English wife, Daphne, was a charming lady. We came across them again in later years. Lech Mintowt-Czyż, a pilot, was one of the two flying Poles in Aden, the other a navigator. His elder brother, Jan, lived in Kampala and held a high post in the Uganda Government as a Coffee Officer. Lech and Halina had six children, four were in English schools and the two youngest boys with them at home. They were very bright and Pat was amazed at their ability to converse with ease in two languages, one for her and one for me.

We gave a cocktail party in our spacious flat for over sixty people, to repay in small measure many kindnesses from our fellow Aden sufferers. The new Commanding Officer, Gp Capt. Vicary and his wife were the first to arrive; they had another invitation for the same evening and took us on first. There were hardly any free evenings at home for them, it was part of a CO's duty to be sociable. A good way to get to know your men is to drink and play cards with them. Our CO had many opportunities to do the former but not much the latter, I crossed swords with him over a bridge table on a number of occasions in the hot season, but no blood was spilt. Mohammed, as major domo, acted splendidly and supervised the food and drinks departments run by his helpers, insisting that we left everything to him and enjoyed the company of our guests. We asked a small group of close friends to stay behind and carried on merrily until beyond midnight. Mohammed assured us the party was a success.

One shop in Maala was selling padded, waterproof garments made in Hong Kong. They were taking orders for direct despatch from their factory to England or any other country. We sent seven winter coats to Poland, one each for my mother, three brothers and their wives, selecting appropriate sizes and colours. We had tried to assist them over the years but, of necessity, concentrated on my mother. Glad news came several months later that everything had arrived in a good state before the onset of winter.

One day we drove to Lahej with a picnic lunch. The road led through empty desert, and after a while the strange thought came into my head that we were driving towards the end of the world, where the sand would end and the road run into nothing. My morbid vision was shattered by shouts from the boys.

"Stop! Please stop! We want to climb those sand dunes."

I obliged and took an excellent photograph of the two of them climbing on all fours up a steep ridge of virgin sand. Further along the road we saw a mosque built of mud bricks, the only building for miles, and not a soul in sight. Near Lahej the sand gave way to cotton fields and a large banana plantation where water was flowing freely through irrigation canals. We had our picnic there, photographed the bananas on the trees and made the acquaintance of a little Arab girl who followed us wherever we went.

Lahej was a strange town with a few simple shops, selling locally made baskets and other crafts, a blind-folded camel walked around in circles grinding grain. Earthenware pots of all shapes and sizes were stacked in pyramids, a number of camels rested in a paddock and several tribesmen armed with rifles and knives walked proudly about their business, quite unlike the town dwellers who were a different breed of people.

In Aden town Arabs chewed Qat, a mild narcotic plant grown in Abyssinia, in ever increasing quantity. Daily supplies were flown in and quickly distributed throughout Steamer Point, Maala and Crater. The addiction was widespread, making people drowsy, disorientated and conspicuous by their inability to concentrate. A taxi driver chewing Qat was to be avoided.

There was hardly a corner of the colony we did not explore. We wandered by the ancient salt pans, the few remaining windmills, Turkish fortifications, paddled in the shallow water, which covered miles of coast between Crater and Khormaksar and, of course, we went to the Aden Races – an annual event celebrated for its camel race.

We also visited Sheikh Othman several times, a noisy, rowdy, bustling Arab town of considerable size and commercial importance. It had a most unhappy looking zoo with animals devoid of energy, as if they were about to drop dead, except for the monkeys which were determined to be entertaining. The town's pride and joy were the gardens maintained by much effort and care as well as constant irrigation. The result was an oasis of green grass, flowers, shrubs, and tall trees, the only public gardens within ten miles of Aden, and so refreshing to see. The open market had everything, including local pottery of every shape and size piled up in an eye-catching display at one end. The potters shaped their pots by walking around them; they had heard of the potter's wheel but this was the way it had always been done here.

Aden had a surprising variety of birds, and the places to see them were the tidal shallows and mud flats near the salt pans, at dawn, at Sheikh Othman dump, and on one side of Little Aden Causeway. There were white-winged black terns, gull-billed terns, curlew, sandpipers, dimlin, plover, Asiatic golden plover, green shank, spoonbill, avocet, flamingos, godwits, terek sandpipers, marsh sandpipers, gulls, and, near the refuse dump, Egyptian vultures and African tawny eagles. The gardens of Sheikh Othman with its tall trees, shrubs, and grass, were the home for a lot of small resident or migrant birds such as redstarts, great reed warblers, little green bee-catchers, red-throated pipits, and Nile Valley sunbirds.

Once a year in the hot season, families of Servicemen of all ranks were entitled to a two week holiday at the NAAFI Silver Sands Camp near Mombassa, in Kenya. We went in July. Air transport, provided by the RAF, was free. The camp was situated in lush woodlands near the beach of very fine silver-white sand, huge palm trees leant over along its edge. We had two bedrooms and a bathroom in a banda built for two families. The climate was sheer heaven and the first hot bath after over a year was bliss. Two large buildings on opposite ends of the camp provided common facilities, one for Officers and one for Other Ranks families.

Within the first two days we had arranged a safari trip to Tsavo National Park with a young Army family of three, in a large station wagon. The plan was to stop for the night in Kibo Hotel at the foot of Kilimanjaro, start very early next morning so as to arrive at the gates of the park at the first glimmer of dawn. Then to proceed through the park in the direction of Mombassa spending the best part of the day in it, seeing as many wild animals as possible, and returning to the camp in time for dinner.

There was a red glow of first light in the sky as the gates were opened for us and we drove slowly into Tsavo Park. Our first encounter with the wild life were hunting dogs with big, almost round, ears. A snarling, growling pack was milling around their dead victim, tearing it apart within a few yards of the road. It was an ugly sight and we watched mesmerised by the way things were ordained in nature.

Then came the elephants. A large herd of about twenty-five, led by a giant bull with enormous tusks was walking nonchalantly on a converging course. The leader turned his head towards us, trumpeted, quickened his pace and broke into a trot, the herd following dutifully. Our driver's black skin turned grey, he left the road and drove fast across rough land covered with dry grass towards a lane not far away, praying for a flat stretch without pot holes or large stones. We left the elephants behind and watched them at a safe distance slowing down to a walking pace again. Apparently they do not like intruders, and particularly not before breakfast.

Tsavo Park must be, at a guess, about sixty miles across. It has several lodges with food and drink, dotted around every twenty miles or so. Roughly in the middle there are Mzimi Springs with a hippo pool and another lodge where we had lunch and stretched our legs, watching the hippos and chasing impertinent monkeys. Our driver was also our guide and tried to show us as many animals as he could. Lions were a 'must' of course, and he found two sleepy specimens after a long search. We saw gazelles, giraffes, buffaloes, water bucks, zebras, wildebeest, baboons, monkeys, secretary birds, etc. and photographed everything we could.

We spent many hours wandering about in Mombasa's old town, Fort Jesus, and the modern part that welcomed visitors with two vast arches over the road in the shape of elephant tusks. It was a marvellous break from the heat and humidity of Aden.

Back in Aden it was soon time for Pat and the boys to start packing for their homeward journey in September. We felt sad at saying good-bye for six months. To make matters worse their departure was delayed by engine problems and we spent several hours waiting at the airport. On landing at Stansted their bus to London broke down. They should have stayed in Aden with me all the time. I had a guilty conscience about it for a long time.

I moved back to my old single quarter in the Mess. There were a number of new faces about and I was pleased to see Peter Sheridan (ex Skubała) whose wife Muriel was expecting a baby in the UK, their first, at last. He was convinced it would be a boy and was already planning his education,

Once a week I played bridge with two half-Colonels and a lady Major. We took turns to be hosts which entailed providing four glasses and a bottle of whisky. They were amusing companions and our bridge sessions were usually followed by good conversation until the bottle was finished. I met one of them ten years later and was delighted to learn that the Army had made him a Brigadier.

Some of my Arab chaps divorced their wives, marrying again, and having domestic problems, *Allah Karim!* (Allah is merciful!). There was a period when two or three ex-wives squatted outside the airmen's Mess waiting in ambush for their ex-husbands, demanding outstanding settlements with angry scenes. This was not conducive to good order, discipline, or efficiency, and the ladies were advised to lay their ambush at another point which, *imshallah!* (God willing!) could be easily by-passed. The fellows approved the manoeuvre wholeheartedly in true Arab fashion and throwing in several *taijib! taijib! Allah Akbar!* (Good! good! God is great!) for good measure. Quite frequently I addressed a short sentence in Arabic to the men piling potatoes and vegetables on plates as the queue of Servicemen moved along - *lah tah gib katir* (don't give too much) which always produced a smile and several *taijibs*. They were getting the message at last, I thought, *Allah akbar!*

Ramadan was a problem month. They practised their religion faithfully and did not take any food or water during daylight. Those of them who worked in the kitchens became dehydrated much quicker than the others, becoming dizzy and fainting in the late afternoon. I wanted them to have frequent short breaks in the air-conditioned area but "*lah*" (no), that smacked of cheating, *Allah karim!* they would have nothing to do with it. I could only admire them for sticking to what they believed was right. Their observance of daily prayer times and devotion to Allah was most praise-worthy. I made a point of greeting them with "*Salaam aleikum!*" and always had a cheerful and loud "*Aleikum salaam!*" fired back at me with a grin. The few Arabic words

I learned and brandished about all the time helped to establish a degree of rapport between us, and mutual respect. They were not bad fellows and worked as well as they could if properly treated, and learned willingly if a genuine attempt was made to teach them something. They could also teach some of us a thing or two - faith in God, to start with.

I sold the car for ninety pounds and blew it all on another East African holiday by agreement with Pat before she left. I accepted an invitation to visit Jan and Lulu Mintowt-Czyż in Kampala, and the Carltons in Nairobi again, but first I shared expenses for a two day safari to Amboseli Park, about a hundred miles from Nairobi. There were a great number of species in a comparatively small area with a lodge and over-night accommodation in native-type huts in the middle of it. I was woken up several times throughout the night by animal noises of growling, thumping and scratching on the wall outside the hut, and did not get much sleep. My companions, an Anglo-Polish couple, had no sleep at all in the adjacent hut. The large Yorkshire lass was terrified of being devoured by lions or trampled to death by elephants and had hysterics. As there was no communication between the huts and the warden, they had to sit it out until day-break and were both exhausted. After early breakfast we went for a tour of the park with a warden in his Land Rover until lunch. This was most successful. A few hundred yards from the lodge we found a superb male lion resting in the middle of the road. The warden drove around him a couple of times whilst we were taking photographs. His family of six cubs were nearby, quite unconcerned - they must have had their breakfast already. We came quite close to a rhino, saw a cheetah silhouetted against the sky, standing motionless like a statue - too far for my camera unfortunately - a great variety of other animals but always in small numbers. Amboseli is close to Kilimanjaro, has a lot of water, trees and vegetation, and the mountain towers above it all with snow covered peak, a superb setting.

I stopped the second night with the hospitable Carltons and boarded the train for Kampala early in the morning. The journey took twenty-four hours through magnificent country at an ambling pace of 25-30 miles per hour. It was the nicest train journey of my life; I had the compartment all to myself, the food was excellent and the bed very comfortable. Waking up at dawn I had the first glimpse of Lake Victoria, the dam at Jinja and the Nile at its source. I was surprised to meet a Polish lady in the restaurant car, she was on her way to visit her married daughter in Entebbe. We talked and she told me that her odyssey had taken them from Poland to Russian labour camps, then Iran with General Anders, from where a group of families were sent to Kenya and they had been amongst them.

My hosts met me at the station, took me home, and laid before me their plans for a combined business with pleasure trek across Uganda instead of my intended flight from Entebbe to Murchison Falls, where the river Nile plunges through a rock-bound cleft barely six yards wide. I agreed with pleasure, on the understanding that I would share all expenses. Next morning we made an early start for the Queen Elizabeth National Park in the first instance. It was a fascinating journey through lovely country dotted with large and small coffee plantations, farms, woodlands, rivers, volcanic crater lakes, through villages and small towns, with an odd restaurant and a hotel for travellers. We crossed the equator at a well marked point, saw a road-sign near a car-wreck reading: 'Elephants have the right of way', and arrived towards evening at a camping site, where we spent the night inside an empty hut with strong doors shut and bolted. Next morning we drove to the heart of the park, the Mweja Safari Lodge standing high on a peninsula surrounded by the waters of Lake Edward's and the Kazinga channel. We took a trip on the channel with other people, which enabled us to get very close to the animals on both banks. There were elephants feeding and blowing fountains of water, buffaloes taking a drink or staring at us, hippos on land and dozens of them in the water playing games close to the boat, and a fantastic number of water-birds particularly near Lake Edward - pelicans, cormorants, yellow-bill and marabou storks, flamingos, herons, Egyptian goose, kingfishers and more.

We left Mjweja Lodge after lunch and continued across the park, running close to very large herds of buffaloes, some water bucks, Uganda kob - which forms the badge of Uganda National Parks - hartebeest known also by their Swahili name 'Kongoni', and the birds - the beautiful crested cranes, and a solitary secretary bird whose local Acholi name '*Labong-cula*' means 'He who wanders in the wilderness'. Towards the evening we reached our furthest point, the Kiko tea plantation at the foot of the Ruwenzori mountains, run by an English couple - good friends of Jan and Lulu and kind hosts to me.

The remaining months of my Aden tour of duty ticked away much slower than I would have liked, but in the end the time came for me to say "*Salaam aleikum!*" to Aden, shake the dust off my feet and hurry home.

Pat took me for an 'Eastern Gentleman' at first, before she recognised me at Waterloo Station. It was a happy reunion and we hurried home where the boys gave me a warm and noisy welcome of their own. It was good to feel loved and wanted.

All our possessions arrived safely, including a demi-jon (two gallons) of red wine, supplied unofficially by the French in Djibouti to Aden, which I declared on the customs' form as 'one large bottle of wine'.

Two weeks at home passed in a flash and on 27th April 1964 I reported to Headquarters Technical Training Command at Brampton, near Huntingdon, for Staff duties as number two to Wg Cdr Gledhill, the Command Catering Officer. Pat and the boys stayed at Merrow and we became a week-end family again, but this time I could get home every Friday evening by about 9 p.m.

For the next two years I was deputy controller of catering standards and efficiency at twenty-five RAF stations and three hospitals, inspecting, advising, writing reports and instructions. I also liaised with building contractors and architects on the design of catering premises, and originated some building conversions and improvement schemes. I travelled by road, rail, and air, all over England meeting many old friends and making some new ones. This was an interesting job with a challenge and scope for initiative - I enjoyed it.

In the spring of the next year my brother wrote with some anxiety and asked me to come for a visit as soon as possible. He said it was our mother's wish, she wanted to see me before she died. As far as I knew no Poles serving in the British Forces had visited Poland as yet, however I wrote the usual "Sir, I have the honour...," letter saying exactly what my brother had told me. I was granted fourteen days leave eventually, with instructions to travel both ways by air. I made all arrangements through the Poland State Travel Agency'. They gave me an application form for a visa which had sixteen questions with up to three sub-questions to most of them. It was a detailed life story, revealing all.

"Why three copies?" I asked.

"Ah well... one will probably follow you to Poland."

I flew to Poland in Russian-built four engine aircraft of the Polish Air Line LOT, via East Berlin where we stopped for a while. Before we boarded the aeroplane again I saw a guard of honour lined up on the tarmac with a military band playing the Polish National Anthem. A state visit from the

Polish People's Republic was in progress. I stood to attention, it was my National anthem, they were the usurpers, they betrayed it.

I did not see Warsaw from the air nor did I see much of the countryside either. The airport terminal was a conglomerate of temporary buildings. I went through the customs very quickly and was met by a young man.

"Excuse me" he said, "Is your name Kornicki?"

"Yes, and who are you?"

"Antoni, your nephew, welcome to Poland!"

We shook hands smiling at each other and moved to a quiet part of the terminal, talking about my train to Hrubieszów which was due at midnight, and the immediate plans for the rest of the day. Toni was a technician in Gdańsk shipyard, planning to start a degree course in ship-building and engineering, a bright young man, son of my middle brother Felek. We took a bus to the city and Toni invited me to his room in 'Dom Chłopa' - a large, cheap hotel for Poles, but not for foreign visitors, where we talked at length about the family. There was no time for any sight-seeing and we made arrangements to meet in Warsaw on my return, when I intended to spend a few days exploring the city and calling on my school friend who lived in the suburbs. We had dinner together in a restaurant in the 'Old Town', looked up a couple of bars in the square and went by taxi to the station. There was nobody in my compartment and I was fast asleep before the train pulled out. I woke up when we reached Zamość in the morning, and was surprised to see two policemen with sub-machine guns standing on the platform facing passengers descending from the train. This seemed to be routine at all stations - what, or whom, were they afraid of? From Zamość onwards I was glued to the window filling my eyes with Poland.

As the train was squeaking to a halt in Hrubieszów I saw my three brothers standing on the platform - older, very much older, and worn more than when I last saw them. I felt a big lump in my throat as we smiled, shook hands, and hugged one another. They had a station-wagon which belonged to the state farm where my nephew worked.

Some twenty kilometres later, as we reached the top of a rise near the big woods, within about eight hundred yards of the village, I looked eagerly expecting to see the estate buildings, the cottages, and the tall flour-mill behind them, but there was nothing there, absolutely nothing, except the mill and a bungalow nearby -

"All gone, burned to the ground, and the village too, there is nothing left of Wereszyn. The few houses you will see were built after the war" said Władek, "the seven farms which were around here, this side of the village, have all gone and so have the people. The wooden house on your left, the only one here and the unfinished out-buildings, belong to me. I live here as if I was on an island."

We proceeded in silence towards the big lake. All estate buildings had disappeared, there were a few heaps of rubble and broken bricks, the big house was in ruins, part of it had straw where the roof was, not a single house could be seen on the other side of the lake, all the Jewish shops near the bridge were gone, and every house that ever stood in the village. All I could see was an empty space with some trees, a few shrubs, grass and weeds. Were it not for the lake I would not have known where I was. As we progressed and passed the site of the non-existent village we arrived at two wooden houses with some modest out-buildings nearby.

"This is my place" said Felek, "And the other one belongs to Janek."

We stopped outside Janek's house, got out of the car, and there she was. My mother, standing in the drive, slightly stooping, shrunken, eighty-eight years old, shawl over her shoulders and smiling. I kissed her hands, looked at her dear face, tears rolling from her eyes, skin creased; I took her into my arms, our tears met, she was whispering "My boy, my boy" and I was unable to say a word. A bottle of vodka was needed urgently and Janek led us quickly inside where three families were assembled to say "hello" to me.

The first two days were a bit chaotic, we were all catching up with our past, it was not easy, I wanted to know about my father, about his life after I left Poland until he died. Janek took me for a short walk to the big lake on the village side. We were walking along a mud road overgrown with weeds towards the area where the last few houses stood nearest to the dam, when Janek stopped and pointing to an old lilac bush said -

"Here. This is where our father sat down, under this bush, feeling unwell, and died."

On the third day I went by bus to Hrubieszów where I had to report to the police. They checked my passport and asked me to fill in a form which contained several questions including: "What is your occupation?" My answer, "RAF Officer", caused a bit of a commotion. They wanted to know precisely what I meant by that and when I explained they kept me waiting for a while and then allowed me to leave. I was asked politely that I should call again before departure.

I walked through every street of the town, most of it intact, but looking terribly neglected. The Jewish quarter, their shops and businesses were no more. The whole area was flat and turned partly into a bus terminal with a few new buildings on the edges. The house where Helka lived with her parents, sister Balka, and younger brother Chaim was standing firm, as was the rest of the street, exactly as I remembered it. Joseph, the barber, had his shop on the opposite side of the street but on a higher level; he was open for business as usual. I went in wondering whether he would be there. He was - and recognised me instantly. He had two assistants, looking very prosperous, talked about the future of the country, development plans for the town, democracy, unity of purpose in the new Poland, like a good Party member and the local commissar that he obviously was. I wanted to know about people - barbers used to know everybody - so I invited him for a drink, but Joseph did not tell me very much and would not give any details on the liquidation of the Jews either. I left him and wandered as if in a dream towards my school. As I stood on the pavement looking at it, Professor Jopyk who taught me German came along and we talked for a while. I was shocked by his appearance. He had always been impeccably dressed, how was it possible that he presented such an unbelievable picture of neglect? His trousers had no creases at all, shabby jacket, no tie, open-neck shirt none too clean, and above all he had not shaved that morning. By comparison Joseph the barber, dressed in a good suit, looked the model of smartness.

The head of my old school was a lady, the doctor's daughter where I lived for my last school year, helping her brother Władek. She was the only one of the family left in Poland; her parents had died, elder sister - a barrister - and her cavalry officer husband, both prisoners of war, liberated by the Allies, lived in Canada, and Władek, also ex prisoner-of-war, married a rich Dutch widow–. She gave me his address. She was well dressed in a masculine sort of way, and had lost her softness and femininity that I so well remembered.

Stasio Michalski, who shared digs with me at one time, was a barrister and luckily I found him at the District Court. We had a long talk. He swore at the new rulers of Poland, the local party chiefs, the red tape, the graft, the inability of having anything done unless you were one of THEM. But he was not despairing, he believed they would never get the people to follow them like sheep. I left Hrubieszów feeling sad at what I had seen and heard.

Four kilometres from my brother's house was a vast State Farm specialising in cereals and seeds. Władek's two eldest sons worked there. Wiesław, married with four children was the accountant, and Roman, also married but no children, was a driver. Wiesław asked me to lunch and Roman offered to pick me up, but I preferred to walk through the fields and woods. I passed the source of the stream, that fascinating bubbling spring I remembered so well. I stopped there a long time thinking of my childhood and the many packed lunches I had there with my father during harvest time. It was all so clear in my mind and still is.

I was welcomed warmly by the two families, their hospitality was overwhelming, they must have gone to no end of trouble to provide a feast like that. I knew times were hard and would have rather they offered me a sandwich instead, but that was not the Polish way. We had not quite finished lunch when Wiesław was called to the office nearby to take an urgent telephone call. He returned a different man, very frightened, wondering what the Security Police (Polish KGB) wanted with him; he had had no problems with them for years. They were on their way, arriving shortly. His brother and the two wives were terribly shaken and I was shocked by the effect the mere mention of Security Police had on them.

"They are not coming to see you" I said, "They want to see me. Don't worry, calm down, we will both meet them outside, you invite them in for a drink, offer them food and let us see what they want of me, not you, and I don't think they are after my blood either."

That helped to restore the equilibrium as it seemed that I might be right and they all relaxed a bit. When the car drove to the house two officers stepped out, Wiesław greeted them and introduced me as his uncle from England.

"Ah, yes! Nice to see you. How is your wife, Pat, and your sons, Peter and Richard?" "They are all well, thank you. You seem to know a lot about me, but I am at a disadvantage, I know nothing about you, might I ask who you are?"

"We are Security Police, I am Major 'X' and this is Captain 'Z'." They clicked their heels and bowed slightly; I bowed back.

"We would like to have a little chat with you, nothing serious you understand, we are curious about a few things and perhaps you could help us."

"Gladly, if I can."

At this point Wiesław suggested vodka and food and we all went inside, the two officers behaving in a friendly and jovial manner, drinking, eating and talking as if we were on the best of terms. A good half hour later they offered me a lift to Wereszyn.

"We will take you back by car to your mother and chat with you on the way. All right?"

"Yes, fine. I am ready when you are."

I wanted to get them out of my nephew's house as soon as possible and end their ordeal. They took me the long way around, stopping at an inn where they ordered a bottle of vodka and three glasses.

"Good stuff this, you must miss it in England."

"I don't drink much. Can't afford it really but when I do it is usually beer, or occasionally gin or whisky."

"But they pay you well now, don't they? You are a Major, you should be all right?"

"I am not complaining."

"Why did you join the RAF?"

"I have to work for my living and I prefer a job in the RAF rather than in civilian life."

"So, it is just a job, you are in the RAF for money only?"

"No. The RAF is also a way of life which appeals to me. As you know, I was in Dęblin and a regular officer in the Polish Air Force first."

"What about loyalties? You are a Pole. Can you be loyal to England and Poland at the same time?"

"I am a British citizen living and working in England. I have the same rights and obligations as any ethnic British person. The British did not do any favours to Poles who chose not to return to Poland by granting them these rights, we earned them. As a Pole I have the interests of Poland at heart and would do anything I could to help my country. Should there be a serious conflict of loyalties I would have to make a choice and declare openly what I stand for, but I don't think this is likely to happen. Of course, your concept of a free Poland differs from mine and that is why I stay in England."

We went on and on for about two hours. The Captain was slowly getting drunk and hardly said a word, but it was the Major and I who were crossing swords all the time. I drank my share of vodka but it had no effect on me. I felt clear-headed, alert and in control. We covered my job in detail, past service, the way I was treated in the RAF, social life, chances of promotion, and then came the big question -

"Would you work for us?"

"No, I would not."

"Well, it doesn't matter really, you don't know much do you?"

"You are quite right, I do not."

They dropped me at my brother's house, wished me a pleasant holiday and drove away.

In 1939 my three brothers were, respectively, thirty-eight, thirty-three, and twenty-eight years old. The youngest, Janek, was the only one called to the colours by the general mobilisation orders just before the war started. The mobilisation was delayed on the insistence of our Western Allies on the grounds that the Germans would consider it a provocation.

Janek joined the 50th Infantry Regiment in Kowel - a garrison town in eastern Poland. The Regiment was moved to Bydgoszcz, north-west of Warsaw, at first, and then further north to the region of the great forests of Tuchola. The Regiment fought there in the uneven battle and, having suffered heavy losses, withdrew to Puszcza Kampinoska - another forest region immediately west of Warsaw - where elements of several divisions assembled and fought again. Janek was taken prisoner and moved to Sochaczew first, then to Skierniewice and put on a train for Germany with other POWs. Several of them, including him, jumped the train beyond Kalisz, close to the German border, and made their way east. Janek managed to board a goods train and return to Warsaw, from where he walked for seven days avoiding the Germans until he returned home.

Mr Robert Białkowski had died during the winter of 1940 and his son, Tadek, took over the management of the Estate. In 1943 and at the beginning of 1944 marauding Ukrainian gangs were ravaging this remote area and it was no longer safe to sleep at home. People often moved for a night to the neighbouring estate, travelling on horse-drawn carts. On 19th March my brothers left Wereszyn, just in time, as next day the brigands plundered and burned the village, and all estate buildings, except the mill, a day later. They found temporary work, hiring themselves out with a pair of horses and a cart each at an estate run by the Germans. Later they moved to Siemenice. As the Red Army was advancing the Polish AK units were attacking the German lines of communication with the usual reaction from the Army and SS which included retaliation on the civilian population. My brothers and their families spent some time hiding in a forest, then the Germans retreated and the Red Army arrived in on the 22nd July 1944. The bewildering New Order came into being. The brothers split, two moved to Hrubieszów trying their luck in town, and Janek lived with his in-laws and our mother. In 1947 a land reform was introduced allocating seven hectares to individual farmers. My brothers returned to Wereszyn, took over the disused mill as their temporary home and started farming. They rebuilt the roof of the bungalow near the mill and converted it into three one-room flats for their families, using the mill as stables, livestock accommodation, storage for crops and anything else which needed protection against the elements. It took them ten years to build their own houses, outbuildings and wells, not a mean achievement by any standards.

On Sunday we went to the old wooden church in the next village where I had made my first communion. I was pleased to see the village had escaped destruction as most of it was still standing. The church filled up with people of all ages, whole families were obviously worshipping together. I made a comment to Janek about it, to which he replied -

"Oh, this is nothing. Some years ago when there was a lot of anti-church propaganda and intimidation this church was packed solid. People who never went near the church flocked to it, whereas now only those who want to pray come."

I met the priest after the service and asked him to say Mass for my father the following Tuesday, to which he readily agreed. All the family came. Janek harnessed two fine horses to his spruced up cart and brought mother in style. It was a solemn occasion, we were united in prayer and in remembrance of a good man, my father. After Mass we went to the cemetery where we laid a few flowers on four family graves: Władek's first wife, Victoria, and her baby daughter, my brother Kazik, and my father.

There was a great farewell family party in Władek's house before I left, twenty-two in all, including children. The place was charged with good will, mutual respect and affection. They had their differences but they always stuck together in good and bad times. I had no fears for any of them, they were stronger than I had anticipated and I was certain that in a crisis they would rally to each other's side and survive. As a family they were quite a force and I was proud of them and loved them all. The party ended with a sing-song of old favourites and 'one for the road'.

Early next morning I said 'good-bye' to my mother. She was calm, thanked me for coming to see her, sent her love to her daughter-in-law and two grand-sons whom she had never seen, told me to take good care of them and not to worry about her. As the car was pulling away she stood on the edge of the road waving and wiping away her tears until we were gone out of sight. We both knew it was good-bye for ever this time.

My brothers and nephew Romek drove me off to Hrubieszów where I boarded a bus for Warsaw. I thought I would see more of Poland that way, stopping in towns and villages on the way. We shook hands and hugged one another in Polish fashion, few words were said, I waved and the bus rolled on. It was not a comfortable journey but I certainly saw a good slice of the country, three hundred kilometres of it, trying to lock in the 'Polishness' of it, to store inside me for a rainy day, something I could fall back on. I stopped at the Bristol Hotel in Warsaw, a well-known place for its high standards before the war but not so then. An old school friend with whom I had corresponded over the past several years was expecting a telephone call from me and when I rang he invited me and my nephew for lunch on the following day. He had fought in the AK and having failed to reveal all to the authorities, and particularly his AK assumed name, found himself in jail for the best part of a year. He lived in a lovely small villa with a garden beyond it, close to a suburban railway station and pine woods, with his charming wife and a school-teacher son. Unfortunately he had lost a leg in a motor-cycle accident and felt the consequent restriction acutely. Both he and his wife had full-time jobs and in their spare time cultivated their garden. There were vegetables, soft fruit, apples, as well as lilac trees, philadelphus and other shrubs, also flowers everywhere. We talked about old times, friends and places, some stories were joyful, some very sad, there were too many lives cut short too soon.

I stayed three nights in Warsaw, had Toni as my guide for most of the time, took sight-seeing and other conducted tours of the City, visited St John's Cathedral, Łazienki Museum, the monument on the site of the Jewish Ghetto, prayed at the little street shrines where executions had taken place, browsed in book-shops where sales ladies were interested in everything except customers. Perhaps they were not keen on Russian books, and books about Russia. I walked in the parks and wherever my feet took me, photographing everything I wanted to remember.

I flew back in a BEA Comet. Just as I was about to be checked into the departure lounge I was met by the ex Commanding Officer of 315 Squadron, a POW, and now a Polish Air Line (LOT) Navigation Officer. He had a Security Police 'guardian angel' with him, who did not talk but would not leave us alone. He enquired about many people and hoped to visit England one day as he had been granted a passport recently, which meant he could apply for a visa. I was very pleased we met, he must have been looking through passenger lists for old friends and he had obviously arranged this brief encounter, plus the compulsory eaves-dropper. It was good to see him, but I hated that silent young man and his patronising smile.

I arrived home with a small amber gift for Pat and typical tourist shop items for the boys, and was met by a barrage of questions. My home de-briefing lasted for a couple of week-ends and included a commentary on my slide shows. I had been switched on to the Polish language again so completely that I frequently broke into it when talking to Pat. At night I dreamed of Poland and talked Polish in my sleep, being awakened by Pat who wanted to know what I had been talking about. It took quite a while for the pent-up sensations, impressions and feelings to simmer down and fall into the perspective of my every-day life in England.

Our boys' education was well mapped out. A year earlier, thanks to Pat's determination and perseverance, the Surrey Education Authority agreed to transfer them to St George's, a good Catholic Public School in Weybridge and pay the education fees. It was all her idea, she saw the headmaster first, obtained his agreement in principle, and attacked the education authority with letters and a telephone call.– They did not have a chance and gave in gracefully. In September 1964 our sons became day-boys at St George's, travelling by bus and train, and being assured of boarding places should I be posted overseas.

It was shortly after my forty-ninth birthday when I asked Pat whether she would like to go overseas again. It would have to be soon as I was due to be retired compulsorily in less than six years and the last tour of duty was, as a rule, a home tour. She was quite keen.

"Another adventure! Yes, please. It would be good for the boys and their 'A' levels to stay put and not to waste time on travelling daily. Where might they send us?"

"It could be Germany, Cyprus, Malta again, Gibraltar perhaps, or Hong Kong. They wouldn't waste a chap of my talents on anything smaller than that."

I applied and was posted to RAF Akrotiri in Cyprus as Station Catering Officer with effect from 28th March 1966. The Caterers at the Ministry of Defence told me that the Station commander, Air Commodore North-Lewis, was a holy terror. "Watch it!" they said. I rather liked the sound of him, I always got on well with tough commanders and was looking forward to working for yet another one.

I went to Cyprus on my own while Pat stayed behind to tie up loose ends - dozens of them - arranging boarding for the boys, handing over maisonette keys to an agent, and joining me as soon as possible. She came in May, landing at Nicosia at the crack of dawn. I met her with our new (£325) Renault 4L, which I bought with the kind permission of our bank manager, and took her to our lovely Married Quarter on the edge of the camp. It was a fine three bedroom house with a huge open fireplace set in a wall faced with local stone. A veranda led to a good size garden with lawns, a mimosa tree, a geranium bush five feet tall by the kitchen window, flower beds, and a few other shrubs and trees. We brought with us only the necessary minimum, having put most of our precious possessions, including books, into storage. I took a week's leave and whisked Pat on a quick sight-seeing tour of the island, showing her something different every day and ending with the perilous drive to the top of Troodos mountain, some 5,500 feet high, where the RAF had a radar station in the shape of a golf ball.

It was at about that time of the year that we changed to the pleasant 0700 to 1300 hours summer routine. It did not follow that nobody worked after 1300 hours. It all depended on the nature of each set-up - flying, refuelling, maintenance, air movement of freight and passengers, air traffic, air surveillance, signals, air sea rescue, guards, police, etc. the work went on around the clock and people needed food around the clock - which was my business.

Akrotiri had quite a punch with its five Canberra squadrons, elements of one Lightning squadron, Argosy transport, and a Helicopter Flight. Close to the Base were two signals units and a first class modern Hospital, then there was a Marine Craft Unit in Limassol and the radar station in Troodos. Akrotiri was the main element of the RAF Near East Command, Malta and Idris being the other two. The command was part of the Central Treaty Organisation (CENTO) set-up and had its Headquarters at Episcopi, less than ten miles away, much too close for our liking, we thought, as there were too many staff wallahs breathing down our necks.

I had two large Airmen's Messes for about eight hundred men, with capacity to cater for more than double that figure should the need arise, and a separate in-flight and ground meals centre for Transport Command passengers and Air Crew staging through, night stopping, or terminating in Akrotiri. The Centre was part of my organisation, it produced on average 20,000 in-flight meals a month and at least three times as many ground meals and refreshments. In addition there were some sixty men in Troodos who were liable to be cut off every winter by heavy snow falls and had to have long-life reserve rations.

An important aspect of our work were 'Base Alerts' ordered periodically by the C-in-C at any time of the day or night, putting us on a war footing. All men living in the camp area and those accommodated with their families about fifteen miles away in Limassol had to report immediately to their units. Squadrons were armed and in readiness, all supporting units organised for work around the clock, nobody was allowed to leave the base and I gained about 50% more customers demanding meals day and night, in the Messes and at their places of work. The performance of all specialist units and sections was carefully measured with the view to increasing efficiency and above all reducing the time from the words 'Alert' to 'Ready for Action'. Akrotiri was the biggest RAF peace-time station, and in my time had the right man in command, a confident and inspiring leader, tough but fair.

We were on the island by courtesy of the Republic of Cyprus Government, which leased to Britain part of its territory as a 'British Sovereign Base' for something like twenty million pounds sterling per year. Thus the Army had Dhekalia, the RAF had Akrotiri, and the two Command Headquarters Episcopi. We were by no means the first foreign military forces on the island.

Looking back no further than, say, 1450 BC the island had been ruled by the Egyptians, Assyrians, Persians, Egyptians again, Romans, Byzantines, Arabs, Byzantines again, English Knights Templar, Lusignanians, Venetians and Turks before, in 1926, becoming a colony of the British Empire. In the late 1950s the Cypriot Greek population took to arms for four years, fighting for union with Greece - Enosis. Their underground fighters, EOKA, were led by the ex Greek General George Grivas, 'Dighenis', with the support of his Beatitude the Archbishop Makarios III who, after a spell of enforced exile in the Seychelles, signed the London Agreement together with Dr Fazil Kuchuk representing Cypriot Turks, granting Cyprus the status of an Independent Republic as from 16th August 1960. The two leaders became the President and vice-President of the Republic respectively.

The ten strong council of Ministers had three Turks. The population ratio of Greeks to Turks was four to one. The Greeks wanted it all their own way. The Turks would not have it and refused to co-operate. The country divided into two hostile parts with isolated villages and towns on the wrong sides. The capital Nicosia had barricades between the Turks and the Greeks with armed guards on either side. Guns came out and UNO forces were brought in to keep the peace. Their presence on the island was also a source of considerable income to the local economy, which was reflected in the budget. The story went that the Greeks were arranging small 'fireworks' at regular intervals so that UNO would extend the presence of its forces for another six months, and another, ad infinitum. This was the situation in 1966.

Pat and I went to Paphos one day to see the site of a palatial Roman Villa discovered in recent years, where beautiful mosaics depicting mythological scenes were still in their full glory and in a perfect state. I asked the guide whether anybody was digging in the area.

"Yes, Professor Michałowski and his two assistants, they live in that old cottage over there" he said, pointing to a stone building about a hundred yards away.

I decided to call and after a few words in Polish we were invited inside warmly by young Mr Daszewski. Another assistant joined us and then the Professor himself. He was the head of the Faculty of Mediterranean Archaeology at Warsaw University. They all spoke English and we had a lively session in two languages, eating fresh cherries and being shown a few of their finds, among them the bottom half of a small, but unmistakably, male statue. I told Mr Daszewski that I knew an officer in 303 Polish Squadron by the same name who was killed in action. Yes, he knew him, it was his uncle.

We were determined to visit a couple of ancient places in the Cypriot Turkish territory. It was not advisable to go there without UNO Forces escort, but we went just the same, trusting to our luck. Armed men in uniforms stopped us several times but let us pass. We saw a military training camp run by the Turkish Army and several sections being drilled and marching about. A few Turkish words came in useful and produced a grin on solemn faces of the young soldiers. They saw we were a family on a sight-seeing tour and made no more fuss than they had to. The ancient Vouni Palace and Soli Theatre were well worth seeing and we had good guides in both places.

About ten miles from Akrotiri was a perfectly preserved and restored Roman theatre at a place called Curium. It was built in the usual semi-circular fashion on a hillside which was sloping gently down to the sea. The British forces were allowed to use the theatre for concerts by Army Bands, and once a year a local amateur dramatic company gave us a taste of Shakespeare. The performances were geared to the full moon shimmering on the sea below, whilst we sat on cushions, Roman style, with wine, food, and fruit ready to hand. The finale of the military band concerts was usually the 1812, culminating in gun-fire from an adjacent hill.

There was a great deal of tension on the island lasting several weeks and it looked as if a Turkish Army invasion was imminent at one time, but fortunately tempers cooled off and the two communities went back to their normal and acceptable state of hostilities. The British Forces were not involved and, taking no sides, sat tightly watching developments.

We had a pleasant family routine in the summer at Akrotiri. Almost every evening after supper we strolled along a rough country lane and lay down on our backs on the warm sun-burned grass and watched falling stars. Brilliant short flashes on the background of an almost jet black sky covered with millions of twinkling stars.

There was a cloud burst one autumn and several inches of rain fell within a short time, flooding lower areas, roads, hangars, workshops, houses, and covering the runway with tons of stones, gravel, and mud. The airfield was out of action for about forty-eight hours. Even a heavy bombardment would not result in a complete shut down of the base for so long. The clearance of the runway was top priority. The Air Commodore led the assault team on the stones and mud personally, with spade in hand, followed by bull-dozers and fire engines washing the stuff away. One of my large Messes had a foot of water inside and a huge lake outside.

Before Christmas 1967 several Greek and Turkish villages had a fierce shooting argument again. When the boys flew out from England to join us for the holiday, the road from Nicosia airport was cut off by the hostilities. A small 10-seater Pembroke aircraft made a couple of round trips from Akrotiri to reunite all the children on the flight with their parents. Our two, being older, had to wait for the second trip, and were happy to do so, enjoying the hospitality of the Officers' Mess at Nicosia in the mean time.

There were several stark tragedies on the base. Road accidents were one cause. I visited several men from my unit in hospital with broken bones and went to the funeral of one. A Canberra crew ejected at very low altitude to avoid an accident and certain death. Their broken bodies were flown by helicopter to the RAF Hospital only a couple of miles away. One was patched up reasonably well, the other had a long and painful road to recovery and never flew again.

An engineering fitter was virtually beheaded in a terrible accident whilst servicing a hydraulic platform which collapsed on him. An officer who was an amateur skin-diver volunteered to search for a lost out-board engine belonging to the water-skiing club and was killed, while snorkelling in shallow water, by one of the last boats which was returning to base at speed and rode over him. Every year several crosses were added to the Services cemetery at Dhekalia, and some wives went home widows.

The Akrotiri runway was in a bad state and required major works and re-surfacing. The former RAF Station at Nicosia was still open with a handful of airmen who provided some services to the Civil Airport Authority. Arrangements were made to close Akrotiri for two months and move the sharp end to Nicosia, making it a joint Military/Civilian airfield. Several existing empty buildings had to be adapted for the new purposes, water and power had to be brought in, walls licked with a quick brush of paint in newly created kitchens and Messes and a lot of equipment installed. About half of our men stayed and worked there. There were problems and all units and sections dealt with their own headaches as they came.

Shortly after the re-opening of Akrotiri I took four weeks leave, packed the family into a second-hand, Renault 16, plus our camping gear, and we embarked on a ship for Greece. After seeing as much as we could of ancient Athens, we worked our way round the sites of Greece, from Delphi to Olympia; Tyrins and Mycenae. At Megalopolis, in the middle of the Peloponnese, we found a remote camping site, far off the road, in an orchard with woodlands and a wild gorge curving around on one side, and an old church on the other. We arrived late but managed to put up the tents before darkness enveloped the empty site. Next morning a Christening was taking place. When the service was over a feast had begun. Several tables had been placed together in a long line outside the church and were laden with food and bottles of wine. Pat had brewed some tea and we were resting after our labours when a nice woman came along and speaking in a very good American English, invited us to join the party, which we gladly accepted. She was a schoolteacher and a charming interpreter during this hilarious celebration. There was plenty of excellent food and we tucked in heartily, but the wine was a problem. They poured Retsina into our glasses and neither the boys nor Pat could drink it, its flavour characterised by the tar-lined barrels in which it traditionally matures. The boys and Pat were pretending to sip it, but were discreetly pouring it onto the grass beneath the table, only to have their glasses filled again. An SOS to the interpreter with a warning that somebody's feet may get wet produced a lot of laughter and a bottle of ordinary plonk which went down well. A village elder wanted my opinion on the right-wing Colonels then in power after a coup. What did I think of them? I asked the interpreter to tell him what he would like to hear, after all I was a guest and did not wish to offend him. With a twinkle in her eye she did it so well that the old boy shook my hand and beamed from ear to ear. We admired the baby, clapped hands to their singing and dancing and thanked them warmly for their marvellous hospitality when the party broke up in late afternoon.

At the north end of the Bay of Navarino is a most beautiful lagoon, almost circular, with a narrow opening to the sea and a strip of sand around it. The access to the lagoon from the main road was by a two mile long lane which stopped some way short. Pat and Richard left the car and walked to the sea, while Peter and I drove beyond the road (against their advice) down to a flat, grey ground, following old wheel marks of a vehicle, in order to get nearer to the lagoon. We entered marshland and within fifty yards the front drive wheels sank. We tried everything we could to no avail, the spinning wheels covered the family with muddy sand and sank deeper. There were no stones, nor planks of wood to jack up the car; we were stuck and there was not a soul to be seen. Peter volunteered to seek help. He set off for the main road, flagged down a (German) car and explained the predicament by comparing the vocabularies at the back of the English and German editions of the Blue Guide to Greece. That got him to a police station where he put his knowledge of Greek to the test. Unfortunately, it was only ancient Greek that he had been studying. The police had to off-set for the accent and the antique language, before they could even try and guess at the significance of 'The wheels of my father's chariot have become stuck in the sand by the wine-dark sea'. But they got there and their response was marvellous. Promptly they found a tractor with a trailer, put Peter on it, and another three men, and the party sped to our rescue. The tractor pulled us out with a long rope in no time at all, everybody treating it as a huge joke. I was very relieved and grateful and wanted to pay for their help but they refused to take any money until I persuaded them that they must at least have a drink on us. We had ours some time later, in a restaurant on the road to Kalamata, sitting by a large window as the sun set over the bay. As the colours of the sky changed from dark red to purple, they were reflected by the sea in an unforgettable picture.

Once the boys had left for England again our routine was simple but pleasant. Pat had had a clerical and typing job in the General Engineering Flight for the best part of two and half years. The Flight was part of Sqn Ldr Reg Mitchell's empire, a capable man whose name appeared in the Honours List for his work at Akrotiri. He and his wife were our friends and we went out occasionally to Limassol, a large town fourteen miles distant from Akrotiri. Arif's kebab place was a regular haunt. Although devoid of any frills, just tables and chairs as in most of Turkish establishments, it was as good as anywhere on the island

After Christmas and New Year festivities at home and in the Officers' Mess, attended by three generations of our family, Pat gave up her job and we packed and despatched our crates and boxes of accumulated loot to the RAF depository in the UK, pending our return. Our plan was to drive back in March 1969 via Athens, Patras, by ferry to Brindisi, and all the way home through Italy and France, but that was not what was written.

On the morning of 8th February Pat fainted outside the camp cinema whilst walking home after a doctor's appointment for a fibrositis complaint. She was taken by ambulance back to the same doctor who had taken her blood pressure and told her to rest. They called me and when they eventually found me about noon, I took her home and put her to bed and stayed with her. She had several more fainting spells until about 9 p.m. when we both realised something was seriously wrong. I contacted the same doctor, described the symptoms and an ambulance was immediately called and the hospital alerted. By the time he reached our house Pat was vomiting blood.

The hospital chief physician, Gp Capt. Kelly and his brilliant assistant, Sqn Ldr Flynn, kept her on blood transfusions for four days hoping that the haemorrhage might cease by itself, but it did not. During those four days several doctors, including a group from Dhekalia Army Hospital came to examine Pat - an interesting medical case, they called her.

"It sounds as if an express train is rushing through a station" said Gp Capt Kelly putting aside his stethoscope. The others nodded, smiled and thanked Pat politely then went.

At about 6 p.m. I was sitting by Pat's side with a nurse in the room when the crisis came very suddenly. She was vomiting blood again and went into shock. Alarm bells sounded, nurses ran, and Pat's bed was pushed at high speed to the lift and the operating theatre. It was a long operation, I waited and prayed. When it was over Gp Capt. Williams, the surgeon, saw me alone in a small room.

"She is alive" were his first words. "We had to remove the best part of her stomach - a partial gastrectomy - she is very weak but, God willing, she will be all right. They will give you a bed here, you had better stay in the hospital."-

There was no improvement in Pat's condition for the next four days and on the 16th February, at about 9 p.m. a second crisis came - another massive haemorrhage. She was losing blood at such a rate that two doctors were employed in frantically pumping pints of blood into her by a hand-driven pump whilst the chief Surgeon was called and the theatre prepared. The second operation was performed at speed, a number of balls of clotted blood were removed, the bleeding stopped, and she was brought back to the intensive care area, her face pale and lifeless, as if she was cut in marble. The surgeon said she had a strong will to live, there was a lot of fight and courage in her, and that was good. He looked very serious, had little more to add - except that there was always a chance. I had a note passed to me from the Commanding Officer - was there anything he could do?

I said "Yes, Pat ought to have her family around her, please get the boys out here." and gave him their school addresses. They arrived the next day and so did her parents. The RAF looks after its own; I will never forget that.

The next few days were touch and go. She had the best possible attention and care the hospital could give her, we had to wait. Slowly, very slowly, she started picking up. The sight of the boys and her parents was good for her and she fought back, determined to win. Sqn Ldr Flynn brightened up a bit and although he continued to say -

"She is not out of the woods yet" each morning, it was the way he said it that mattered.

There was always a risk of infection after surgery and sure enough she had one. Her wound burst open one day in three places ejecting accumulated fluids. Then came pneumonia, keeping Sqn Ldr Flynn busy with his terrifyingly long draining needle, but there was no more internal bleeding and Pat, still very weak, began smiling a little - she was winning. Her next serious difficulty was digesting food and absorbing all essential elements, it took years for her system to adjust.

Weeks later, when she was almost 'out of the woods' and no longer on the danger list her parents went back and so did the boys. My posting to the Ministry of Defence in London was ideal for our circumstances, we could live in Guildford whilst I commuted to London. Pat would not be alone any more as this was my last job before being compulsory retired from the RAF at the age of fifty-five. Pat was strongly in favour of my going to England alone, re-opening our home and taking up my appointment. She would return later when ready, she felt safe in hospital and this was the sensible thing to do. I consulted the chief Physician and he agreed with her, he would send her home on the 'Casualty Evacuation' flight when she was fit enough. I shipped our car to England, went back myself full of doubts as to whether I was doing the right thing, re-established our home with the help of the boys during their Easter break, took up my appointment and towards the end of April met Pat at the RAF hospital at Wroughton when she returned to England, with tears in her eyes.

Just before Pat's return I had a letter from my brother telling me that our mother had died peacefully on 27th March at the age of ninety-two.

"Why didn't you write for so long?" he asked.

It was not easy for Pat to pick up the threads of normal life again. Now that she was back home everybody assumed she was fully recovered and there was no longer any physical or other problems - why then was she so depressed? Why could she not sleep? Why was she so thin and losing weight? Why could the doctors not *do* something? They did. Barbiturates and anti-depressants were in vogue at the time and a panacea for all ills. They prescribed buckets-full for her until she rebelled, threw them away gradually and fought her own battle to normality.

The Ministry job was very interesting. I worked for the Director of Victualling, which was a Royal Naval Department run by Civil Servants and dealing with food for the three services - policy, ration scales, cash entitlement, supplies, contracts, the lot. I was in the policy section to do with tri-service policy matters such as rules and regulations, analysis and assessment of proposals and requests, rationalisation projects, submissions to the Treasury, occasional visits to Service establishments, etc. I worked in harmony with my Civil Service colleagues and respected them for their diligence, impartiality, and ability. The Chief Executive Officer, John Bone, had a very shrewd, logical and analytical mind. There was very little he missed when he looked at a problem and his letters and minutes were fine examples of concise and clearly argued papers. Some of my clumsy expressions became a joke. Sometimes, when concluding an analysis, I would begin by writing "We have a choice…" Once I overheard my chief saying to *his* chief with a chuckle "Frank says we have a choice."

"Oh good" came the reply, "I was getting worried as to whether we had any."

As it happened my choices were not too bad on the whole and a fine working relationship developed between us in time.

Six months before my retirement from the RAF in January 1972 we sold our maisonette, moved temporarily to RAF Married Quarters at Kenley and then bought, jointly with Pat's parents, a large single-storey property in Bracknell, close to the RAF Staff College.

In the meantime I had passed 'O' level in Principles of Accounts and attended a six week's Business Management Appreciation course at the School of Management Studies, Central London Polytechnic, designed for Senior officers about to retire. At the end of the course I gained the right to wear a special tie - black with crossed sword and umbrella in gold. I now wish I had attended a House Maintenance course at Aldershot instead, which was most popular with high ranking officers and known in the trade as 'the plumbers' course', but I was ambitious. As soon as I collected two hundred copies of my curriculum vitae I started applying for jobs, my RAF pension of £1,440 a year was not enough to keep the family going. But it was either "No, thank you" or no reply at all to about a hundred of my applications. Then I met Peter Sheridan, ex Skubała, of Aden times, who worked as an accountant for the Gas Industry Training Board in Grosvenor Crescent. They needed an administrative assistant, a lowly post of a dogsbody, but better that than nothing. I applied and was called for an interview. They showed considerable interest in my catering background.

"Could you produce a cold lunch for about thirty on the premises with the help of a 'tea lady', doing your own buying in Harrods, or anywhere else, and appropriate wines of course? We have a spacious kitchen, crockery, cutlery, the lot."-

"No problem, would enjoy it, how much a head?"

"We are not worried, you would have a free hand."

I got the job and although the pay was poor, the address was excellent, and within a short walk from the RAF Club in Piccadilly of which I was a member and where I read my daily papers and Country Life.

I left the RAF on 8th January 1972, a civilian for the second time. It was like taking a cold shower in Iceland. I was fifty-five years old and needed a job for ten years.

CIVVY STREET

The Gas Industry Training Board had a Director - an ex RAF Officer, a Secretary - my chief, an Accountant, and organisers of managerial and technical training courses. They had several young and beautiful secretaries, some married, some single, mostly university graduates, and the charming but tough Kay - the queen of the General Office. She made me tremble with fear when I first met her. Within a week of taking up the post we were informed of the government decision to disband all Industry Training Boards, but our jobs were safe - for at least one year.

A couple of weeks later the Civil Service Commission offered me a job as a Linguist Officer, having rejected me once after a successful examination but not so successful an interview. The starting date would be in August at the earliest and the pay under £1,500 a year, the lowest in the grade, as if I had come straight from University having studied Polish as a foreign language. I decided to haggle. After all, Polish was my native tongue, my service experience must count for something, I needed more money than a young graduate to discharge my responsibilities, and my present salary was higher. I could not afford to work for less. In the end they added a few increments, I climbed down a bit and in the good old Arab fashion we agreed the price of my future labour.

With my next job secured I relaxed a bit, planted roses for Pat to see from the kitchen window, and a lavender hedge along the path. There were cabbages in the vegetable garden. The beautiful flowers by the main gate were tended lovingly by Pat's father.

At work I built up my reputation as a caterer rather than an administrator. They liked my Harrod's lunches with an array of salads, which included my own green version and a French dressing. I enjoyed shopping and arranging everything on a long, help-yourself table, but clearing and washing up was the devil of a job. Fortunately all the secretaries rallied to my help. I usually bought a little extra for the 'washing-up brigade' and there was always a bottle or two opened in the last minute and almost full which had to be finished. The washing-up sessions were a riot!

Glancing through the correspondence column of the weekly publication of the Hotel and Catering Institute, of which I had been a full member for years, I came across a letter written by a pillar of the industry complaining that it was difficult to find men or women with adequate qualifications and experience for executive posts. I sent them my curriculum vitae, and a break-down of my job applications, the number of negative replies without a single invitation for an interview, and number of 'no replies' at all. At the same time I resigned from the Institute and suggested that the esteemed correspondent's lament was not fully justified. I had a nice letter from the editor expressing surprise at my plight, he simply could not understand how that was possible, but then neither could I really. Perhaps I was expecting too much too quickly.

I was a bit sad to leave my lowly job. I had enjoyed the friendship and camaraderie of my fellow workers, the long walks in Hyde Park with Peter Sheridan and our snack lunches in the dungeon of the RAF Club. When the time came to part I said my warm farewells with a gallon of my best homemade wine, sent some flowers to the beautiful secretaries and joined a bunch of strange Civil Servants in the Ministry of Defence.

The department was like the tower of Babel with a confusion of many tongues and was then nick-named 'The Polish Mafia', on account that the head, his deputy, one senior, and one almost senior were all Poles. I was the fifth and the junior, miles behind the lot of them. The job was sedentary and painstaking. I dealt with somebody else's thoughts and words, but never my own, and I was not required to make any decisions except selecting appropriate words from Roget's thesaurus when I got stuck - it was an automaton's job. But with Pat's health still causing problems, I was glad of an undemanding post. I plodded on, passed my probation period, and thought hard of how to get out of it. I almost succeeded, at least I thought so. when I had two interviews, one for the post of Officers' Mess Manager at the RAF Staff College Bracknell, a stone's throw from my home, and one at the Navy Department at Empress State Building where I had worked before, at double my MOD salary. I was well qualified for both but it was not written, *Allah karim*!

I made two very good friends at the Ministry, Mietek Gigiel-Melechowicz, my boss, known to all as MGM, and Tom Vybiral, an outstanding war-time Czech fighter pilot, one of the handful of Czechs who disobeyed Hacha's order to surrender to Hitler and made their way to France and England where they formed the Czech fighter Wing comprising 311 and 312 Fighter Squadrons. Tom had risen to command 312 and ultimately the Wing. He fought with great distinction in France and England, returned to Czechoslovakia in 1945 to command Prague airport, married Gita, the beautiful Prague Opera soprano, and when the communists took over they both escaped to England.

Tom was a socialist and a genuine admirer of Harold Wilson. His faith in socialism, the British version, was somewhat shaken after the series of conflicts between the Trade Unions and the successive Labour Governments. MGM, on the other hand, was the bluest of blue Tories, while I was just blue, in spite of being an undisputed member of the Polish proletariat. The two of them had endless political arguments, sometimes both calling for my support which I gave to the chap who was losing, to fan the flames a bit. Tom and I talked about our two respective countries, the past, the present, and the future. He thought that the Russians had put an end to the traditional Czech's leanings towards them for protection against the Germans, and that this should help our two nations to get together at last.

MGM was sixteen when war broke out. His father, a Colonel commanding an Infantry Regiment in Lwów was taken by the Russians and perished, either in Starobielsk or Ostashkov, the two infamous sister camps of Katyn. It was known that in Katyn 4,143 bodies were discovered, shot in the back of the head, but the fate of 3,920 and 6,500 respectively in the other two camps was not established until several decades later. MGM and his mother reached the West via deportation to Russian Labour Camps and then the Middle East, where he sustained dreadful injuries following the explosion of a grenade in a Military Training Camp. He survived, read Russian at Glasgow University, and at London for a higher degree.

The time had come to reassess our position. Of my brothers in Poland only one, Janek, was still alive. I was in my sixty-second year and my engagement had been extended for one year already. Civil Servants normally retire at sixty and I could only hope for a maximum of three more years if I was very lucky. I was not earning a fortune. What the paymasters gave, rampant inflation and British Rail's frequent fare increases took away. Four hours a day commuting was getting very wearing. And then we heard about the Government Job Release Scheme, the essence of which was that men over sixty-two years of age who gave up their jobs to the younger generation would be paid £2,000 a year until they qualified for a State Pension, on condition that they did not take any other job, or earn more than a few pounds a week by any other means.

"Retire on the scheme" said Pat, "Nine years of commuting is enough, why subsidise British Rail any more? You need a change"–

"And so do you" I said .

And so we retired, first to Cornwall, then finally settling in Findon, West Sussex – after 32 moves in 35 years of marriage.

In October 1980 we went to Rome to see the Pope. The expedition was organised by the Polish Air Force Association, a world-wide organisation of old warriors, with its Headquarters in London. About one hundred and fifty of us made the trip. Most of the wives were Polish but there was also a sprinkling of English ladies who in their youth had failed to listen to their mothers and had bravely married Poles. Tadek Anders, the Chief Organiser, had to console one English wife in distress as the group gathered at Heathrow.

"My husband forgot his passport" she announced, "What shall we do?"

"Have you got yours?"

"Yes, but what about him?"

"Why don't you leave him behind and come on your own? We will look after you."

(He came without passport, was detained in Rome, and joined his wife two days later.)

This was the first time Pat had been amongst so many Poles for a fortnight and, not speaking Polish, was at a disadvantage, but everybody was courteous to her - except two Polish ladies who obviously disapproved of 'mixed marriages'. When I politely reminded one of them that Pat does not speak Polish, she snapped back "It is her own fault" and this from a woman who, after thirty-three years in England, barely spoke pidgin English.

The trip mixed the tourist pleasures of Italy with some more serious days. We visited Monte Cassino, finally taken by Polish troops after an assault with horrific losses.

From the courtyard of the monastery we could see the Polish cemetery on a gentle rise below, facing the Abbey. One thousand and one hundred graves, with the same number of gravestones detailing name, unit, date and place of birth, and date of death, on each of them. May they rest in peace. This was a pilgrimage, a Holy place to every Pole, where we went to pay homage and mourn, and which we left strengthened in our resolve never to give up. They did not die in vain, the fight goes on.

I walked among the terraces of graves and saw the name Hrubieszów, the town where I went to school. Among the crosses were Jewish and Mohammaden stones, all sons of Poland. I was overwhelmed; Pat saw it and walked away.

On Wednesday 15th October we attended the Pope's general audience in St Peter's Square where several thousand people from many nations assembled. Of the Poles there was our own group, and several bus loads from two Parishes in Poland.– We joined forces in the privileged area close to the Pope. At the end, the Pope talked for a while to representatives of all groups. It was then that Gp Capt. Gabszewicz, the Chairman of the Association and former Commanding Officer of 131 Polish Fighter Wing presented His Holiness with the Association's plate depicting the Holy Mary of Ostra Brama and the Polish Air Force Eagle emblem, in company with two other officers, Andersz and Lasota.

Next day, on the second anniversary of Cardinal Wojtyła's accession to the Papal throne, our group had a special audience in a magnificent hall with a splendid ceiling, wall paintings and pictures. After a few words of introduction by Cardinal Rubin, our Chairman addressed the Pope briefly, who replied impromptu in beautiful Polish and a strong, clear voice. He acknowledged the Polish Air Force war effort and sacrifices, spoke of the links between Poles abroad and at home and thanked us for coming to see him. In the end we prayed together, he blessed us, posed for photographs and chatted to people for quite a while before he left. There was an aura of gentleness and strength about him. One felt that there stood a righteous man who knew what he was about and would not deviate an inch from the road that was his. His election was a blessing to Poland and to Poles throughout the world. Many a faint heart started beating stronger when he was elected. He became a focal point for our hopes and aspirations, a defender of human rights. He spoke for us, he cut through the jungle of lies, the chains of oppression, reaching for the minds, trying to awake the will to resist evil. He was a great man and half Europe owes him an enormous debt for its freedom.

POSTSCRIPT

The official Standard of the Polish Air Force was returned to Warsaw in 1992. It had been sewn in secret in occupied Poland in 1940 and smuggled to Britain where it was held in turn by each Polish squadron. After the war it was kept in Britain until it could be taken back to a free country, the country we fought for and lost in 1939, fought for and lost again in 1945, and then waited two generations to see finally free. And now, some 60 years after the war, Britain is suddenly full of young Poles again. Bringing the same energy and determination that their grandfathers brought. But this time free to come, and free to go home, at a time of their own choosing.

I am now 91, and it is 24 years since we moved to Findon. There are racing stables on the Sussex Downs nearby. The village echoes to the clip of hooves. It is a deep pleasure for me to see and hear the passing horses – as much now as it was in my boyhood in Wereszyn, when I rode the lead horse of the team, harvesting the corn in a world about to be swept away.

APPENDIX

12th Entry, Polish Air Force College, Dęblin

Name	Date of Birth	Passing Out Place	Specialisation	First Unit	War Casualties & Survivors
1. Aduckiewicz, Marjan	1917	70	Navigator	55 E(B)	Canada
2. Aleksandrowicz, Henryk	1915	75	Navigator	No. 5 Regiment	U.S.A.
3. Anders, Bohdan	1915	82	Pilot	132 E(F)	U.K.
4. Andruszko, Michał	1917	94	Pilot	151 E(F)	U.K.
5. Andrzejewski, Stanisław	1917	128	Pilot	151 E(F)	U.K.
6. Augustyński, Julian	1915	73	Navigator	212 E(B)	Uruguay
7. Babiański, Mieczysław	1917	119	Pilot	152 E(F)	k.a. 4.4.1940 - France
8. Bagiński, Czesław	1914	138	Pilot	No. 5 Regiment	m. Katyri
9. Bećko, Stanisław	1915	74	Navigator	55 E(B)	k.a. 5/6.9.1941 - Flt. Training Unit
10. Białoskórski, Jerzy	1916	158	Navigator	212 E(B)	U.S.A.
1 l. Bilecki, Kazimierz	1917	116	Pilot	64 E (B)	U.K
12. Blicharz, Tadeusz	1915	125	Pilot	No. 2 Regiment	U.S.A.
13. Bondar, Józef	1916	20	Pilot	151 E(F)	k.b. 28.6.1941- 303 Squadron
14. Borowski, Kazimierz	1914	110	Navigator	42 E (B)	New Zealand
15. Bożek, Wtadysław	1914	87	Pilot	123 E(F)	k.b. 28.7.1941 - 303 Squadron
(Bronowicz, Jerzy	1914	Released - P.A.F. College Order No. 130/1937)			
16. Brzozowski, Władysław	1916	146	Pilot	24 E(B)	k.b. 8.9.1941 - 301 Squadron
17. Brzostowski, Lucjan	1917	66	Pilot (B)	No. 1 Regiment	k.b. 17.9.1939 - 221 Esk
18. Buchowiecki, Zdzisław	1916	120	Pilot	No. 4 Regiment	U.S.A.
19. Bukowiecki, Grzegorz	1916	159	Pilot	No. 2 Regiment	k.b. 3.4.1942 - 307 Squadron
Chwalbiński, Tadeusz	1917	(Died in Flying accident 19.6.1936; P.A.F. College Order No. 134/1939)			
20. Cierpiłowski, Wacław	1915	136	Pilot (B)	No. 1 Regiment	k.b. 7.9.1939 - 216 E
21. Cieliński, Stanisław	1918	142	Pilot	No. 2 Regiment	k.a. 18.4.1943 - Training Unit
22. Ciołek, Jakób	1917	154	Navigator	55 E(B)	k.b. 5/6.8.1942 - 301 Squadron
23. Chciuk, Władysław	1915	100	Pilot	121 E(F)	U.S.A.
24. Choms, Wiesław	1913	155	Pilot	161 E(F)	k.b. 14.8.1941 - 306 Squadron
(Chłapiński, Erazm		(Navigator) (died in Flying accident 19.7.1939 No. 1 Regiment Order 139/1939)			
25. Czajkowski, Franciszek	1916	24	Pilot	141 E(F)	k. 25.10.1942 (Torquay hospital bombed)
26. Czternastek, Stanisław	1916	97	Navigator	No. 2 Regiment	k.a. 5.2.1941 - 615 Squadron
27. Cybulski, Jan	1916	46	Navigator	51 E(B)	k.b. 6.9.1939-51 Esk

Name	Date of Birth	Passing Out Place	Specialisation	First Unit	War Casualties & Survivors
28. Danek, Antoni	1919	29	Pilot	123 E(F)	k.b. wounds, died 18.3.1940 - Poland
29. Dąbrowski, Tadeusz	1915	163	Pilot	55 E(B)	k.a. 25.10.1940 - Training Unit
30. Drecki, Władysław	1915	149	Pilot	112 E(F)	k.a. 13.9.1943 Italy- 152 RAF Squadron
31. Drybański, Zygmunt	1916	122	Pilot	141 E(F)	Australia
32. Drzazga, Michał	1915	135	Pilot	No. 4 Regiment	U.K.
33. Dzięgielewski, Antoni	1916	52	Pilot	162 E(F)	k.b. 19.5.1943 - 307 Squadron
34. Dziubiński, Tadeusz	1916	113	Pilot (B)	No. 2 Regiment	k.b. 11.1.1941 -301 Squadron (Colision, Ops. flight)
(Feifer, Walerian	1916	Released - P.A.F. College Order No.28/1937)			
(Fishering-Jampolski, Jerzy	1916	Released - P.A.F. College Order No.122/1937)			
35. Gąsowski, Wacław	1917	48	Navigator	No. 4 Regiment	d. 1949 Belgium
36. Gębicki, Stefan	1916	101	Navigator	21 E(B)	U.K. (Davis)
37. Gierycz, Czesław	1914	171	Pilot	No. 4 Regiment	d. U.K.
38. Gil, Józef	1914	32	Pilot (F)	No. 1 Regiment	k.b. 31.12.1942 - 306 Squadron
39. Gnyś, Władysław	1910	26	Pilot	121 E(F)	Canada
40. Goldhaar, Jerzy	1915	63	Navigator	No. 1 Regiment	k.a. 20.2.1945 (Gander)
41. Górecki, Wacław	1917	23	Pilot	217 E(B)	k.b. Poland
42. Grandys, Wacław	1914	34	Navigator	22 E(B)	k.b. 3.9.1939
43. Groyecki, Zbigniew	1918	91	Navigator	22 E(B)	U.S.A.
44. Grudziński, Władysław	1917	27	Pilot	122 E(F)	k.b. 23.11.1941 - 315 Squadron
45. Hebda, Józef	1915	4	Navigator	211 E(B)	d. Canada
46. Jaksztas, Ludwik	1915	103	Navigator	No. 5 Regiment	k.b. 7/8.7.1944 - 305 Squadron
47. Janicki, Zbigniew	1917	57	Pilot	No. 1 Regiment	k.b. 13.6.1944 - 56 Gr. 61 Squadron U.S. Air Force
48. Janik, Józef	1916	131	Pilot	No. 2 Regiment	South Africa
49. Jaroszka, Witold	1915	106	Pilot	132 E(F)	k.b. 122.9.1939
50. Jasiński, Tadeusz	1917	152	Pilot	No. 2 Regiment	U.K.
51. Jasiński, Zygmunt	1916	162	Pilot	No. 5 Regiment	k.b. 16.8.1944 - 305 Squadron
52. Jaugsch, Leon	1914	109	Pilot	142 E(F)	U.S.A. (died 8.4.1984)
53. Jeleń, Józef	1917	13	Pilot (B)	No. 2 Regiment	k.b.3.9.1939 - 23 Esk
54. Juraszek, Konrad	1918	117	Pilot	No. 4 Regiment	U.K.
55. Kabat, Alfons	1915	121	Pilot	131 E(F)	Poland
56. Kalpas, Rajmund	1916	42	Pilot	113 E(F)	k.b. 1.6.1940 - Lyon, France
57. Kamiński, Leszek	1915	31	Pilot	No. l Regiment	Poland
58. Kandziora, Adam	1913	60	Navigator	32 E(R)	k.b. 4.9.1939
59. Kaniewski, Zdzisław	1917	61	Navigator	65 E(B)	k.a. 19.9.1941 - Training unit
60. Kędzierski, Stanisław	1916	164	Pilot	152 E(F)	Argentina

Name	Date of Birth	Passing Out Place	Specialisation	First Unit	War Casualties & Survivors
61. Klimek, Jan	1916	8	Navigator	22 E(B)	k.b. 3.9.1939
62. Klocek, Jan	1915	124	Navigator	41 E(B)	k.b. 28.9.1942 - 301 Squadron
63. Kobierzycki, Zbigniew	1918	72	Navigator	No. l Regiment	U.K.
64. Koczor, Ryszard	1916	85	Pilot	121 E(F)	k.a. 4.12.1940 - 308 Squadron
65. Kogut, Stanisław	1914	28	Pilot	142 E(F)	k.a. 5.6.1940 - Lyon, France
66. Kolczak, Stanisław	1916	78	Navigator	216 E(B)	U.K.
67. Koń, Stanisław	1918	38	Navigator	64 E (B)	Argentina
68. Kornicki, Franciszek	1916	3	Pilot	162 E(F)	U.K.
69. Kortus, Florian	1916	11	Pilot	131 E(F)	Poland
70. Kowalski, Edward	1917	89	Pilot	No. 3 Regiment	k.b. 12.12.1942 - 316 Squadron
(Kowalski, Franciszek	Released P.A.F. College Order No.9/1937)				
(Kowalewski, Seweryn	Released P.A.F. College Order No.122/1937)				
71. Kozłowski, Franciszek	1917	18	Pilot	122 E(F)	k.b. 13.3.1943 - 316 Squadron
72. Kramarski, Edward	1915	1	Pilot	161 E(F)	k.b. 2.9.1939
73. Kratke, Tadeusz	1917	137	Pilot	123 E(F)	d. l984 Canada
74. Kulesza, Bogusław	1915	134	Pilot	No. 4 Regiment	U.K.
75. Langhamer, Zdzisław	1918	30	Pilot (F)	No. 4 Regiment	d.U.K. 19.2.1984
76. Laska, Edward	1916	141	Navigator	21 E(B)	d. U.K. 13.1.1979
77. Latawiec, Michaś	1915	36	Pilot	64 E(B)	k.b. 24/5.5.1944 - 305 Squadron
78. Łopacki, Ryszard	1916	144	Pilot	162 E(F)	d.U.K.
79. Łucki, Jan	1915	150	Navigator	51 E(B)	k.b. 16.10.1941 - 305 Squadron
80. Łukaszewicz, Marian	1916	22	Pilot	151 E(F)	k.b. 23.11.1941 - 315 Squadron
81. Maciejewski, Stefan	1917	51	Pilot	31 E(B)	Australia or New Zealand
82. Maciński, Janusz	1916	95	Pilot	112 E(F)	k.b. 4.9.1940- 111 Squadron R.A.F.
(Majkowski, Stanisław	Transferred to Army College, P.A.F. College Order No. 148/1937)				
83. Makowski, Bohdan	1914	129	Navigator	42 E (B)	k.b. 4.9.1939
84. Malarowski, Anddrzej	1911	104	Pilot	161 E(F)	U.K.
85. Malinowski, Mieczysław	1917	10	Navigator	41 E(B)	Poland
86. Maliński, Jan	1917	19	Pilot	132 E(F)	U.K. & Poland
87. Malczewski, Ryszard	1917	148	Pilot	34 E (B)	Poland
88. Maliszewski, Eugeniusz	1914	166	Pilot	No. 4 Regiment	d. U.K.
89. Makarewicz, Władysław	1915	64	Pilot	31 E(B)	k.a. 26.11.1940 - No. 12 OTU
90. Marcisz, Stanisław	1914	115	Pilot	32 E(B)	U.K. & Poland
91. Marciniak, Janusz	1916	111	Pilot (F)	No. 1 Regiment	k.b. 23.6.1944 C.O. 306 Squadron
92. Martusewicz, Tadeusz	1916	44	Navigator	51 E(B)	U.S.A.
93. Mazak, Feliks	1916	7	Pilot	212 E(B)	Poland

Name	Date of Birth	Passing Out Place	Specialisation	First Unit	War Casualties & Survivors
94. Mączyński, Józef	1917	80	Navigator	No. 1 Regiment	k.b. 10.1.1942 - 304 Squadron
95. Mielecki, Leopold	1911	105	Pilot	217 E(B)	k.a. 22.11.1945
96. Mierzwa, Bogusław	1918	145	Pilot	114 E(F)	k.b. 16.4.1941 - 303 Squadron
97. Miksa, Włodzimierz	1915	107	Pilot	114 E(F)	U.K.
98. Malinowski, Zenon	1917	114	Pilot	51 E(B)	m. Katyń
99. Murawski, Bolesław	1914	39	Pilot	211 E(B)	k.b. 1/2.2.1941 -301 Squadron
100. Nowakowski, Jan	1915	17	Pilot	No. 1 Regiment	POW in Germany 1939 missing
101. Nowakowski, Władysław	1918	43	Pilot	No. 1 Regiment	???
102. Nowak, Mirosław	1917	47	Pilot	131 E(F)	Poland
103. Olewiński, Kazimierz	1918	9	Pilot	132 E(F)	k.a. 29.7.1940 (OTU)
104. Olszyna, Marian	1916	67	Pilot	211 E(B)	k.b. 1/2.1.1940
105. Ołpiński, Tadeusz	1916	165	Navigator	211 E(B)	Interned U.K. during war, then U.S.A.
106. Oparenko, Michał	1915	172	Navigator	No. Regiment	U.K.
107. Osiatyński, Włodzimierz	1917	168	Navigator	211 E(B)	Spain
108. Ostrowski, Michał	1915	35	Pilot	212 E(B)	d. 29.7.1972 Poland
109. Ośmlaiowskl, Leon	1916	2	Navigator	41 E(B)	k.b. 31.8.1943 - 300 Squadron
110. Owczarski, Tadeusz	1918	71	Naviga-tor/Pilot	No. l Regiment	U.K. & Poland
111. Pankiewicz, Stanisław	1916	153	Pilot	No. 4 Regiment	k.a. 17.12.1942 (Malta) 138 Sqn
112. Pfleger, Włodzimierz	1916	99	Navigator	42 E (B)	k.a. 27.9.1941 - 307 Squadron
113. Pietruszko, Stanisław	1916	151	Pilot	24 E(B)	k.a. 23.6.1941 - 301 Squadron
114. Piotrowski, Józef	1916	156	Pilot	No. 3 Regiment	k.b. 14.1.1944 - 308 Squadron
115. Piwowarek, Bolesław	1916	45	Navigator	216 E(B)	d. 22.7.1981 France
(Piechocki, Tadeusz	Released, P.A.F. College Order No. 2207/1937)				
116. Pniak, Karol	1910	118	Pilot	142 E(F)	d. 17.10.1980 Poland
117. Pokorniewski, Fabian	1916	81	Navigator	41 E(B)	d. 21.6.1943 - 300 Squadron
118. Polek, Antoni	1916	83	Pilot (F)	No. Regiment	U.S.A.
(Pomierski, Józef	1914	Released, P.A.F. College Order No.208/1937)			
119. Pruchnicki, Henryk	1915	139	Navigator	No. 1 Regiment	?
120. Przywara, Stanisław	1911	93	Pilot	211 E(B)	d. August 1969 Poland
121. Pudelewicz, Jan	1916	5	Pilot	132 E(F)	?
122. Radomski, Jerzy	1915	88	Pilot	113 E(F)	d. 17.12.1978 U.K.
123. Radwański, Władysław	1913	96	Pilot	41 E(B)	U.K.
124. Rajchert, Karol	1917	127	Navigator	No. 1 Regiment	U.K.
125. Ranoszek, Ginter	1917	126	Pilot	No. 3 Regiment	m. Katyń
126. Reda, Wacław	1915	12	Navigator	53 E(R)	k.b. 22/3.1.1942 -301 Squadron
(Reymer Edward	Released P.A.F. College Order No. 117/1938)				

Name	Date of Birth	Passing Out Place	Specialisation	First Unit	War Casualties & Survivors
(Rostowicz, Kazimierz	Released P.A.F. College Order No. 117/1938)				
127. Rozwadowski, Mieczysław	1915	37	Pilot	No. 1 Regiment	k.b. 15.8.1940- 151 Squadron RAF
128. Ruszel, Piotr	1918	14	Pilot	161 E(F)	k.b. 2.9.1939
129. Ryński, Józef	1916	140	Pilot	No. 5 Regiment	Poland
130. Ryżko, Władysław	1907	49	Pilot	No. 1 Regiment	k.a. 11.8.1963
(Rybicki, Witalis	1915	Released, P.A.F. College Order No. 122/1937)			
131. Salski, Jerzy	1915	173	Pilot	131 E(F)	U.S.A.
132. Sikorski, Marian	1915	143	Pilot	No. 4 Regiment	k.a. 12.9.1941
133. Sierpiński, Stanisław	1915	157	Pilot (B)	No. 1 Regiment	k.b. 12.9.1939 - 211 E
134. Siuda, Witold	1915	40	Navigator	42 E (B)	Australia
135. Skarpetowski, Franciszek	1916	161	Pilot	55 E (R)	Poland
(Skowroński, Henryk	1916	Released P.A.F. College Order No. 117/1938)			
136. Siwiec, Jan	1915	77	Navigator	55 E(B)	k.b. 23/3.12.1941 - 305 Squadron
137. Słomski, Zygmunt	1914	79	Pilot	151 E(F)	k.b. 29.7.1942 - 315 Squadron
138. Smolik, Zygmunt	1917	130	Navigator	22 E(B)	k.a. 25/6.10.1941 -No. 18 OTU
139. Sobczak, Kazimierz	1918	132	Pilot	No. 3 Regiment	k.b. 3.9.1939-34 Esk
140. Sobański, Michał	1916	21	Pilot	No. 1 Regiment	m. Katyń
141. Srzednicki, Tadeusz	1918	68	Navigator	216 E(B)	k.b. 25/6.7.1941 -301 Squadron
142. Stadnicki, Jan	1915	41	Navigator	217 E(B)	Canada
143. Stefankiewicz, Henryk	1918	53	Pilot	113 E(F)	k.b. 22.6.1944 -315 Squadron
144. Stoga, Wiktor	1915	169	Pilot	114 E(F)	k.b. 6.9.1939
145. Stutzman, Ferdynand	1918	142	Navigator	21 E(B)	Poland
146. Suwalski, Roman	1917	98	Pilot	No. 4 Regiment	k.a. 26.1.1942 - No. 57 OTU
147. Surma, Franciszek	1916	55	Pilot	121 E(F)	k.b. 8.11.1941 - 308 Squadron
148. Szabuniewicz, Juliusz	1917	58		No. 3 Regiment	k.a. 18.5.1941 - Training unit
149. Szajkowski, Janusz	1916	86	Pilot	No. 1 Regiment	Canada
150. Szumelda, Zygmunt	1916	84	Navigator	64 E (B)	U.S.A.
151. Tuszyński, Tadeusz	1916	6	Navigator	41 E(B)	U.K.
152. Waltoś, Antoni	1915	123	Pilot	65 E (B)	k.b. 19.8.1942-87 Squadron RAF
153. Wapniarek, Stefan	1916	15	Pilot	132 E(F)	k.b. 18.2.1040 - 302 Squadron
154. Waszkiewicz, Mieczysław	1917	160	Pilot	152 E(F	k.b. 16.4.1941 -303Squadron
(Wesołowski, Kazimierz	1915	died, P.A.F. College: Order No. 43/1938)			
155. Weyman, Wiktor	1916	167	Pilot	34 E (B)	k.b. 6.9.1939
(Węgrzyn, Antoni	1916	moved to 13th entry, P.A.F. Order No. 95/1939)			
156. Widawski, Ludwik	1915	162	Pilot	No. 1 Regiment	d. 23.11.1973 Poland
157. Wilczak, Rudolf	1917	50	Navigator	21 E(B)	k.b. 2.9.1939

Name	Date of Birth	Passing Out Place	Specialisation	First Unit	War Casualties & Survivors
158. Wiśniewski, Andrzej	1915	76	Navigator	217 E(B)	k.a. 18.5.1942 - No. 18 OTU
159. Witke, Edward	1915	59	Navigator	217 E(B)	U.K.?
160. Własnowolski, Bolesław	1916	102	Pilot	122 E(F)	k.b. 1.11.1940 - 213 Squadron RAF
161. Wodzicki, Mariusz	1915	92	Navigator	22 E(B)	k.b. 30.10.1942 - 138 Squadron RAF
162. Wojtal, Wacław	1915	90	Navigator	21 E(B)	U.K.?
163. Wojcieszek, Wiktor	1914	33	Pilot	216 E(B)	Poland
164. Wójcik, Józef	1915	65	Pilot	217 E(B)	k.b. 14.10.1942 - 300 Squadron
165. Wróblewski, Zbigniew	1914	133	Pilot	114 E(F)	U.K.
166. Wrzesień, Henryk	1915	170	Pilot/	No. 4 Regiment	Poland
167. Wyciślok, Walter	1916	69	Navigator	21 E(B)	k.b. 10.9.1939
168. Wyrożemski, Ksawery	1915	Ki	Navigator	217 E(B)	d. 12.2.1967 accident U.S.A.
169. Zieliński, Benedykt	1915	147	Pilot	No. 4 Regiment	U.K.
170. Zwierzawski, Stanisław	1916	108	Navigator	211 E(B)	Interned U.K. during war. then USA
171. Żegałło, Włodzimierz	1915	56	Navigator	No. 5 Regiment	d. U.K.
172. Żmichowski, Stefan	1913	54	Navigator	34 E(B)	Poland
173. Żychowicz, Henryk	1916	25	Navigator	34 E(B)	Poland
(Maćkowski, Tadeeusz	1912	Pilot - Released P.A.F. College Order No. 24/1937)			
(Grzanka, Kazimierz	1914	Pilot - died P.A.F. College Order No. 95/1938)			
(Oleksik, Władysław	1914	Pilot - died in flying accident, P.A.F. College Order No. 163/1938)			

Abbreviations
k.b.	-	Killed in Battle
k.a.	-	Killed in flying accident
E	-	Eskadra (Flight)
E (B)	-	Eskadra (Bomber)
E (F)	-	Eskadra (Fighter)
E (R)	-	Eskadra (Recce)
m.	-	Murdered
d.	-	Died of natural causes, etc.
U.K. U.S.A. etc.	-	Settled in, after the war
OTU	-	Operational Training Unit

Pilots 114.
Navigators 59
Authority: CWL No. 11, l.dz. 988 p.f. z dnia 25.8.1939

War losses of 12th Entry:
Killed in action:
19 in Poland
1 in France
40 in Great Britain
Murdered in Katyn   4
Killed in flying accidents: 2 in France
20 in Great Britain

Total   86 out of 173

BILIOGRAPHY

Anders, Wladyslaw ,Bez Ostatniego Rozdzialu,Gryf Publications Ltd. 1959
Bullock, Alan ,Hitler,Penguin Books Ltd.
Conquest, Robert ,The Great Terror,Macmillan 1968
Cynk, J.B. ,History of the Polish Air Force 1918 - 1968,Osprey Publishing Ltd. 1972
Deshner, Gunther ,Warsaw Rising, Pan/Balantine
Dziewanowski, M.K, Poland in the 20th Century,Columbia University Press New York, 1977
Fitz Gibbon, Louis ,Katyń, TomStacey, 1971
Fuller, Maj. Gen .J.F.C. ,The Conduct of War 1789-1961, Eyre & Spottiswood, London 1962
Halecki, Oscar, A History of Poland, Routledge & Kegan Paul Ltd., 1978
Leitgeber, Capt. Witold, It Speaks for Itself (Selection of Documents 1939 - 1946),
    Polish Forces Press Bureau
Maczek, General Stanisław, Od Podwody Do Czolga,Orbis Books (London) Ltd.
Mee, Charles L. Jr., Meeting at Potsdam, Andre Deutch
Piłsudski, Jozef, Rok 1920, M.I. Kolin (Pubs.) Ltd. 1941
Piłsudski, Jozef, Pisma Wybrane, M.I. Kolin (Pubs.) Ltd. 1943
Raczyński, Count Edward, British - Polish Alliance, The Melville Press Ltd., 1948
Shirer, William L., The Rise and Fall of the Third Reich, Pan Books Ltd., London
Smogorzewski, Casimir, About the Curzon Line, Free Europe Pamphlet, London, 1944
Stevens, Stewart, The Poles, Collins/Harvill, London 1982
Urbanowicz, Witold, Początek Jutra, Published in Poland
Urbanowicz, Witold, Swit Zwycięstwa, Published in Poland
Wankowicz, Melchior, Bitwa O Monte Cassino, Polish Second Corps Press, Rome, Milan 1945
Wandycz, Piotr, Soviet Polish Relations 1917 - 1921, Harvard University Press 1969
S. Wilmont, Chester,The Struggle for Europe, Collins 1952
Zawodny. J.K., Nothing But Honour, Macmillan, London Ltd. 1978
Bellona, Polish Military & Historical Quarterly Nos. 1 & 3, 1958
Destiny Can Wait, The Polish Air Force in the Second World War,William Heinman Ltd. 1949
Archives of the Polish Institute and General Sikorski Museum, 20 Princes Gate, London, S.W.7

Further reading:
Cynk, Jerzy B. The Polish Air Force at War. The official history, Schiffer, Atglen 1998
Gretzyngier, Robert, Poles in Defence of Britain, Grub street, London, 2001
Olson, Lynne & Cloud, Stanley, For Your Freedom and Ours, Heineman, London 2003

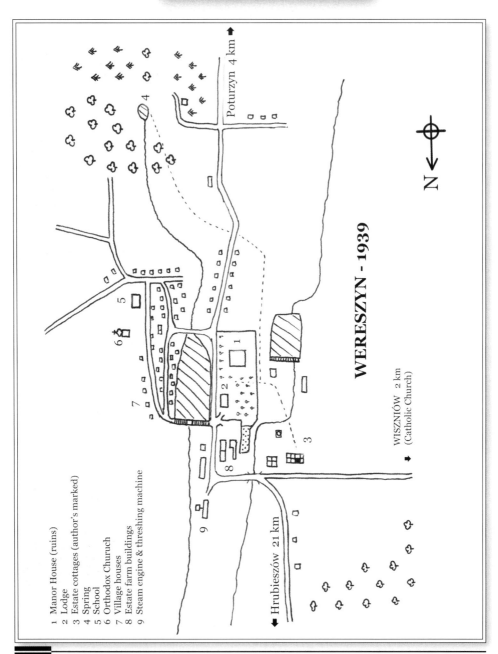

WERESZYN - 1939

1 Manor House (ruins)
2 Lodge
3 Estate cottages (author's marked)
4 Spring
5 School
6 Orthodox Churuch
7 Village houses
8 Estate farm buildings
9 Steam engine & threshing machine

Poturzyn 4 km

WISZNIÓW 2 km
(Catholic Church)

Hrubieszów 21 km

Pupils and a teacher of Stanisław Staszic Grammar School in Hrubieszów (1931-1936). Author is to the upper left of the teacher's hat.

Author with Czajka glider during flying training at Goleszów in 1935.

The Polish Air Force College at Dęblin.

PAF College instructors. At far left is Capt. Józef Ostrowski, C. O. of the 12th entry class, known to his cadet officers as 'Tata', meaning 'Dad'.

PWS-26 trainers during formation flying practice.

Author in the cockpit of the trainer aircraft, PWS 18, produced in Poland under Avro licence.

PAF College cadet officers. Left to right: Drzazga, unknown, Wodzicki, Dzięgielewski, author, Marciniak.

PAF College cadet officers during fighter pilot training at Ułęż. In the middle is instructor Lt Janusz Żurakowski. After the war he became a test pilot of the highest repute in Britain and Canada.

PAF College cadet officers. Left to right: Waszkiewicz, author, Suwalski.

PAF College cadet officers at a skiing camp in Zakopane. Left to right: author, unknown, unknown, Babiański, Suwalski, Dzięgielewski, Marciniak, Waszkiewicz.

PZL P.7 fighter, used for fighter pilot training at Ułęż.

PZL P.11c fighter of a Lwów-based 6 Air Regiment's squadron.

The Struggle

2nd Lt C. Głowczyński from 162nd Squadron with the PZL P.11c of Capt S. Morawski commanding III/6 Wing.

P.11c of Lt J. Dzwonek of the 161st Squadron, by the PZL P.11c adorned with his personal "turkey" emblem.

Briefing of III/6 Fighter Wing pilots at Basiówka airfield near Lwów before the move to Łódź, 30 August 1939. In the background (with his shirt in his hand) author.

Squadron pilot quarters near Łódź-Widzew airfield.

The PZL P.11c of Lt T. Jeziorowski, III/6 Wing Tactics Officer, shot down on 4 September 1939 at Łódź-Widzew.

Aircraft shown from the other side.

Evacuation. Posing with the Opel car, left to right: Dzięgielewski, Wiśniewski, author.

Private quarters at Tulcea. Left to right: unknown, Vasilica, author, the hosts, Wiśniewski, Dzięgielewski, unknown.

Author and Wiśniewski crossing Danube.
Author's passport photo taken in Bucharest for the false papers.

Busy streets of Bucharest.

Author, Rumanian policeman and his wife, Wiśniewski, Dzięgielewski.

S/S 'Patris', the ship on which the author and his friends left Rumania.

Marseille, as the Polish airmen saw it when their evacuation ship reached France.

The author's mishap during conversion training on the Caudron CR.714 Cyclone.

Morane-Saulnier MS.406 fighter and Bloch MB.131 bomber at Lyon-Bron, the Polish Air Force training centre in France during 1939-1940.

Having good time at Juan Le Pins in April 1940. Left to right: Dyrgała, Stabrowski, author, Peterek, Jastrzębski, Jakubowski.

S/S 'Arandora Star', the evacuation ship that took Polish airmen, including the author (far right in the bottom photo) to Britain.

'Thank God we've arrived here' - the first Mass in England.

Ready to fight: 315 Squadron pilots at Northolt. Left to right: Grudziński, Jasionowski, author.

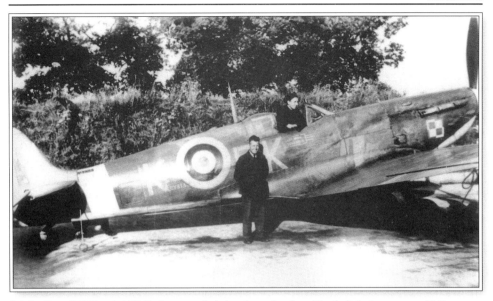

Spitfire II no. P7855 coded PK-K, flown regularly by the author from Northolt during summer 1941.

315 Squadron pilots with one of their Spitfire Vs at Northolt in late 1941. Left to right: Blok, Matus, two unknown, Chudek, author, Falkowski.

Author and his two ground crew with the Spitfire V coded PK-I that he usually flew in late 1941.

The dwarf emblem on one of 315 Sqn Spitfires was a favourite motif for souvenir photos.

Author with Ailsa Paterson and her mother at Ormskirk near Southport. 315 Squadron Day party - author singing with others.

Author (in the middle, under the propeller blade) taking over command of 308 Sqn from S/Ldr Walerian Żak (standing under the propeller spinner).

Author (middle) as commander of 317 Squadron, with F/Lts Weber (adjutant, left), and Wróblewski (A Flight commander). Author (right) and George Radomski.

Visit of Gen. Ujejski (3rd right, back to camera), to decorate pilots and ground crew of 315 Squadron, 1942.

Author decorated with the Silver Cross of Virtuti Militari in the autumn 1943.

Author (far right) during his studies at the Polish Air Force Staff College at Weston-super-Mare.

Polish Wing's base at Ghent following surprise German attack in the morning of 1 January 1945.

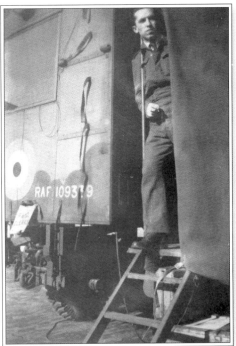

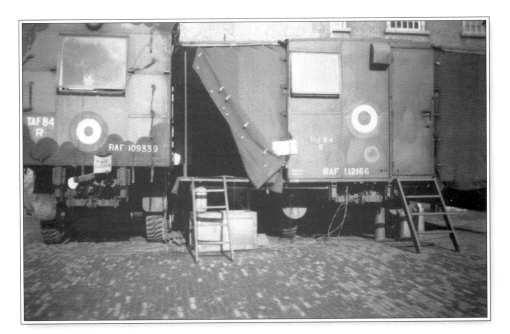

HQ 84 Group (Rear): living and working in the mobile home.

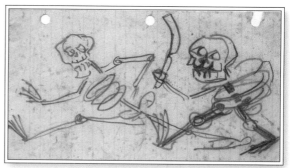

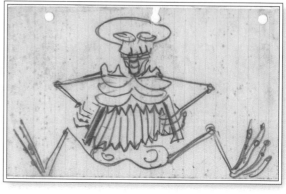

Author's war nickname was "Korniszon" or "Gherkin".

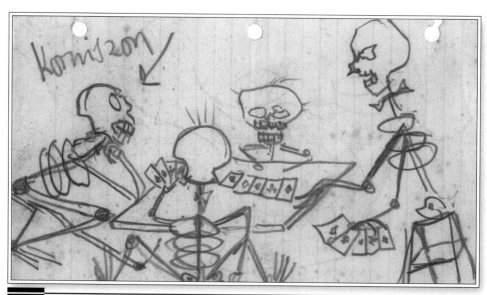

Occupation: author's quarters in former German Gas School.

Author and 131 Wing's F/O Jodidijo and G/Cpt Gabszewicz among German wrecks.

On 6 March 1948 the author married Pat Williams.

Polish Resettlement Corp's Hotel and Catering course in 1947.

Pilots' Navigation Course at RAF Shrewsbury in 1952. Author seated at far left.

With the RAF on Malta in mid-1950s. Author on right.

Officers Work Organisation Course at RAF School of Catering, 1959. Author standing at far right.

HM the Queen at the RAF College Cranwell in 1961.

Polish Air Force veterans meeting at the Polish Air Force Association HQ in London in the 1980s.

50th Anniversary of Northolt Airfield. Left to right: unknown, author, Janus, Bienkowski, Sulerzycki, Gabsze-wicz, unknown, Trzebiński, Drobiński

Polish Air Force veterans reunion in Warsaw in 1992 - Poland independent at last! Author front row, 2th from right.

Ditto. Author 2nd from left

Warsaw, 3rd September 1992, return of the Polish Air Force Colours. Front row: former squadron and wing commanders; author 3rd left

Polish AF veterans during 1997 reunion. Left to right: Sawicz, author, Pilkington-Miksa, Kwiatkowski.

Memorial at Perranporth - one of many places in Britain where Polish fighters served.

*Author reunited with the Spitfire VB BM597 which he had flown in 315
Squadron in 1942. Chailey Airfield, August 2004.*

© Ian Le Sueur